The Truth About HTML5

Luke Stevens
RJ Owen

Apress®

The Truth About HTML5

ISBN-13 (pbk): 978-1-4302-6415-6

ISBN-13 (electronic): 978-1-4302-6416-3

President and Publisher: Paul Manning
Lead Editor: Ben Renow-Clarke
Technical Reviewer: Andrew Zack
Editorial Board: Steve Anglin, Mark Beckner, Ewan Buckingham, Gary Cornell, Louise Corrigan, Jim DeWolf, Jonathan Gennick, Jonathan Hassell, Robert Hutchinson, Michelle Lowman, James Markham, Matthew Moodie, Jeff Olson, Jeffrey Pepper, Douglas Pundick, Ben Renow-Clarke, Dominic Shakeshaft, Gwenan Spearing, Matt Wade, Steve Weiss
Coordinating Editor: Kevin Shea
Copy Editor: Kim Wimpsett
Compositor: SPi Global
Indexer: SPi Global
Artist: SPi Global
Cover Designer: Anna Ishchenko

Distributed to the book trade worldwide by Springer Science+Business Media New York, 233 Spring Street, 6th Floor, New York, NY 10013. Phone 1-800-SPRINGER, fax (201) 348-4505, e-mail orders-ny@springer-sbm.com, or visit www.springeronline.com. Apress Media, LLC is a California LLC and the sole member (owner) is Springer Science + Business Media Finance Inc (SSBM Finance Inc). SSBM Finance Inc is a Delaware corporation.

For information on translations, please e-mail rights@apress.com, or visit www.apress.com.

Apress and friends of ED books may be purchased in bulk for academic, corporate, or promotional use. eBook versions and licenses are also available for most titles. For more information, reference our Special Bulk Sales–eBook Licensing web page at www.apress.com/bulk-sales.

Any source code or other supplementary material referenced by the author in this text is available to readers at www.apress.com. For detailed information about how to locate your book's source code, go to www.apress.com/source-code/.

Contents at a Glance

Contents

About the Authors

Luke Stevens is a Sydney-based designer who cut his teeth with PageMill in the 90s, wrangled Content Management Systems in the 00s, and switched to web apps in the 10s. With a passion for design, some brief formal print design training, and more than a decade of insatiable curiosity about new web technology, he has built sites of all shapes and sizes for clients all over the world, usually with ExpressionEngine. Currently in-between client work he tweets nonsense @lukestevens and works on his web app at AnalyticsExplorer.com which he will, he swears, release in 2014.

RJ Owen is an experienced front-end developer who has worked in a variety of technologies on the Web for more than ten years. He is a frequent speaker at industry events such as SXSW and Adobe's Max conference. RJ started his career as a Flash developer before moving to the open Web and then to design and customer insight work, which he totally loves. When not working or writing, RJ spends time chasing his children or enjoying the mountains of Colorado, where he lives and works.

About the Technical Reviewer

Andrew Zack has been at the forefront of implementing successful Internet marketing strategies since 1996. He has authored a book and been a technical reviewer for numerous industry publications. Mr. Zack's industry expertise includes business development, IT project management, Internet marketing, SEO implementation, operational software, and web site development and coordination.

Foreword

HTML5 is a mess. It's also one of the most exciting technological advances perhaps ever (a big claim, especially for something I just described as a mess).

There are quite a few books, most of them excellent, on HTML5. Some cover the markup exclusively. Some cover markup and JavaScript APIs. Others still focus on a specific development challenge, such as games.

This book is a little different. Rather than simply looking at the *what* and *how* of HTML5 (though it does that as well), it endeavors to explain the *why* and *why* not of HTML5.

And it's a passionate, informed, opinionated critique of much of HTML5 to boot.

Along the way, you'll learn a great deal about HTML5 markup and additional HTML5 features such as the new audio and video elements, the Canvas element, the History API, and related features such as SVG.

But ideally, most of all you'll learn to think critically about HTML5 as a tool and adopt the good parts, for good reasons, and ignore the less than useful parts, for the right reasons as well.

Luke Stevens has written a book all web designers and developers who care about their code should read. So go ahead and read it!

John Allsopp
Author, Developing with Web Standards
Cofounder of Web Directions
Web evangelist

Introduction

Introduction From RJ

Hi. I'm RJ, your average HTML developer. I've been working with code since I was a kid and quickly gravitated to the instant gratification that comes from making beautiful things for computers, especially online.

I did the updates and revisions for the most recent version of this book, and I have to tell you, you are in for a wild ride. A year ago I was just like you—a person who hadn't read this book. I came into it thinking HTML5 was pretty neat. I had done a few "HTML5" sites, read a few blog posts, enjoyed the fancy logo, and maybe even bought the official HTML5 T-shirt (yeah, I did). I liked the new elements because they were, you know, semantic. I liked evolving beyond Flash. I liked (the idea of) SVG.

Wow, did I have a lot to learn. What follows from here is a journey into a strange and unbelievable world. If you're like I was, then very little of what comes next is going to be what you expect, and even less of it will seem reasonable. HTML5 is not what you think it is. Buckle up: Luke Stevens is taking us all to school, and between you and me he drives a little like a maniac.

Introduction From Luke

Hi. I'm Luke, your average, garden-variety web designer. I've been building web sites for more than a decade, use ExpressionEngine as my CMS, and have enjoyed both working in-house and full-time freelancing.

I thought it would be fun to write a short book about HTML5. I thought HTML5 would be simple. I thought writing about it would be straightforward. And I thought the respected voices in the design community would be telling everyone what it is (and what it isn't) simply and clearly, particularly with the plethora of other HTML5 books out there.

I was wrong.

Fortunately, this book (and I hope your experience as a reader!) is infinitely better for it. And I hope once you've read it you'll share my concern about the strange direction basic markup has taken and my excitement for the new HTML5 (and related) technologies that are coming soon to a browser near you. That includes Internet Explorer —Microsoft, finally, truly gets web standards.

What seemed impossible just a few years ago—a far-fetched, almost utopian ideal of *all* browser vendors, including Microsoft, competing tooth-and-nail to support bleeding-edge web standards—is now a reality. Innovation in web standards is happening at break-neck speed, and my hope is this book gets you up to speed not only with the fundamentals of HTML5 but with the broader picture of where the Web as a whole is heading, especially as we look toward a post-Flash future.

As you make your way through the following chapters, please keep in mind this book is as much of a *critique* as it is an explanation of HTML5. By taking a critical look at *why* things are the way they are, my hope is you save hours by not having to worry about things that don't matter (particularly when it comes to basic markup) and your eyes are opened to how the HTML5 sausage gets made. It may not always be pretty, but if you spend your days in the trenches building web sites, knowing *why* things are the way they are will help guide your design and development decisions in a very direct way.

That said, there's plenty of exciting technology in and around HTML5 too, so be sure not to miss the later chapters on graphics technologies like Canvas and SVG, the state of audio and video in HTML5, and the more developer-oriented HTML5 features including a new way of handling something as fundamental as a page request.

(Also note we will be focusing almost entirely on HTML5 as defined by the HTML5 spec, with the addition of SVG and a few other related initiatives such as Schema.org and WebGL. "HTML5" has become a buzzword that can mean everything from the HTML5 spec itself to CSS3 and modern JavaScript to just "cool and new and not Flash." We'll be mostly sticking with the features in the actual HTML5 specification.)

I love the web design community because it's filled with smart, excitable, curious, opinionated folk who will call you on your BS. This is an opinionated book, not a dry explanation of the technology, and I'll be stating my views pretty strongly. I look forward to you doing the same. Passionate, considered debate makes us all smarter.
So please, write it up on your blog, send me happy/sad/angry e-mails (luke@itsninja.com), talk to me on Twitter (@ lukestevens), or whatever you like.

I look forward to the discussion.

And now I'd like to ask a couple of favors.

First, if you enjoy my writing, then please tell your friends, colleagues, Twitter followers, blog readers, and pretty much anyone who will listen about this book. Like a lot of authors, I rely on readers like you to spread the word (and the links). If you can help me out by spreading the word about this book via good old-fashioned word of mouth, I'd *really* appreciate it. Thank you.

And second, if you use Google Analytics and want to get more out of it, I'd love you to check out my web app Analytics Explorer (http://analyticsexplorer.com). Analytics Explorer brings all the great data that Google Analytics buries to the surface through a simple, elegant interface, and combines it with great tips on improving your site. You can add your clients, send them nicely designed regular reports, and focus your work on improving metrics that matter, not just making the proverbial logo bigger. My hope is it will make your own design practice (and your client's sites) more productive and profitable. After all, all the HTML5 in the world won't help you if your conversion rates are lousy and your bounce rates are sky-high. (We'll return to this theme in the final chapter of this book when we look at Performance Based Design.) Check it out: http://analyticsexplorer.com.

CHAPTER 1

■ ■ ■

A Somewhat Sensationalized History of HTML5

We all know that HTML5 is the great hope for the Web—that's what everyone tells us, so it must be true. It's a beautiful shining Utopia where all citizens can browse in peace and harmony with pages loading smoothly and quickly, layouts looking the same across browsers, and not a plug-in in sight. That's what they'd have you believe, anyway. There's no doubt that HTML5 contains a lot of good, but it also contains a lot of... well, we'll get to that. It's time to learn the truth about HTML5.

How Architecture Astronauts and the W3C Tried to Kill HTML

Murder is always interesting, so let's start there.

As you may know, HTML has a strange and sordid past. Between 1989 and 1990, Tim Berners-Lee wrote the first specification for the HTML language along with the client and server software to make it go. By 1996 he helped form the World Wide Web Consortium (W3C) to take over maintaining the HTML specification with input from browser manufacturers. At this point HTML would be pretty recognizable to any modern developer, and things were looking up.

In 1997 the W3C published a Recommendation for HTML 4.0. And two years later it was more or less completed in the form of HTML 4.01. (Don't remember? Well, you were probably too busy worrying about the dreaded Y2K "bug" wiping out civilization.)

And that was pretty much it for plain old HTML.

So, what happened between HTML being "finished" in 1999 (in every sense of the word) and HTML5's emergence today?

A long, aborted march to "XMListan."

The W3C published the eXtensible Markup Language (XML) 1.0 specification in 1996 (`www.w3.org/TR/1998/REC-xml-19980210`), which it hoped would become a more flexible, machine-readable, stricter, and more extensible way to mark up documents and other data. And it was soon being used to do just that. But the W3C believed the *Web itself* would eventually move to XML.

One of the first baby steps toward making HTML a language machines as well as people could understand was XHTML—an XML formulation of HTML 4.

You Probably Use XML

XML may sound foreign, but if you own or even subscribe to a blog, then you're already using it. The RSS or Atom feed that blogs generate to syndicate their content is just one form of XML. If you look at the source of an Atom feed, you can see tags such as `<author>`, `<published>`, `<category>`, and `<summary>`. These are *specific tags that accurately describe the content they represent*. These tags aren't part of a formal XML schema, but rather defined for that Atom

1

format. This flexibility is just one example of the "extensible" part of XML that allows machines (parsers, RSS readers, and so on) to do interesting things with the content.

Now, imagine a world where we could describe our web pages in a similar way. That was the W3C's plan for the Web—that *all* the future content on the Web should be described in more accurate terms than just <div>s, <span>s, <p>s, and <h1>s. And with XML, we could do it.

HTML would still exist as a legacy format. But the future was XML, baby.

XHTML Is Born, But What Does It Mean?

So if HTML was the past and XML was the future, how would we get there? With the interim step of XHTML.

By reformulating HTML 4.0 to stick to XML's rules, XHTML was born. And in January 2000, having barely survived the Y2K apocalypse, the XHTML 1.0 spec was adopted as a W3C Recommendation (www.w3.org/TR/xhtml1/). We were on the road to XMListan.

In early 2002, Jeffrey Zeldman published the landmark XHTML article "Better Living Through XHTML" on A List Apart (www.alistapart.com/articles/betterliving/), describing XHTML as follows:

> *[T]he standard markup language for web documents and the successor to HTML 4. A mixture of classic (HTML) and cutting-edge (XML), this hybrid language looks and works much like HTML but is based on XML, the web's "super" markup language, and brings web pages many of XML's benefits, as enumerated by the Online Style Guide of the Branch Libraries of The New York Public Library.*

Those benefits enumerated on the New York Public Library web site (http://legacy.www.nypl.org/styleguide/xhtml/benefits.html) included this:

> *The web is moving to XML, a powerfully enabling technology. Writing well-formed, valid XHTML pages is the easiest way to begin this transition. All it takes is learning a few simple rules of XHTML markup.*

Web designers took heed of this call to begin the transition to XML via XHTML. In 2003 Dave Shea wrote a post called "Semantics and Bad Code" (www.mezzoblue.com/archives/2003/08/26/semantics_an/) where he said this:

> *The move from HTML to XML requires a huge shift in developer mindset. There are a lot of obstacles to overcome yet, not the least of which being solid browser support. We've only started down the road, and XHTML is how we'll get there.*

Shea's view was a popular one at the time and certainly reasonable given our faith in the experts in the W3C.

But we never made it to XMListan. The car ran out of gas, the wheels fell off, and the engine exploded about two blocks down the road.

Draconian Error Handling (Or: Why Don't I Just Punch You in the Face?)

Those of you building web sites back in the early '00s may remember how important it was to have a *valid* web page. People even put dinky little "Valid XHTML" badges on their sites to show off just how forward-thinking they were. (They now put equally silly HTML5 badges on blogs—and books.) Design nerds would even run *other people's* markup through the HTML validator and write a snarky blog post or e-mail if it failed. (Back then there was no Twitter to bitch publicly in 140 characters.)

Yes, having valid HTML is a good thing. But as web designers adopted XHTML, it became—in theory, if not practice—life or death. If you had so much as a single error in your XHTML, your browser would reach out and *punch you in the face.*

OK, Not Really. But Your Browser *Would* Punch You in the Face

Well, your browser would punch you in the face if you set up your server to tell the browser to adopt XML's strict XHTML parsing rules, as Mark Pilgrim described in 2003 (`www.xml.com/pub/a/2003/03/19/dive-into-xml.html`), which hardly anyone did. Internet Explorer, right up to and including version 8, didn't even support these strict XHTML parsing rules. (Ironically, IE9 now does, just as everyone stopped caring.)

Why didn't anyone do it? Because they didn't want to inflict the "draconian error handling" (`www.w3.org/html/wg/wiki/DraconianErrorHandling`) on their users (or themselves). And it really was draconian—one invalid character, such as & instead of &, would generate a fatal error that destroyed the entire page. And as a user, all you got was a hideous error message—no content, no nothing.

In light of this, the web standards community adopted the *theory* of XHTML without its harsh realities (or true XML nature), preferring to stick with the warm, cuddly, and vastly forgiving HTML parsing from the early days.

XHTML turned out to be a baby step toward a baby step. What should have been the first move toward a strict XML formulation of the Web, where we could use more descriptive (that is, semantic) tags, was just a step toward stricter, old-style HTML. It was two steps forward, one step back—back to the HTML the W3C had declared finished and was hoping to make obsolete.

XHTML Still Meant Better HTML

Nevertheless, XHTML gave the web standards community something to, well, standardize on. It allowed everyone to be a bit more serious, and dare I say *professional*, about the markup we were writing. Jeffrey Zeldman wrote this on his blog in 2009 (`www.zeldman.com/2009/07/07/in-defense-of-web-developers/`):

> *XHTML's introduction in 2000, and its emphasis on rules of construction, gave web standards evangelists like me a platform on which to hook a program of semantic markup replacing the bloated and unsustainable tag soup of the day. The web is better for this and always will be, and there is much still to do, as many people who create websites still have not heard the call.*

For much of the '00s, web sites built with web standards continued using XHTML. Designers got serious about separating presentation from content and tried to write more semantic markup. Using XHTML also triggered standards mode on the major browsers of the time. All good things.

But in the W3C's grander scheme of things, XHTML ultimately proved to be a bit of a stepping-stone to nowhere.

But the Crazy Had Only Just Begun

XHTML served a useful purpose for web standards—albeit not the one originally intended. But now we step into the mad, mad, mad world of XHTML 2.0.

While we were all happily using and advocating XHTML in web standards land (though some stuck to HTML 4.0), the W3C was working on XHTML 2.0. Sounds like a harmless update of the 1.0 spec, right?

It wasn't.

XHTML 2.0 was day zero for the Web. It wasn't backward compatible with HTML or even XHTML 1.0. It was a *whole new thang.*

And nothing was safe.

Among the list of sweeping changes, plain old forms would be replaced with fancy XML-style XForms. Even the <img> element was on the chopping block at one point, as the W3C re-envisioned the Web as a more XML-ified place.

In an April 2011 blog post on software development, Joel Spolsky described what he calls "Architecture Astronauts" (www.joelonsoftware.com/articles/fog0000000018.html):

> When you go too far up, abstraction-wise, you run out of oxygen. Sometimes smart thinkers just don't know when to stop, and they create these absurd, all-encompassing, high-level pictures of the universe that are all good and fine, but don't actually mean anything at all.
>
> These are the people I call Architecture Astronauts.

And XHTML 2.0 was a classic case of Architecture Astronauts at work.

Here's how Bruce Lawson, HTML5 evangelist for Opera and author of *Introducing HTML5* (New Riders, 2010), describes it (http://news.cnet.com/8301-17939_109-10281477-2.html):

> XHTML 2 was a beautiful specification of philosophical purity that had absolutely no resemblance to the real world.

As far as HTML was concerned, this is what the W3C—the custodians of the language that underpins much of our relationships, business, and government in the 21st century—worked on from 2002 to 2006 over eight drafts. Not only would it have broken backward compatibility, it would also have sent all the talk of "forward compatibility" and "future-proofing" in the web standards community up in smoke. (You can read more about XHTML 2.0 in Wikipedia: http://en.wikipedia.org/wiki/XHTML#XHTML_2.0.)

XHTML 2.0: Unloved and Alone

While the W3C toiled away on XHTML 2.0, what did web authors, standards advocates, and browser vendors think of it?

Not much.

There was zero interest in implementing it. Even members of the working group were deeply unhappy with it. (See Jeffrey Zeldman's thoughts on XHTML 2.0 in 2003 under "XHTML 2 and all that": www.zeldman.com/daily/0103b.shtml.)

What was dopey about XHTML 2.0 wasn't so much the spec itself (which would be fine if we could go back in time and rebuild the Web from scratch). It was the idea you could do something as revolutionary as breaking backward compatibility with millions of existing documents and create a whole new tier for the Web. But that was the path the W3C set itself on way back in 1998 (see it for yourself in "Shaping the Future of HTML" at www.w3.org/MarkUp/future/).

But what if the next evolution of HTML was just that—evolutionary rather than revolutionary? One that built on the world as it was and not some utopian world we could only hope for?

HTML5: A New Hope...We Hope

HTML5 began as a reaction to the W3C's descent into markup madness. The problems with the W3C's direction had not gone unnoticed.

In 2004, the so-called Web 2.0 movement took off in a big way, and web *applications* became a big deal. The Web was no longer just a collection of text and images on pages connected through links. It was becoming a platform for applications that could run anywhere, OS be damned.

Compared to the '80s and '90s, when your OS determined what applications you could use, running applications through a browser on any OS was a revolutionary idea.

No one really predicted this (certainly not the W3C), which isn't surprising when you think how bad we are at predicting the future in general. (Where *is* my flying car?) We're much better at reacting and evolving when the future arrives, which is what some people suggested we do with HTML.

In 2004, members representing Opera and Mozilla (with Apple "cheering [from] the sidelines," as Ian Hickson recalls: www.webstandards.org/2009/05/13/interview-with-ian-hickson-editor-of-the-html-5-specification/) presented an alternative to the W3C—a spec focused on web applications. (See the original "Position Paper" here: www.w3.org/2004/04/webapps-cdf-ws/papers/opera.html.)

The W3C Says Go to Hell

HTML needed to adapt to the future of web *applications*, rather than a utopian world of perfectly marked-up XML-ified web *pages*. So, this new group suggested an alternative direction for HTML based on backward compatibility: no more draconian error handling (the one-error-and-you're-dead problem of XHTML as XML), new features for web applications, and an open process, which was in stark contrast to the way the W3C operates.

Essentially, the group's philosophy was that HTML was here to stay, so we should concentrate on evolving it. (This may sound completely obvious now, but back then it wasn't a view shared by the W3C.)

Anyway, the group members pitched their ideas to the W3C, and the W3C told them to go to hell. (Actually, they lost by only two votes—11 to 8 against. But this *is* the somewhat *sensationalized* history of HTML5.) WHATWG was formed after a proposal from Mozilla and Opera on "Web Applications and Compound Documents" was voted down on June 2nd, 2004 (www.w3.org/2004/04/webapps-cdf-ws/papers/opera.html). Among the founding members of WHATWG were representatives from Apple, Mozilla, and Opera, including Hickson (http://en.wikipedia.org/wiki/WHATWG).

With the W3C being less than accommodating, those interested in evolving HTML and adding features for web applications, who were backed by (and worked for) the browser vendors, decided to press on and work outside the W3C. They formed the Web Hypertext Applications Technology Working Group (WHATWG) and set up shop at http://whatwg.org on June 4th, 2004.

The WHATWG Is Born

And so the WHATWG was born. Here's how Hickson explains it all (www.thechromesource.com/interview-html5-standards-author-ian-hickson/):

> So [after the W3C rejection] we opened a mailing list called the WHATWG to continue work on Web Forms 2.0 in public, and later that year started a new draft called Web Applications 1.0 into which we put many features aimed at writing Web apps, including a new version of HTML that we jokingly called HTML5, and a bunch of other features that later became Web Storage, Web Sockets, Server-Sent Events, and a variety of other specs. [...]
>
> Later, around 2006 or 2007, the W3C basically realized they had made a mistake, and they asked if they could work on HTML5 as well, so we renamed Web Applications 1.0 to HTML5, and the WHATWG and the W3C started working together. Web Forms 2.0 got merged into HTML5, and most of the bits of HTML5 that weren't really HTML got split out into separate specs.

It's ironic, isn't it? The establishment (the W3C) was the utopian revolutionary, and the rebel outsiders (the WHATWG) were fighting for incremental conservatism. Go figure.

It's a Whole New World

It's worth noting several points here:

- The W3C failed dramatically at maintaining HTML (which is kind of scary when you think about it).

- Web standards are incredibly haphazard. There was—and is—no unifying vision of "HTML5." It was just a bunch of separate specifications bundled up and given the name "HTML5," and those specifications came about only as a reaction to the W3C's failures.

- Big, bold ideas such as the march to XML for the Web—which had many people excited a decade ago—can fade to nothing. We should learn from this and retain some skepticism toward big, bold ideas, including some of the changes in HTML5.

- The balance of power now rests with the browser vendors.

In truth, the balance of power has *always* rested with the browser vendors. If they don't implement something, *by definition* it's a nonstarter. Hickson says this (www.webstandards.org/2009/05/13/interview-with-ian-hickson-editor-of-the-html-5-specification/):

> *The reality is that the browser vendors have the ultimate veto on everything in the spec, since if they don't implement it, the spec is nothing but a work of fiction. So they have a lot of influence—I don't want to be writing fiction, I want to be writing a spec that documents the actual behavior of browsers.*
>
> *Whether that's too much, I don't know. Does gravity have too much influence on objects on earth? It's just the way it is.*

Nevertheless, the fact an independent standards body—*our* independent standards body—failed miserably is more than a little concerning.

To HTML5 and Beyond!

To cut a long story short, the WHATWG kept working on its own vision of evolving HTML—the *only* vision of evolving HTML. And in 2006 Tim Berners-Lee, father of the World Wide Web and director of the W3C (read more about him here: http://en.wikipedia.org/wiki/Tim_Berners-Lee), sucked it up and announced the W3C would work with the WHATWG, saying this (http://dig.csail.mit.edu/breadcrumbs/node/166):

> *The attempt to get the world to switch to XML, including quotes around attribute values and slashes in empty tags and namespaces all at once didn't work.*

Berners-Lee left the door open to switching to XML by saying "all at once." But in reality it looks very much like "The attempt to get the world to switch to XML...didn't work."

And that's fine. We need big ideas and bold directions to try and work toward, and if they don't work out, so be it. Sometimes good ideas just don't happen.

With the WHATWG having so much momentum (and the backing of the browser vendors), the W3C had no choice *but* to work with the WHATWG on HTML5. In 2007 the W3C formed a group that worked with the WHATWG on developing HTML5. And in January 2008 the W3C released its first HTML5 Working Draft (www.w3.org/TR/2008/WD-html5-20080122/), adopting the work the WHATWG had been doing for several years.

HTML5 Is the New Black or Hotness or Something

By the late '00s web technologies were exciting again, and after years of stagnation and dead ends we finally reached a point where the bowels of innovation were loosened. (That's a horrible image—sorry.)

Starting in the early '10s and continuing to the present, things are looking even better. In fact, there continues to be a veritable Cambrian explosion of web technology taking place. Google, Mozilla, Apple, and Microsoft are competing to make the best *standards-compliant* browser (with new versions coming thick and fast—Google Chrome releases so quickly it's not even worth tracking its release schedule). There's a whole bunch of new and interesting technology around. And web developers, designers, software companies, and app developers are all interested in the new and shiny tech in and around HTML5.

To think browser makers—including Microsoft—are now trying to outcompete and even out-market each other with their *web standards support* is pretty incredible. It wasn't that long ago (late '90s) that we faced the threat of them all going their own nonstandard ways. Hats off to all involved.

Is HTML5 Hype, Substance, or Both?

But back to the HTML5 specification. Two questions:

1. What exactly *is* HTML5?

2. Who's in charge now that there's a (decidedly uneasy) working relationship between the establishment (the W3C) and the rebels (the WHATWG)?

Let's deal with what HTML5 *is* first. There's:

- HTML5, the all-encompassing marketing buzzword

- HTML5, the bit that's actually about HyperText Markup

- HTML5, the new functionality available through JavaScript for web applications

- HTML5, the behind-the-scenes stuff that's really important and documents a whole lot of stuff browsers actually do (but you're probably not interested in)

All this comes from a technical specification that runs for hundreds of pages.

For us web designers, HTML5 is currently a confusing mix of hype *and* substance, which we'll try to sort through in the coming chapters.

In many ways, HTML5 is, to put it bluntly, a mess. But it's the most ordered mess we've had in a long time. (For instance, a big part of HTML5 is written for browser vendors to ensure implementations are consistent and we can trust all browsers to do the same thing. And that's never been done before.)

Perhaps the biggest problem is everyone thinking that if HTML5 is cool, then *all* of it (at least according to the web design community) *must* be great, and we should adopt it post-haste without too much critical thought. And that's something I'm keen to dispel in the rest of the book because while HTML5 certainly has some great ideas, it's not as great as you may think, and without a lot of critical thought we're likely to wind up in a great deal of trouble.

Hixie or Bust

For a long time, both the WHATWG and W3C versions of the HTML5 spec (the differences between the two are minor) were edited by one person: Ian Hickson. In September 2012 the W3C introduced a larger team of editors to oversee what went into the actual HTML5 spec and what was divided into other specs, but it still largely pulls from the WHATWG specification, which is authored solely by Ian Hickson.

HTML is essentially in the hands of one man.

The W3C's working groups tried building consensus and got absolutely nowhere with HTML. It was closed but democratic. The WHATWG, on the other hand, has an open process but with an editor-has-the-final-say approach.

And that editor is Ian "Hixie" Hickson.

Hickson helped start the WHATWG when working for Opera and now works full-time for Google developing the HTML5 spec. Currently, he is the HTML5 (and now just "HTML") editor for *life*. Theoretically, the browser makers can veto him or kick him out at any time, but that seems highly unlikely. This has not gone unnoticed in the community and is (rightly, in my opinion) a cause of some concern.

It's a classic "glass half-full/glass half-empty" situation. If Hickson flat out refuses an idea (which is known to happen), then having a single person in charge may seem like utter madness. But for those who saw the W3C's democratic processes get nowhere with XHTML 2.0, having someone who can take the reins, push things along, and actually make decisions would seem wonderful.

Of course, this invariably polarizes people.

Here's John Gruber of Daring Fireball fame (`http://daringfireball.net/linked/2009/07/01/hickson-codecs`):

> *Let it be said that Ian Hickson is the Solomon of web standards; his summary of the situation is mind-bogglingly even-handed and fair-minded.*

And here's Kyle Weems, creator of the CSSquirrel comic, who has been following HTML5's development for several years (`http://twitter.com/#!/cssquirrel/status/58559284224589824`):

> *Also… why oh why is @hixie still the editor for any world-altering spec like HTML anymore? Ego doesn't even begin to describe his antics*

As you can see, Hickson has his fans and his detractors.

I imagine editing a spec the size of HTML5 for as long as he has, with all the controversy that surrounds it, would be a pretty thankless task. But Hickson seems to go about it in a cheerful, dispassionate way.

If there's one overarching theme here, it's this: pragmatism rules.

The W3C had the "pure" spec of XHTML 2.0 and failed—it wasn't pragmatic. It also had its rules, membership, and democratic processes but was mired in politics and failed (with HTML at least)—it wasn't pragmatic.

The WHATWG put an editor in charge, and while this approach terrified and/or infuriated some people (including me from time to time, as you'll soon see), it *was* pragmatic (as was its approach to the spec). It got things moving (and, more importantly, shipping). And as long as it remains pragmatic, it's probably how the WHATWG will stay.

XHTML 2.0 Is Dead and Everyone Is Happy

So, what happened to XHTML 2.0? It was pronounced dead after being taken off life support in 2009 (`www.w3.org/2009/06/xhtml-faq.html`). I hear the death of XHTML 2.0 will soon be fictionalized in an upcoming episode of *Law & Order: Web Standards Unit*.

And what about XHTML 1.0 and its various flavors? Considering it's essentially just HTML, it will keep working pretty much forever. (There's actually a continuing XML serialization of HTML5 called XHTML5, but the chance of you actually needing to use it is practically zero.)

HTML5 … er … HTML, wait … HTML.next?

To show how things have come full circle with the HTML spec, the WHATWG declared in January 2011 that its HTML5 spec would be a "living standard" and renamed it to just HTML. (See the announcement at `http://blog.whatwg.org/html-is-the-new-html5` and the rationale at `http://wiki.whatwg.org/wiki/FAQ#What_does_.22Living_Standard.22_mean.3F`.)

And what of the future of HTML? The WHATWG insists it—and particularly Hickson—will maintain the HTML spec as a "living standard" indefinitely, while the W3C is sticking with the snapshot process and is simultaneously wrapping up "HTML5" while working on the next version, previously called "HTML.next" and now titled "HTML5.1." (See some of the ideas here: `http://www.w3.org/wiki/HTML/next`.)

(A W3C member gave a personal presentation that captures the differing approaches to the future of HTML quite nicely: `www.w3.org/2010/11/TPAC/HTMLnext-perspectives.pdf`.)

Will the W3C come up with another pie-in-the-sky path to nowhere (echoing 1998's "Shaping the Future of HTML" workshop; `www.w3.org/MarkUp/future/`)? Will the W3C try to work with the WHATWG or fork HTML5 and do their own thing? Who knows. Some have been asking if the W3C should even exist.

Should We Just Kill Off the W3C Altogether or Embrace It?

In September 2011, a debate broke out about the purpose of the W3C, and three broad views emerged: reform, destroy, and embrace.

Before we get to those three views, let's consider why debate about the W3C is still continuing just as it seems to have its house in order, having adopted the WHATWG's successful HTML5 specification.

In short, it's because the world kept turning. The WHATWG began its work on what became HTML5 in the mid-2000s, and the details of HTML5 (and related specifications) are still being nutted out in the 2010s. Mobile is exploding, "apps" are taking us back to the platform-specific software world of the '90s, and standards development is still slow, even in this new wow-stuff-is-actually-happening environment we now enjoy.

Can the Web keep up in the face of resurgent, platform-specific app development? Has the W3C outlived its usefulness, or is it now finally back on track after years in the wilderness? Here are three perspectives, all from September 2011.

Reform

In "Things the W3C Should Stop Doing" (`http://infrequently.org/2011/09/things-the-w3c-should-stop-doing/`), Alex Russell, who works for Google on Chrome, argues the W3C needs to drop all its XML and enterprise stuff and refocus solely on the Web. Essentially, drastic reform can save the W3C from irrelevance.

> *The time has come for the W3C to grab the mantle of the web, shake off its self-doubt, and move to a place where doing good isn't measured by numbers of specs and activities, but by impact for web developers.*

Destroy

In "Web Technologies Need an Owner" (`http://joehewitt.com/2011/09/22/web-technologies-need-an-owner`), Joe Hewitt, who worked on early versions of Firefox, created Firebug, and was responsible for the iPhone Facebook app, argues the Web is just another platform but without anyone taking responsibility for it (unlike Windows, Android, and iOS).

> *Let's face facts: the Web will never be the dominant platform. There will forever be other important platforms competing for users' time. To thrive, HTML and company need what those other platforms have: a single source repository and a good owner to drive it. A standards body is not suited to perform this role. Browser vendors are innovating in some areas, but they are stalled by the standards process in so many areas that is impossible to create a platform with a coherent, unified vision the way Apple has with Cocoa or the way Python has with Guido.*

Therefore, we should destroy it, as Hewitt tweeted (`https://twitter.com/joehewitt/status/116292923288592384`):

> *[D]issolve the W3C, and run the web like an open source project. No more specs, just commits. Does Linux need a standards body?*

Embrace

Finally, in "The Web is a different problem" (`www.webdirections.org/blog/theweb-is-a-different-problem/`), John Allsopp, longstanding web evangelist, writer, and speaker, argues that while standards development certainly stalled in the '00s, we've seen an "explosion of innovation at the browser level" in the last few years, particularly with CSS3 and more modular specs, and are we really now going to throw the baby out with the bathwater?

> *So, to put it bluntly, I think the problem is overstated. We seem to have arrived at an approach that both enables the exploration and implementation of novel features in browsers, which are also widely adopted across browsers. [...]*

> *[But] the web is a different problem. It makes little if any sense to compare innovation of the web ecosystem with that of iOS, Android or other platforms. The web faces challenges far far greater (and has goals far more important). [...]*

> *So, rather than generally criticising the W3C, or going so far as calling for its dissolution, we should focus on how well in many ways it has done an almost impossible task—getting companies which are fierce commercial rivals to sit down, work together and agree on core technologies they will each, and all, implement, even while at the same time, these same competitors are involved in significant legal conflicts with one another.*

Whatever we may wish for, sheer inertia is likely to see the W3C maintain its role as the home of web standards development in the coming years (for better or worse), especially now that it has brought the WHATWG and HTML5 inside the W3C tent.

How Does New Stuff Get Added to HTML5 Now?

How will HTML5 evolve from here on out? How will the WHATWG implement new HTML features in its "living standard"? The WHATWG says new HTML features should first appear in browsers (experimentally at least) and *then* be codified into the spec, assuming there's a reasonable use case for them and the editor approves. (See the WHATWG FAQ for more: `http://wiki.whatwg.org/wiki/FAQ#Is_there_a_process_for_adding_new_features_to_a_specification.3F`.)

This means the HTML spec will capture features as they emerge, rather than dictate new features from scratch—a somewhat odd stance given the amount of innovation the WHATWG did in the HTML5 spec before *any* browser implementation.

How long will the WHATWG/W3C relationship last? Your guess is as good as mine. Hickson has been openly hostile to the W3C's process at times (`http://lists.w3.org/Archives/Public/www-archive/2012Jan/0032.html`), and his decisions and refusals continue to be a source of considerable friction on the W3C mailing lists.

At the end of the day, either party can dream up all the specs they like. What really matters is what the browser vendors choose to implement. As far as HTML is concerned, the WHATWG's extremely close relationship with the browser vendors means it'll probably be calling the shots for the foreseeable future.

WHATWG and W3C Diversions

In September 2012 the W3C introduced its own team of editors, deposing Hixie as the king supreme of HTML5, at least in theory. The W3C explained the decision as one made at Hickson's request in a blog post in April 2012 (http://lists.w3.org/Archives/Public/public-html/2012Apr/0204.html):

We have reached a point in the HTML WG where the W3C process and community expects to finalize the HTML 5 Recommendation-track specifications. For the last several years, Ian Hickson has been the editor of the HTML 5 spec. At the same time, we all recognize that work will begin on 'what will come after HTML 5.' As Ian is already working on proposals for this work, he has asked the chairs if someone else could volunteer to take the HTML 5 spec to REC. Today, we are announcing the following changes:

* W3C is starting a search for editors to begin the REC level work on HTML5 and HTML Canvas 2D Context. We anticipate this search will take 30 days.

* Anyone is welcome to contribute proposals that could be used as input for future products of the HTML WG, either based on the work of Community Groups, or based on proposal drafts created in an HTML WG Task Force or the HTML WG itself.

* Ian will continue editing the WHATWG HTML specification, which we anticipate will be one such proposal.

* Editors of Recommendation-Level specifications and authors of HTML.next proposals are encouraged to work together to avoid introducing contradictions, but are free to make their own changes directly.

* W3C has started the process of extending the W3C HTML WG charter to jump start the work on HTML.Next in parallel to completing the current Recommendation track work. Once the HTML WG is re-chartered then the W3C will review proposals for HTML.Next work, and seek additional editors or co-editors for HTML.Next work.

* As W3C proceeds with its work on follow-ons to HTML 5, W3C and the WHATWG plan to continue their partnership in developing the right features for the future web.

In July, the W3C's new editorial team was announced, and now in 2013 it's been expanded (with Ian Hickson still listed as a participating editor).

So, by the W3C's explanation, HTML5 needs to be standardized and set in stone. WHATWG is working on a living standard that will never be finished, so the W3C needed to break away, take a snap shot, and lock down HTML5. HTML development will continue as "HTML.next" (referred to as HTML5.1 by late 2013) and continue drawing inspiration and ideas from the WHATWG specification.

In September 2013 the W3C gave itself a new charter for the HTML5 spec that lasts through July 2015, specifying its license for distributing the HTML5 spec and redeclaring its intention to publish a formal and finished HTML5.0 specification in 2014 (www.w3.org/blog/news/archives/3253). None of this is mirrored by the WHATWG, though Hickson's involvement in both is intended to keep the two groups from diverging too far.

In the year since the W3C and WHATWG diverged, little has changed in the W3C spec. The W3C has focused on breaking the single, large HTML5 spec proposed by the WHATWG into several smaller specs. Isolated differences have emerged, but both the W3C and WHATWG, groups that are publishing specifications about how HTML5 *should* work, frequently affirm that nothing matters until the browsers implement a feature. Let me say that again: in 2013, the W3C and WHATWG are again working on different specifications, and both agree that only the browser makers' decisions really matter. See the following two URLs for more info:

```
http://html5doctor.com/interview-with-robin-berjon-html5-editor/
http://dev.w3.org/html5/decision-policy/html5-stabilization-plan.html
```

So, after all that, we're back in a familiar place. The W3C has a group of editors working on a spec, the WHATWG has an editor working on their spec, and the major browser companies are involved in both and implement whatever they think works best. There's more cooperation and commitment on all fronts this time, but it still feels eerily familiar. We're back to HTML.

That wraps up our somewhat sensationalized (and highly condensed) history of HTML5. Or HTML. Or... you get the idea.

TL;DR

In summary, the W3C tried to kill HTML and took us on a decade-long journey to nowhere; some people from browser vendors formed a group interested in web apps and evolving HTML's forms; they worked outside the W3C on what became HTML5; the W3C realized they were screwed and agreed to use their work; browser vendors are implementing it (or their existing implementations of certain features have been standardized); web standards have become a *Microsoft* marketing buzzword; hell has not frozen over.

What We'll Be Focusing On

HTML5 is a massive specification, filled with mind-numbing detail for browser vendors.

But that detail is actually the best thing about it. Removing the implementation ambiguities has led to more predictable behavior, which is good news for designers and developers alike. (Before that, browser vendors were looking over each other's shoulders to see how parts of the spec were interpreted.)

It's not sexy work but rather years of careful documentation and clarification by the WHATWG that we can all be grateful for.

The other parts of HTML5 very much reflect its origins as Web Applications 1.0 and Web Forms 2.0. We'll touch on the web app stuff in Chapter 12 and look at the web forms in Chapter 8.

As designers, the biggest point of interest are the changes and additions to the actual markup side of HTML. And that's what we'll focus on: semantics, forms, graphics, and audio/video.

We'll also touch on the new features for web apps in HTML5, which we'll hopefully see in our content management systems sooner rather than later.

Most importantly, though, we'll be looking at the *ideas* in markup and the practical—sometimes critical—dos and don'ts of HTML5 along the way.

Let's jump in and look at how we start a document in HTML5.

CHAPTER 2

■ ■ ■

The Truth About a Basic HTML5 Web Page

Let's start with the first line of a web page. It's now just this:

```
<!doctype html>
```

That's it. It's short, it's memorable, and it triggers standards mode in all major browsers (including IE6). It's also case insensitive. In HTML5 the opening `<html>` tag has also been simplified to `<html lang="en">`.

Browsers will cope without the `lang` attribute, but it's good practice to specify the page's primary language, especially for non-English pages. (See this helpful article on declaring languages in HTML5: `http://nimbupani.com/declaring-languages-in-html-5.html`.)

Next comes the `<head>` tag, which will contain our `<title>`, `<meta>`, CSS, and JavaScript tags as per usual. You don't actually need to specify `<head>` tags if you want to be ultra-minimal (see Bruce Lawson's minimal HTML5 document discussion here: `www.brucelawson.co.uk/2010/a-minimal-html5-document/`), but we will.

Inside our `<head>` tags we have this:

```
<meta charset="utf-8">
```

This specifies the character encoding for the page. Again, it's been reduced to the simplest form possible in HTML5. You should *always* specify this for security reasons (there's a technical discussion at `http://code.google.com/p/doctype-mirror/wiki/ArticleUtf7`), and it should come before the `<title>` tag.

```
<meta name="description" content="My HTML5 Website">
```

This hasn't changed. Google and other search engines sometimes use this tag in their search results pages, but not for rankings. (You can forget all about `<meta content="keywords">`, though. Search engines have been ignoring it for years. We'll look at markup and SEO in Chapter 6.)

For more on meta tags Google does understand, see `www.google.com/support/webmasters/bin/answer.py?answer=79812`.

The `<title>` tag hasn't changed

To link CSS and JavaScript files, we can just use this:

```
<link rel="stylesheet" href="styles.css">
```

and this:

```
<script src="myscript.js"></script>
```

There's no need to specify type="text/css" or type="text/javascript" anymore—the browsers assume it anyway.

We can start using these techniques now. There's no harm in them; they just make it simple enough to start writing our documents from memory. (The old techniques will continue to work, though—probably forever.)

So, a basic HTML5 page (with basic body content) looks like this:

```
<!doctype html>
<html lang="en">
<head>
    <meta charset="utf-8">
    <meta name="description" content="My HTML5 Website">
    <title>My HTML5 page</title>
    <link rel="stylesheet" href="mystyles.css">
    <script src="myscript.js"></script>
</head>

<body>
    <h1>My HTML5 Page</h1>
</body>
</html>
```

As you can see, it's pretty much what we're used to, just simpler.

Formatting Changes in HTML5

Here are a few things to note about how we write HTML in HTML5:

- **Quotes are optional.** You no longer need to quote attribute values, so you can write `<meta charset=utf-8>` or `<div class=myclass>` if you like. I prefer quoting values, but HTML5 leaves it up to you.

- **It's case-insensitive.** You can write your markup in upper or lowercase, or even in a mix like `<DiV ClAsS=VaLuE>` if you really hate your co-workers and/or feel nostalgic for YoUr WaCkY MySpAcE days.

- **Closing slashes are optional.** You no longer need to close stand-alone tags with a closing slash (for example, `<meta charset=utf-8 />`). As you probably guessed, this was a relic of the move to XML. Likewise, `<br>` and `<br />` are both perfectly valid—it's up to you.

If you're a stickler for XHTML's stricter syntax (always writing in lowercase, quoting attribute values, and closing stand-alone tags), you can keep doing it—it will always be happily supported.

What About an HTML5 Shim and CSS for the New Elements?

HTML5 introduces new elements such as `<nav>`, `<header>`, `<article>`, `<section>`, and so on. These sound fine in theory but are terrible in practice.

To support these elements in IE6–8, others suggest you include a small script that tells IE6–8 these elements exist and to use whatever styles you specify for them (it will leave them unstyled otherwise). I don't recommend using these new elements, so we don't need the HTML5 shim. (If you really want to use them, here's the code to do it: http://code.google.com/p/html5shiv/. But seriously, don't use the new elements. You'll thank me later.)

You also need to set the new elements to `display: block;`, as shown in this `HTML5doctor.com` boilerplate: `http://html5doctor.com/html-5-boilerplates/`. Again, don't use these elements. (You'll see why in the next two chapters.)

What About the HTML5 Boilerplate and Modernizr?

If you want an everything-and-the-kitchen-sink boilerplate for new HTML5 pages, check out `http://html5boilerplate.com/` and the markup documentation at `https://github.com/h5bp/html5-boilerplate`. (There's more documentation in the wiki.)

While I appreciate the effort put into the HTML5 Boilerplate, if you're just finding your way with HTML5, it's pretty intense. I prefer to start simple and work with my own bare-minimum approach. But if you prefer the start-with-everything-and-delete-what-you-don't-want approach, the HTML5 Boilerplate may be right up your alley.

Modernizr (`www.modernizr.com/`) is a handy script for detecting support for HTML5 and CSS3 features. (It doesn't *add* support; it only *detects* it.) It's become a staple for designers who live on the bleeding edge and experiment with new features, so if that's what you're interested in, check it out. (We'll talk more about Modernizer, and the merits of *feature* detection rather than *browser* detection, when we look at HTML5's web application features in Chapter 12.)

Well, that was easy. Almost *too* easy. Now let's take a big left turn into the proverbial ditch that is the new structural tags.

CHAPTER 3

■ ■ ■

The Truth About Structuring an HTML5 Page

One of the most common tasks web designers do is mark up page structure, which usually consists of a header, footer, navigation, sidebar, and content area. It's the sort of thing you can probably do blindfolded and handcuffed to your chair after being spun around for five minutes.

HTML5 introduces a handful of new elements to help us define the structure of a given web page, such as `<section>`, `<article>`, `<main>`, `<nav>`, `<aside>`, `<header>`, and `<footer>`.

We shouldn't use most of them. All but `<main>` were made up on a whim by (probably) *one guy* in 2004, and even *he* seems to have forgotten what their purpose is. `<main>` was made up later by a different guy, and all that the W3C and WHATWG agree on about it is that it doesn't do much of anything.

If that's all you needed to know, great. Keep using `<div>`s with meaningful class and ID names, and appropriate `<h1>`-`<h6>` headings. They'll be valid forever (more or less), and you're not missing out on anything.

However, I suggest using some non-HTML5 features when marking up documents, such as ARIA attributes for blind and sight-impaired users and such as microdata schemas (when appropriate) for search engine results. (We'll talk more about these in later chapters.)

Nevertheless, we'll tackle these new elements in depth because everyone gets them wrong. And we'll set the record straight on how they found their way into the spec and their real, intended purpose, which involves a radically different way of structuring your pages.

A Little Taste of Pain: The Sectioning Elements

First let's talk `<section>`, `<article>`, `<nav>`, `<aside>`, `<header>`, and `<footer>`—the so-called sectioning elements. (Missing from this list is `<main>`, which is not a sectioning element. We'll get to that later.) Here are just some of the problems these new structural elements introduce:

- They give terms web designers already use (such as header and footer) new uses, while claiming to be just doing what web designers are already doing.

- They introduce a new method of structuring documents that's vague, complicated, and unnecessary.

- They seriously hurt accessibility for some users (specifically those using IE6, IE7, and even IE8 with JavaScript switched off).

- They introduce broad, unclear, poorly defined use cases that will make web standards harder to learn (and harder to teach).

These are serious problems that hurt, rather than help, web standards. Markup should be lightweight, easy to learn, and easy to apply. It should *not* require mental gymnastics to try to work out what to use where.

But these new structural tags have created a strange, quasi-religious experience where you have to consult the high priests (the HTML5 gurus) for their interpretation of vague religious texts (the HTML5 spec) just to mark up a darn web page.

"But, but...these elements are in the official HTML5 spec! Surely there *must* be a good reason for them?" Read on...

Where Did These Elements Come From?

Quiz question: How were the sectioning elements added to the HTML5 spec?

a. Experts considered different use cases, weighed various options and alternatives, and after extensive consultation and careful deliberation included the most important ones.

b. The community of web developers and HTML authors (such as you and me) cried out for certain elements to enable particular functionality, and after much discussion, the community came up with a short list of necessary elements.

c. A scientific, research-based approach was taken, where markup patterns were studied "in the wild" and codified into a bunch of new elements.

d. Some markup wonks thought they'd be a good idea and threw them in the spec seven-plus years ago.

And the answer is...d.

"But I read in [insert HTML5 book of your choice here] that it was more like answer c. The WHATWG studied real-world usage of ID and class names, and that's how they came about!"

We'll get to that.

I was intrigued about who added the sectioning elements, when they added them, and why. So, I put those questions to HTML5 spec editor Ian Hickson, and here's his reply (reproduced with permission):

> *Me and other WHATWG contributors [added them], [in] 2004ish, because they were obvious elements to add after seeing how authors used HTML4. We later (late 2005 early 2006) did some objective research to find out what the top ten HTML classes were and it turned out that they basically exactly matched the elements we had added, which was convenient.*

You may have read about this "objective research" in other HTML5 books, in talks on HTML5, or in blog posts about these new elements. But almost everyone fudges the history. Sometimes they say the research came first—it didn't. Sometimes it's just implied the research came first, which is still a sin of omission.

(Actually, according to the research in question— https://developers.google.com/webmasters/state-of-the-web/2005/classes—the major finding was that around 90 percent of the billion pages sampled had no classes at all. If Hickson and the WHATWG truly followed the research here, they would have abolished classes altogether!)

So, if these elements didn't come about from research, where did they come from?

Exploring the dark recesses of the (thankfully public) WHATWG mailing list, I found Hickson first mentioning these elements in November 2004, when he discussed block-level elements listed on his whiteboard. (See http://lists.whatwg.org/htdig.cgi/whatwg-whatwg.org/2004-November/002329.html.)

In the same week he said "[W]hat I'm thinking of doing is [adding] section elements [that] would be: `<body><section><article><navigation> <sidebar>`." (You can see the full e-mail here: http://lists.whatwg.org/htdig.cgi/whatwg-whatwg.org/2004-November/002362.html.)

Of course, somewhere along the way `<navigation>` became `<nav>`, and `<sidebar>` became `<aside>`.

So, these new, major structural elements that everyone is trying to get their heads around were probably included because Hickson jotted them down on his whiteboard in 2004. They actually serve a much broader purpose for "sectioning" (which we'll get to shortly). But it's worth establishing how they wound up in the spec and how arbitrary they are.

In Chapter 1 we saw that XHTML 2.0 failed for being absurdly ambitious. In HTML5 we instead get a few semantic elements the editor drew on a whiteboard years ago on a whim, with some input from a handful of fellow WHATWG members of the time.

Who Cares?

"Well, who cares?" you may think. "If the research ultimately supported using these elements, then what's the big deal?"

The problem is Hickson was, in my view, being a bit cheeky when he said these new elements "exactly match the elements we…added." While they share the same *name* as elements commonly used, the spec describes their use in *very* different ways to what the web designers and authors would be familiar with. And for a standard these web designers and authors are supposed to use, that's a big problem.

What happens when you take terms people use, redefine how they should be used (and even give them multiple uses), and then tell those same people not to worry because the terms are exactly what they're already using? You put them on a one-way trip to confusion city.

The Contradiction at the Heart of HTML5's New Elements

HTML5 is supposedly about codifying what we're already doing, or "paving the cowpaths." When it comes to these new tags and marking up a basic template, they suggest you can just replace your current `<div>` structural tags with the new tags (for example, replace `<div id="header">` with `<header>`), and you're done.

That was certainly the implication in the December 2007 ALA article "A Preview of HTML 5" (`www.alistapart` `.com/articles/previewofhtml5`), z and the idea has been repeated in books and blog posts since, usually with a graphic like Figure 3-1.

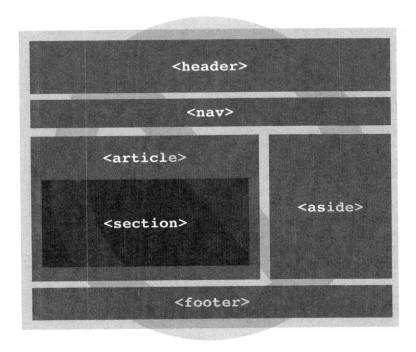

Figure 3-1. *This is wrong. Don't do this*

Swapping the new elements in for our old <div>s certainly looks easy, right? Nice, clean elements replacing a bunch of random <div>s, how lovely!

Unfortunately, there are few problems with this idea:

- **Too few elements.** There aren't enough new elements to do a reasonable 1:1 substitution. Believe me, <div>s aren't going anywhere. So, if you hear anyone say "Finally, I can get rid of my unsemantic <div>s!" you have my permission to pop a cap in their ass with a Nerf gun.

- **Not equal.** While elements are often presented as being equal, they're not. While the "sectioning" elements (<section>, <article>, <aside>, and <nav>) might work the same, the <header> and <footer> elements are intended to work *within* the sectioning elements. This can make a *huge* difference (as we'll see shortly with document outlines), but if you followed most of the discussions about these elements, you'd never know.

- **Not a replacement.** When you dig into the HTML5 spec, you discover these tags *as described in the spec* aren't really meant to be 1:1 replacements for existing tags at all. They're actually meant to be used for creating a new form of *document outline*. A document what? We'll explore this next.

These elements have other problems (they don't add anything for semantics or search engines), but we'll talk about them later when we take aim at those two zombie myths that just won't die. We'll also learn what "semantics" actually means in markup and what search engines really want.

Outline What?

If you try to understand HTML5's new structural elements without understanding *document outlines*, you'll think they're an arbitrary, oddly named bunch of elements with confusing use cases.

However, once you understand *document outlines*, you'll see they are in fact an arbitrary, oddly named bunch of elements with confusing use cases that also have an overarching purpose of questionable value.

Granted, this is esoteric stuff. But bear with me, and you'll see how HTML5 tries to slip in a radical new way of doing something as fundamental as structuring a web page. This isn't so much paving cowpaths as building a new bovine highway to nowhere.

What Is an Outline, and Why Should I Care?

An outline is a sort of hierarchical, bullet-point representation of a document.

We actually make an outline whenever we mark up a document and use heading elements. So, even if you've never heard of a "document outline," chances are you've already made one. Weird, huh?

The reason we never hear about them is because web designers never have to use them. They're mainly used by blind users as a *primary means of navigation*. When it comes to accessibility, outlines are a big deal. So, the best thing we can do to help blind and sight-impaired users navigate documents is provide a good heading structure when using web standards. (We'll explore this a bit more in Chapter 4).

HTML5 tries to radically change how we make these outlines...and maintain the existing way (well, kind of). This new approach to outlines is the reason the new HTML5 tags exist and why Hickson and the WHATWG were thinking about adding "section elements" in the first place.

How We Currently Create Outlines (Even Without Realizing It)

Let's back up a bit and look at our current outlines. In (X)HTML a document's hierarchical structure was dictated through heading levels, using the familiar <h1>-<h6> tags.

So, you might mark up your page like this (as a simplified example), with headings representing the "importance" of each part:

```
<h1>My Sweet Blog</h1>
    <h2>Latest Posts</h2>
        <h3>My Blog Post 1</h3>
        <h3>My Blog Post 2</h3>
        <h3>My Blog Post 3</h3>

    <h3>Blog Sidebar</h3>
        <h4>Blog Archives</h4>
        <h4>Popular posts</h4>
        <h4>Blog roll</h4>

    <h4>Blog Footer</h4>
        <h5>My delicious links</h5>
        <h5>My flickr photos</h5>
        <h5>My social networks</h5>
```

The hierarchy, or "outline," for the document looks like this:

```
1. My Cool Site
    1. Latest Posts
        1. My Blog Post 1
        2. My Blog Post 2
        3. My Blog Post 3
        4. Blog Sidebar
            1. Blog Archives
            2. Popular posts
            3. Blog roll
            4. Blog Footer
                1. My delicious links
                2. My flickr photos
                3. My social networks
```

Uh-oh. We have a problem. All our lower-level headings are "owned" by the heading above them. "Blog Sidebar" shouldn't be a heading under "Latest Posts"—it should start a new section.

If we changed the heading level of "Blog Sidebar" to <h2> (the same as "Latest Posts"), that would give us this:

```
1. My Cool Site
    1. Latest Posts
        1. My Blog Post 1
        2. My Blog Post 2
        3. My Blog Post 3
    2. Blog Sidebar
        1. Blog Archives
        2. Popular posts
```

But now we're no longer representing the importance of a heading. Instead, we're trying to build a logical structure using a limited set of tags (<h1>–<h6>), which have a habit of "owning" everything below them—even when they shouldn't.

Here's another example. Let's say we have a page that says this:

```
<h2>My HTML5 Book Review</h2>
   <h3>Likes</h3>
      <p>It explained some elements of HTML5 well.</p>
   <h3>Dislikes</h3>
      <p>The author had an annoying habit of writing silly, self-referential examples.</p>
   <div class="review-body">
   <p>I bought this HTML5 book for the low, low price of... </p>
   </div>
```

In this document outline, *the entire review* would fall under `<h3>Dislikes</h3>` because the heading "owns" everything underneath it, even though it should really fall under `<h2>My HTML5 Book Review</h2>`. Usually this *structural* problem goes unnoticed. The *visual* problem of having the review text appear under "Dislikes," however, would *not* go unnoticed, so for styling purposes we'd probably introduce a `<div>` so we could visually differentiate between the paragraphs under "Dislikes" and the review body text.

And indeed that's often how we structure our documents—we use `<div>`s to break them up into logical sections. But this has no bearing on the document outline in terms of accessibility; the outline is created by headings alone.

As you can see, headings are flawed for creating outlines. People often use heading levels to display different font sizes (with or without CSS) or to indicate arbitrary "importance" rather than structure. And sometimes they just cut and paste HTML straight into a new template.

When you consider all that, as well as the limitations of using `<h1>`-`<h6>`, it's obvious that most web pages don't have anything *like* a logical outline.

But they *do* have an outline, and using `<h1>`-`<h6>` *at all* gives blind and sight-impaired users a way to navigate our documents, which research shows is common for people using screen readers. (We'll touch on that research in a moment.) So, despite the flaws, for accessibility reasons we need to take headings-for-structure *more* seriously, not less.

(To see the outlines of any site—try your own!—check out the HTML5 Outliner for Google Chrome: https://chrome.google.com/webstore/detail/afoibpobokebhgfnknfndkgemglggomo.)

But what if there was a way to create arbitrary outlines *without* relying on headings? As it turns out, people have been thinking about this for years, if not decades.

"Sectioning" Is an Old Problem

The problem of headings, and how to structure a document, is a long-standing one. XHTML 2.0 proposed a solution in its first draft way back in 2002 (see www.w3.org/TR/2002/WD-xhtml2-20020805/), which involved nesting `<section>` tags and using a generic `<h>` element for headings.

This "sectioning" solution in XHTML 2.0 was initially mooted by Tim Berners-Lee as far back as 1991, as Jeremy Keith pointed out (see http://adactio.com/journal/1683/), when Berners-Lee said this:

> *I would in fact prefer, instead of <H1>, <H2> etc for headings [those come from the AAP DTD] to have a nestable <SECTION>..</SECTION> element, and a generic <H>..</H> which at any level within the sections would produce the required level of heading.*

Yep, a good two decades ago.

HTML5 tries to bring this concept of sectioning into mainstream HTML by following a similar path to XHTML 2.0, while also maintaining some backward compatibility. And the results are, shall we say, *mixed*.

But before we get to HTML5's implementation, let's look at just how important headings are for accessibility.

If We Care About Blind Users, We Should Care About Headings

As we mentioned, with HTML4 it's headings such as `<h2>Blog Sidebar</h2>` (rather than random `<div>`s such as `<div class="blogsidebar">Blog Sidebar</div>`) that create document outlines. And for blind users, these headings are important.

How important? A survey of more than 1,000 screen reader users found the following (where 80 percent of the people were blind and 16 percent were vision impaired):

> *The responses to this question provided one of the greatest surprises to us. It is clear that providing a heading structure is important to screen reader users with 76% always or often navigating by headings when they are available. Use of heading navigation increased with screen reader proficiency with them being used always or often by 90.7% of expert users, 79.3% of advanced users, 69.9% of intermediate users, and 55.4% of beginners.*

(You can see the full results here: `http://webaim.org/projects/screenreadersurvey/#headings`.)

Were you aware of that? I wasn't, and I've been using `<h1>`-`<h6>` willy-nilly for years. I imagine most web designers have some vague idea that `<h1>`-`<h6>` tags are important but not how crucial they are for blind users.

So, we had an established, straightforward, easy-to-implement way of providing outlines for blind and sight-impaired users. That is, until we hit HTML5.

HTML5's "Improved" Outlining Was Dead Before It Ever Shipped

We've established what a document outline is (a bullet-point, table-of-contents style representation of the page), and we've established how they are currently created (with `<h1>`-`<h6>` elements).

Here, in a nutshell, is how HTML5 proposes to create document outlines:

- Each bullet point in the outline, or "section," is defined using one of the four "sectioning" elements (`<section>`, `<article>`, `<nav>`, and `<aside>`) and not the `<h1>`-`<h6>` elements. The intent here is to solve the limitations of `<h1>`-`<h6>`. (We'll explore each of these new elements in the next chapter.)

- There's no generic `<h>` element, as per XHTML 2.0. But in pure HTML5, it's suggested we could just use `<h1>` everywhere as a generic heading element. In fact, *any* heading element in HTML5 will be treated as a generic heading, with its level determined by how deeply it's nested in sectioning elements.

- But there's no such thing as "pure" HTML5, so we need to maintain backward compatibility. Therefore, we should still use `<h1>`-`<h6>` in a logical fashion, which means maintaining *two* somewhat different document outlines in the one document.

That's the general idea. Here's how the spec puts it (`www.whatwg.org/specs/web-apps/current-work/multipage/sections.html#headings-and-sections`):

> *Sections may contain headings of any rank, but authors are strongly encouraged to either use only h1 elements, or to use elements of the appropriate rank for the section's nesting level.*

Please don't use `<h1>` elements everywhere!

In my view, everyone (Hickson in the spec and in public comments, standards advocates in the community, and designers and authors in general) has made a complete hash of communicating this.

This poor communication has meant that designers and developers have been using these HTML5 elements with no understanding of the outlines they have been creating. These elements were supposed to bring about better logical document outlines. Instead, given the haphazard way they've been implemented, they've created HTML5-style document outlines that are even *more* broken than the `<h1>`-`<h6>` outlines they were intended to replace.

HTML5's version of outlining was effectively dead before anyone understood it, much less implemented it properly.

And here's the irony: this approach, which *may* theoretically deliver accessibility benefits in the future (no one knows when, or even if, screen readers will use these outlines), is destroying the page styles for a small group of IE users *now*. So, it's already doing harm yet has no clear future benefit. (We'll look at this more in the next chapter.)

We'll still explore these new HTML5 elements in Chapter 4, but mostly so you can understand just how broken they are. (Remember, the cool HTML5 stuff comes in the later chapters.)

Sneaking in Big Ideas Leads to Dead Ideas

The first problem with this new approach to outlining is the idea that HTML5 is just "paving the cowpaths" and codifying existing practice.

Clearly, introducing a whole new way of structuring documents, however poorly communicated, is not "paving the cowpaths."

You can't then turn around and tell authors and designers, "This is what you've always done!" But Hickson has done just that, saying the new elements are just intended to save common class names. Here are just a couple of examples.

In 2009, Hickson said this (http://lists.w3.org/Archives/Public/public-html/2009Aug/0717.html):

> *They are, more or less, filling the most common requests from Web developers based on what the most common class="" attribute values are. Their main purpose is to simplify authoring and styling.*

And in 2012, he said this (http://lists.whatwg.org/pipermail/whatwg-whatwg.org/2012-January/034506.html):

> *Mostly these new elements make authoring a bit easier.*

So, if HTML5 is going to introduce a big new idea, it needs to communicate that big new idea. Instead, it appears Hickson doesn't remember, or can't be bothered arguing for, the big idea of sectioning he and the WHATWG added to the spec.

HTML5 advocates (as well as the spec itself) need to communicate the purpose of the new elements properly or abolish them.

As it is now, they're just inflicting nonsense on the web design community.

Let me give you an example. The spec says <header> and <footer> elements define areas *within a section* but do not define sections themselves and so won't show up in a document outline. This is something most people get wrong, including those teaching HTML5 through books and blogs, whose examples often show <header> being on par with <section>. The spec also says <header> and <footer> can be used multiple times per page (once per section, for example), but you would never pick that up from most HTML5 resources out there.

These may seem like pedantic, wonkish points. But they illustrate something very serious—the community is trying to implement HTML5 markup in a way that doesn't have much relation to the actual HTML5 spec. It's a weird in-between state of markup limbo that has inadvertently appeared because that's what everyone *assumed* these elements should be used for.

We Forked the Spec

In a sense, the community has forked HTML5, as far as markup goes. That's a big problem. There's the "common (but incorrect) understanding" fork of HTML5, and there's the actual HTML5 spec. But following the "common understanding" and replacing visual areas in our templates with elements that "sound about right" has no benefit for anyone. We just create a weird, broken outline while misusing the new elements. And with so many broken HTML5 outlines there, outlining as a concept is pretty much dead on arrival.

The Exception Is <main> (Sort Of)

So, as you can see, <section>, <article>, <nav>, <aside>, <header>, and <footer> are all something of a misleading disaster. They don't mean what most people think they mean, and they can't be used in the way most people assume they should be used. They weren't created from empirical research or paving cowpaths; they were dreamed up in a dark room and then poorly implemented.

But one structural element in HTML5 does follow the intended path: the <main> element. <main> was added to the W3C spec in 2012 because of the work of Steve Faulkner, who claims to have spoken to "as many implementors..., developers, authors, and users as [he] could" before proposing the spec (http://html5doctor.com/the-main-element/). And he's right: many people were clamoring for a structural element to represent the main content area, including the first edition of this book. Steve did his research and submitted his proposal, and it was accepted.

According to the W3C spec, the <main> element is specifically intended to represent the main content area of a page. In this sense, it is semantic. It's specifically not a sectioning element, so it has no bearing on the page's outline and doesn't get wrapped into the outline mess. It's for styling and providing a logical hook for ARIA accessibility. It means what it says and does what it means; it makes sense.

Unfortunately, <main> is the exception and not the rule, and it's not widely implemented yet. Hickson resisted a <main> element for years, accepting it only after W3C put it in its spec, saying this (http://twitter.com/#!/Hixie/status/8922228541):

> [A]nything that _isn't_ in <header>, <footer>, <aside>, or <nav> is by definition <content>, so we don't need an explicit element.

Hickson eventually accepted <main> under duress, but the WHATWG's definition of the element differs from W3C's and lists it as a meaningless hook for styling. The W3C includes restrictions on when and how <main> can be used; WHATWG does not. W3C sees <main> as an important tag with meaning; WHATWG has grudgingly accepted its existence and little more.

Adoption of <main> has been slow. At the time of this writing, it is supported in Chrome and Firefox but not IE, Opera, or Safari. The only thing everyone in the HTML5 community agrees on is that the browser implementors ultimately decide what is and isn't real. So far, <main> is only half-real.

We'll get into specific implementations for <main> in the next chapter; for now, just remember that it's different from the other elements, was invented for sensible reasons, but isn't consistently implemented by browser manufacturers and isn't fully accepted by WHATWG. It started with the best of intentions, makes a lot of sense, but hasn't broken out yet.

How Should We Structure an HTML5 Page?

All this may seem a bit confusing at the moment, so let's take a step back and look at the general rules of structuring a page in HTML5 (such as they are!), as described in the spec:

- We are supposed to use <section>, <article>, <nav>, or <aside> to create a new *section* in the *outline* (that is, a new bullet point in the document outline). You can see what your outline looks like with the HTML5 Outliner plug-in for Chrome: https://chrome.google.com/webstore/detail/afoibpobokebhgfnknfndkgemglggomo. And yes, the terminology here is clumsy—having multiple elements, including <section>, create a section in the document outline is quite confusing!

- We use <header> or <footer> *within each section* to demarcate the header or footer *of that section*. That section can be anything from the root <body> section down to an individual comment. (An individual comment is supposed to be an <article>, as we'll see in Chapter 4, which would create a section in the document outline.)

We use heading elements (<h1>-<h6>) to give each section a title in the outline and provide backward compatibility. (As I'm writing this, there's no meaningful support for HTML5 outlines anywhere and doesn't seem to be any on the horizon. So "backward" compatibility may actually be "compatibility for the foreseeable future.")

You might think you can just replace all your <div>s with <section>s and create an outline. However, <section>s aren't to be used in cases where you need only a styling hook, so in a true HTML5 document you'll still have plenty of <div>s. In fact, a "correct" HTML5 document would have the following:

- A bunch of <section>, <article>, <nav>, and <aside> tags to create the outline

- A bunch of <div>s for styling

- Redundant use of <h1>-<h6> tags to duplicate the outline as best as possible (this is what screen readers will actually use)

- A <main> for your main content area

- A redundant <div> for the main content area, or JavaScript to tell noncompliant browsers how to handle <main>

- A healthy sprinkling of redundant <header> and <footer> tags within each section that don't do anything.

Simplifying authoring? With two means of structuring a page, two outlines to maintain, and a bunch of redundant tags to add?

I don't think so. And that's before we even consider styling our headings.

Styling Headings HTML5-Style Is Kind of Insane

Let's imagine a pure HTML5 future where we can use <h1> everywhere as a generic heading element, as per the spec's suggestion, and we use the new sectioning elements to create the outline. That is, if we use a <h1> three sections deep, it's essentially an <h3>.

Let's say we want to style this three-sections-deep <h1> as though it was a <h3>. How are we going to pick it out? And can you imagine picking <h1> out everywhere through the cascade to give it a different style for different levels, given four elements can create a section and can be used in any combination? You wouldn't be able to sleep.

Nicole Sullivan touched on the madness that ensues when you try to style HTML5-style <h1> elements through the cascade in the appropriately titled blog post "Don't Style Headings Using HTML5 Sections" (www.stubbornella.org/content/2011/09/06/style-headings-using-html5-sections/) and gave this simplified example:

```
h1{font-size: 36px}
section h1{font-size: 28px}
section section h1{font-size: 22px}
section section section h1{font-size: 18px}
section section section section h1{font-size: 16px}
section section section section section h1{font-size: 14px}
section section section section section section h1{font-size: 13px}
section section section section section section section h1{font-size: 11px}
```

That, however, is the *vastly simplified* version, as Sullivan points out. The true madness sets in when you have to style all your (say) six-levels-deep headlines that may be nested in any combination of <section>, <article>, <aside>, or <nav>. For comedy value, see what such a style sheet would look like here: https://github.com/cboone/hypsometric-css/blob/master/html5/html5-defaults.css#L426. It's utterly insane.

The only option then is to fall back on class names for headings, but avoiding class names when authoring is the very "problem" the WHATWG was trying to solve.

And do you think our clients and colleagues who happily create and edit web pages will ever understand the nuances of sectioning their articles correctly? I doubt it.

No wonder people are confused.

Oh, and to top it all off, the styling of your <nav> (and any other new HTML5 elements) may blow up for ~1 percent of users. (We'll touch on this again soon.)

This is the way of HTML5. And it's a mess.

Not surprisingly, even the most experienced web authors get bogged down in the HTML5 outline quagmire. Read about Roger Johansson's experience here, for example: www.456bereastreet.com/archive/201103/html5_sectioning_elements_headings_and_document_outlines/.

This Is Not Inconsequential: People Have to Teach This Stuff

"OK, maybe the markup wonks got it wrong on this one. Maybe these tags are mostly redundant. So, no one uses them, or they don't do it quite correctly. Who cares, Mister Markup Pedant?"

The thing is, introducing these new elements—and concepts such as arbitrary outlining—into the official HTML5 spec means people *actually have to teach this stuff*. (Heck, some designers even teach their kids this stuff; see Cameron Moll's cool HTML5 whiteboard magnets, for example: http://cameronmoll.tumblr.com/post/10688505696/html5-whiteboard-magnets.)

This is bad for web standards. It makes even basic HTML hard to teach, hard to learn, and hard to implement, and for what? Structuring a web page should be the least of our worries—not a huge distraction for a generation of students and professionals alike.

(A note to those teaching web standards: if you really hate your students, ask them to explain the difference between <article>, <section>, and <main>.)

Where Does This Leave Us?

Hickson and the WHATWG's intentions are good. Theoretically, using these tags could improve accessibility even without considering outlining. (For example, screen readers could skip past the <nav> tag to get straight to the content.) But the vendors making screen readers have shown little interest in HTML5 to date. And there is already support for better alternatives, which we'll look at next.

So, we don't need HTML5's new elements for accessibility. In fact, we should avoid them for the harm they cause another subset of users.

People will still use these tags, mostly because they want to "do the right thing" in the hope the Standards Fairy will leave small change and/or an Apple product under their pillow. But it's just a waste of productive time that could be better spent on more important things.

Remember, what ends up in the spec is often just the idea of a few (or even one) interested, smart, ordinary people from (as of writing) seven-plus years ago. And chances are even they don't remember why they wanted it. So, I think we're allowed to disagree about what's best and pick and choose what we implement.

But what happens to accessibility? Do we just leave visually impaired users with the status quo? No, because fortunately there's a better alternative.

A Sane Approach to Structural Markup for Accessibility

There's a way to add helpers for the blind and visually impaired in our markup *without* wading into the mire of HTML5's new structural elements—ARIA roles.

Actually, it's WAI-ARIA, which stands for "Accessibility People Apparently Don't Do Catchy Acronyms." Or, as sticklers for accuracy may tell you, it's "Web Accessibility Initiative: Accessible Rich Internet Applications." (We'll just call it ARIA.)

It's not part of the HTML5 spec. Instead, it's a separate (and gigantic) W3C spec that's compatible with HTML5, HTML 4, and XHTML 1.*x*.

The secret to ARIA is the role attribute, which can be added to an element like this:

```
<div role="myariarole">
```

The full ARIA spec is big. Really big. (See it here: www.w3.org/TR/wai-aria/.) But we'll be looking at a small subset called *landmarks* (see www.w3.org/TR/wai-aria/roles#landmark_roles).

As an example, here are the four main areas of a simple page:

- Header

- Main content

- Sidebar

- Footer

And here's how we'd mark it up using ARIA:

```
<div role="banner"></div>
   <div role="main"></div>
   <div role="complementary"></div>
<div role="contentinfo"></div>
```

Easy.

We'll touch on the roles we can use when we discuss HTML5 elements and recap in Chapter 4.

ARIA Benefits

ARIA roles have several benefits over HTML5 (or previous HTML versions):

- The roles generally reflect how web authors structure pages. (For example, the header, or "banner," is for the stuff at the top of the page, not for every section on the page, as in HTML5.)

- The roles keep our markup relatively clean because we can use the role attribute as a styling hook for IE7 and newer with attribute selectors, such as div[role="banner"] {border:10px pink;}. (If you need to support IE6 users, you can also include redundant classes.)

- They work right now in screen readers that support ARIA landmarks, such as JAWS version 10 screen reader, NVDA 2010.1, and VoiceOver on iPhone IOS4+. (See www.paciellogroup.com/blog/2010/10/using-waiaria-landmark-roles/ for more information.)

- They don't blow up styling for IE6-8 users with JavaScript off like the new HTML5 elements do.

This technique can help blind users now, doesn't hurt web standards, and doesn't require getting your head around a second way of sectioning your document.

We'll look at the appropriate ARIA landmarks to use as we go through the new HTML5 elements in the next chapter.

Layout Recommendations

Before we finish this chapter, let me recap how I think we should mark up pages in the age of HTML5:

- We *should not* use the new tags. (But we'll look at them next, as well as the ARIA landmarks we should use.)

- We *should* take headings more seriously, given how much blind and sight-impaired users rely on them.

- We *should* use ARIA landmarks for accessibility.

- We *should* otherwise use <div>s with semantic class names or IDs like we've always done. (If you want to scream "BUT THEY'RE NOT SEMANTIC!" make sure you read Chapter 5 on semantics.)

CHAPTER 4

The Truth About HTML5's Structural Elements

What have we done so far?

- We've established the broad (and somewhat obscure) concept that HTML5's structural elements are trying to improve—mostly outlining, which is currently done implicitly with heading tags.

- We've established what an outline is for—to help screen readers, which rely heavily on document headings.

- We've also touched on a better way to help blind users get around our pages with ARIA landmarks.

Let's now look at what the HTML5 specs (both W3C and WHATWG) say about these new individual elements, starting with . . .

<header>

You need to know two things about <header>:

- It doesn't actually do anything.

- Its intended use isn't quite what you think it is.

The <header> element is a good example where a commonly used term has a new meaning in HTML5, while still being used to "pave the cowpaths." You probably use <div id="header"> all the time, so calling it <header> will make it easier to read if nothing else, right? Well, here's one of HTML5's everyone-uses-it-so-let's-change-the-meaning-anyway moments. Here's what the spec says:

The header element represents a group of introductory or navigational aids.

Note: A header element is intended to usually contain the section's heading (an h1–h6 element or an hgroup element), but this is not required. The header element can also be used to wrap a section's table of contents, a search form, or any relevant logos.

The note is instructive—the intended purpose of <header> is to contain a *section's heading*. Remember, sections are created with one of four sectioning elements (article, section, nav, aside) and generate a document outline in HTML5. The <header> element is meant to work *within* sectioning elements. It doesn't create a section on its own (despite how it's often visually represented as another sectioning element), and it doesn't add to the document outline.

Think of <header> as something that wraps the heading of a section, which can be anything from the topmost section of a document, such as the heading inside the <body> tag (that is, the logo and all that "header" stuff we normally consider a header), right down to the header of a comment.

Really, It Doesn't Do Anything

All the <header> element does is say "This is the header of a given section." The trouble is, while that's what your markup might say, at the moment none of the browsers or user agents are listening.

And according to Hickson, *they probably never will be*. Hickson's openly said that these new tags are simply meant to make styling easier and shouldn't ever impact document flow (see Hickson's comment in "Conclusion: R.I.P. HTML5 Structural Tags" later in this chapter). So, this element doesn't do anything now and probably won't do anything in the future. It's the semantic equivalent of a tree falling in a forest with no one around to hear it.

Given the <header> element doesn't modify or add to the document outline, the *actual* heading you see as a bullet point in the document outline (for example, "My Great Blog") is still set by an <h1>–<h6> element. The <header> tags just wrap those heading elements, along with any other header-y stuff, such as a date. So, you could do something like this:

```
<header>
<h1>My blog post</h1>
<p>Published on...</p>
</header>
```

How Can Screen Readers Use <header> When It's Everywhere?

You may think screen readers could skip the <header> element and go straight to the content. But there's no way we (or the user agents) can be sure the first <header> in a document is the main page header. If your markup is in a nonstandard order (the content appears first, followed by the header, footer, and sidebar), the document could have many <header>s, none of which we'd call a typical "header." And so we're back to square one in dealing with the "overall" header for a page.

ARIA Alternative: Banner

Fortunately for blind users, there's an alternative. The ARIA landmark banner demarcates the "header" as we currently know it. Here's how the ARIA spec defines the banner landmark (www.w3.org/TR/wai-aria/roles#banner):

> *A region that contains mostly site-oriented content, rather than page-specific content.*

> *Site-oriented c.ically includes things such as the logo or identity of the site sponsor, and site-specific search tool. A banner usually appears at the top of the page and typically spans the full width.*

It should appear only once per document so screen readers can jump straight there and be fairly sure what it is—which is exactly what we're after.

Recommendation

The `<header>` element is too broad (and too pointless) to be useful. Instead, use the more specific ARIA `role="banner"` on the appropriate element (with a redundant "banner" class for IE6 if need be) for the traditional "header" of a page.

`<nav>`

Here's the spec:

> *The nav element represents a section of a page that links to other pages or to parts within the page: a section with navigation links.*

> *Not all groups of links on a page need to be in a nav element—only sections that consist of major navigation blocks are appropriate for the nav element. In particular, it is common for footers to have a short list of links to various pages of a site, such as the terms of service, the home page, and a copyright page. The footer element alone is sufficient for such cases, without a nav element.*

The `<nav>` element *does* create a new section in your outline and benefits from the following:

- Being somewhat self-explanatory

- Having a seemingly useful purpose

The idea is if we mark up our navigation with the `<nav>` tag, blind people can bypass it and go straight to the content and then jump straight to the navigation links when they want to go somewhere else.

That's a win for accessibility, right?

Good Intentions; Accessibility Disaster

Despite these good intentions, doing it for one minority can potentially screw up the navigation for another: IE 6, 7, and 8 users with JavaScript disabled.

Because of the way IE6–8 handles "unknown" elements, these users won't get any CSS for this element. It could affect one in a hundred users—a higher percentage than people who use screen readers—making the whole idea of using this element somewhat moot for the short to medium term. (This is a problem for all HTML5 elements, which we'll discuss later in this chapter.) Many modern frameworks attempt to work around this by using JavaScript to downgrade the markup to something the user's browser can handle, but that won't work for users with older browsers and JavaScript turned off. Since the new tags won't work in these older browsers at all, there's no way for them to accomplish the only thing Hickson said they're designed for: making the page accessible.

ARIA Alternative: Navigation

Fortunately, we can use the ARIA landmark `navigation` instead by including `role="navigation"` on the appropriate `<div>` (or `<ul>`) to make our navigation more accessible without hurting accessibility for others. The ARIA spec defines the navigation landmark (www.w3.org/TR/wai-aria/roles#navigation) as follows:

> *A collection of navigational elements (usually links) for navigating the document or related documents.*

Recommendation

Use role="navigation". Consider the <nav> element harmful until only a small number of IE8 users are left. (This effectively means Windows XP users because IE8 is the last browser they'll get. We may be waiting a while).

<section> and <article>

These sound the same (everyone gets them confused), but they have different supposed uses. We'll look at each one separately first and then compare the two. Please try to refrain from throwing inanimate objects or small animals while trying to get your head around them.

<section>

Here's the spec:

> *The section element represents a generic section of a document or application. A section, in this context, is a thematic grouping of content, typically with a heading.*
>
> *Examples of sections would be chapters, the various tabbed pages in a tabbed dialog box, or the numbered sections of a thesis. A Web site's home page could be split into sections for an introduction, news items, and contact information.*
>
> *Note: Authors are encouraged to use the article element instead of the section element when it would make sense to syndicate the contents of the element.*
>
> *Note: The section element is not a generic container element. When an element is needed for styling purposes or as a convenience for scripting, authors are encouraged to use the div element instead. A general rule is that the section element is appropriate only if the element's contents would be listed explicitly in the document's outline.*

Let's try to make sense of this. The <section> element is supposed to represent a generic section in a document. So, if this chapter were a web page, we could break it up into chunks with <section> tags. It can also represent different areas of a home page, from news items to contact information. But it shouldn't be used as a generic container element for styling—that requires a <div>.

It also shouldn't be used for the page's content area (and neither should <article>), but we'll get to that in a moment when we discuss the missing <content> element.

Sections == Outlines

Again, the key to understanding <section> is understanding document outlining and the concept of sectioning a document. The spec mentions this (read the last sentence of the second note), but that's not a lot to go on when <section> is the main workhorse for creating a document's outline. As a rule of thumb, as far as creating an outline goes, if it's not an <article>, <nav>, or <aside>, it's probably a <section>.

This is also why you shouldn't use <section> for generic containers to style. If you just throw them in so you can style an area *without* thinking about your outline, you'll get an illogical, broken outline that defeats the whole point of using <section>. It's a common mistake and shows just how poorly they've been explained in the spec, advocated by the experts, and understood by the community (not that I blame the community).

Russian Dolls

Don't forget: you can nest sections (whether created by a <section>, <article>, <nav>, or <aside>). And as we saw in Chapter 3, in pure HTML5 land this determines the true heading level for an <h1>-<h6> element, not the level of the heading you use. In HTML5, the user agent (in theory) just sees them all as generic heading elements when inside a section.

So, we could use <h1>s everywhere, and the user agent would figure out whether they were nested as <h1> or <h101>. However, for screen readers (now, and probably long into the future), we'll need to use <h1>-<h6> headings appropriately, no matter what flavor of HTML we use.

Recommendation

If you want to create outlines the HTML5 way, you'll be mostly relying on <section>s. It took more than 20 years for the element to make it into the spec (recall Tim Berners-Lee's comment in the previous chapter), and it will probably take another 20 years before people understand it correctly.

There's no ARIA equivalent.

<article>

You might think an "article" is like "a newspaper article." Well, shame on you for thinking a new HTML5 element would have an intuitive meaning. Here, it's more like "an article of clothing." Yep, it's another "semantic" term with an unintuitive meaning.

Here's the spec:

> *The article element represents a self-contained composition in a document, page, application, or site and that is, in principle, independently distributable or reusable, e.g. in syndication. This could be a forum post, a magazine or newspaper article, a blog entry, a user-submitted comment, an interactive widget or gadget, or any other independent item of content.*

> *When article elements are nested, the inner article elements represent articles that are in principle related to the contents of the outer article. For instance, a blog entry on a site that accepts user-submitted comments could represent the comments as article elements nested within the article element for the blog entry.*

And here's Hickson on the WHATWG mailing list in early 2012 (http://lists.whatwg.org/pipermail/whatwg-whatwg.org/2012-January/034506.html):

> *<article> covers a wide range of semantics:*
> *-forum posts*
> *-newspaper articles*
> *-magazine articles*
> *-books*
> *-blog posts*
> *-comment on a forum post*
> *-comment on a newspaper article*
> *-comment on a magazine article*
> *-comment on a blog post*
> *-an embeddable interactive widget*
> *-a post with a photograph on a social network*

-a comment on a photograph on a social network
-a specification
-an e-mail
-a reply to an e-mail

In HTML4, a paragraph is a paragraph is a paragraph. In HTML5, an "article" is a forum post is a blog comment is a widget is an actual article. If an element has such broad meaning, how can it be more "semantic"? It's like deciding to call knives, forks, spoons, plates, and televisions all "forks."

This isn't paving the cowpaths.

Again, it's best understood in terms of outlines. The `<article>` element is for creating a section when you don't want to use `<section>`, which is usually when you're wrapping some chunk of content (or "interactive widget," as the case may be).

The spec talks about how an `<article>` could be syndicated as a self-contained element, but how and why this would ever happen is unclear (use RSS!). It's a solution looking for a problem.

Specifications Should Specify

The main problem with `<article>` is it's open to interpretation ("What does 'in principle' mean? Reusable?"). Specifications fail when they leave things up to you to work out. The whole point of a specification is to *specify* exactly what you should do. But here it's open to interpretation, has no clear benefit, and repeats existing functionality (it's `<section>` with a different name).

Nesting <article> for Articles and Comments

You can also nest `<article>`s within `<article>`s when the content is related. The spec suggests blog comments be wrapped in `<article>` tags and then nested in an overall `<article>` for the blog entry. This is the "fork and spoon are all forks" problem. If you have `<article class="post">` and `<article class="comment">`, then article just becomes a more verbose form of `<div>`.

Why not just add a `<comment>` element and at least have basic markup for the standard article-followed-by-comments pattern that just about every blog and publication on the Web uses? Wouldn't that be paving the cowpaths? Not according to Ian Hickson, who injects his own idiosyncratic view on the semantics of the issue: that there is no difference between an article and a comment (http://lists.whatwg.org/pipermail/whatwg-whatwg.org/2012-January/034506.html):

> I think it's anachronistic to consider that the utterances of the site owner are in some way distinct from the utterances of the site readers. What makes them different?
>
> On the contrary, on the Web there _is_ no difference. An article is just a comment that has been hoisted to a more prominent position.

The irony of defining at least one of the differences between these "utterances" and then declaring there is no difference was apparently lost on Hickson.

Of course, this also flies in the face of the oft-stated goal that these elements are mostly to help authors maintain their documents. If ever there was a case where a pattern of markup has emerged—an article, followed by comments—this is it. Yet Hickson, acting as both player and referee, won't budge, asserts his own peculiar philosophical view that all "comment" is equal, and that's that. We're left with nesting `<article>`s in HTML5, and content on the Web, it seems, will be `<article>`s all the way down.

Search Engines Don't Need <article>

Some may think `<article>` could help search engines, but they don't need a tag to know where your content is. Their entire existence relies on them being able to find your content without that sort of help. Even if `<article>` were used widely, how would they know through markup alone whether `<article>` meant blog post, forum post, interactive widget, comment, or whatever? It's too broad to be useful for SEO even if they *did* care what tags you used (which for the most part they don't).

(We'll discuss this more in Chapter 6 when we look at HTML5 and SEO.)

<article> Is Not for the "Main" Part

And `<article>` isn't for denoting the content area of the page. It's worth mentioning that when Hickson dreamed up `<article>`, there *was* no main content element, and he argued vehemently against it. `<main>` wasn't a thing, and `<article>` certainly wasn't `<main>`.

Recommendation

Should you use this? I wouldn't. Instead, I'd put it in the guilty-of-being-useless-until-proven-otherwise category. If a pragmatic benefit appears, go nuts. Until then, pass.

Like `<section>`, there's no ARIA equivalent.

So, What's the Difference Between <article> and <section>?

Here are some things you need to know:

- Articles can be nested within articles.

- Articles can be broken up by section.

- A section can be broken up into articles, which can in turn have individual sections.

- People are terrible at using markup consistently.

Guess what? Apart from the handful of markup über-nerds, anyone who actually uses these elements (and I'd be surprised if anyone does) will just create a huge mess. But hey, maybe I'm wrong.

Personally, I'd rather take a rusty potato peeler to my pinky finger than debate the virtues of `<section>` vs. `<article>`. The very fact there's a debate at all demonstrates a failure in the spec. If you have to debate an element when implementing it, you lose.

Yet thousands of words about this fine distinction have been spilled on blog posts (for example, Bruce Lawson's take: `www.brucelawson.co.uk/2010/html5-articles-and-sections-whats-the-difference/`) and comment threads.

One would have hoped the absurdity of the situation would have dawned on the community when we're left making well-intentioned but otherwise ridiculous *flow charts* just to decide which HTML5 element to use (see `http://html5doctor.com/downloads/h5d-sectioning-flowchart.png`). Alas, it appears it has not. And all this because a WHATWG member or three decided to throw these additional `<section>` flavors into the Web Applications 1.0 spec in 2004.

OK, we've ripped off the Band-Aid and survived the most painful part of HTML5's new elements. But there's still some sticky residue that will sting a bit coming off, so let's look at the last two sectioning elements.

\<aside\>

Question: What do you call a pull quote, parenthetical information, and a sidebar?

If you said, "a pull quote, parenthetical information, and a sidebar," you lose—buh-bow. You call them an "aside." Obvious, huh? Here's the spec:

> *The aside element represents a section of a page that consists of content that is tangentially related to the content around the aside element, and which could be considered separate from that content. Such sections are often represented as sidebars in printed typography.*
>
> *The element can be used for typographical effects like pull quotes or sidebars, for advertising, for groups of nav elements, and for other content that is considered separate from the main content of the page.*

It's hardly obvious why a pull quote, advertising, or a blog's navigation elements (complete with \<section\>s for a blog roll and archive—that's the use cases in the spec) should be called the same thing. But in the bizarro-world of HTML5 structural semantics, they are, and you can happily ignore them.

An Aside Creates an Outline Section in Weird Places

An aside *does* create a section in a document outline, which makes it all the more strange given its broad use cases. (Why should a pull quote be its own section?)

If it was just for a sidebar, or even called \<sidebar\> (as it originally was), that might make sense, but it's not, and it doesn't.

ARIA Alternative: Complementary

The ARIA landmark alternative in this case is complementary, which the ARIA spec describes as (www.w3.org/TR/wai-aria/roles#complementary):

> *A supporting section of the document, designed to be complementary to the main content at a similar level in the DOM hierarchy, but remains meaningful when separated from the main content.*
>
> *There are various types of content that would appropriately have this role. For example, in the case of a portal, this may include but not be limited to show times, current weather, related articles, or stocks to watch. The complementary role indicates that contained content is relevant to the main content. If the complementary content is completely separable main content, it may be appropriate to use a more general role.*

Recommendation

Use role="complementary" on the appropriate \<div\> (or other element) for the sidebar in your template (and anywhere else that's appropriate).

\<footer\>

Remember how \<header\> seemed obvious but wasn't? Well, it's the same deal with \<footer\>. It sounds like it should just be the main footer, but in fact it can mean the footer for any given section. Here's the HTML5 spec:

> *The footer element represents a footer for its nearest ancestor sectioning content or sectioning root element. A footer typically contains information about its section such as who wrote it, links to related documents, copyright data, and the like.*

Contact information for the author or editor of a section belongs in an address element, possibly itself inside a footer.

Footers don't necessarily have to appear at the end of a section, though they usually do.

Footers, like headers, are something you use within a section—they don't create a section in their own right. Again, this is confusing because in the examples in HTML5 books and blog posts the footer appears to be a distinct *visual* section in a template of equal importance to an `<article>` or `<aside>`, when in fact it doesn't appear in the document outline at all. It simply describes part of the parent section, wherever (and however frequently) that section may occur.

Footer Doesn't Do Anything Either

Like `<header>`, `<footer>` doesn't actually do anything. In fact, `<footer>` doesn't even have to go at the end of an element. The spec gives an example in the `<article>` section where the metadata of a comment (comment author and timestamp) is wrapped in a `<footer>` and placed at the—wait for it—*top* of the comment. Apparently the element wasn't confusing enough.

Again, no cowpath paving here. I certainly didn't hear a thousand web designers crying out for a `<footer>` element for every section on a page. Did you?

Fat Footer? Good Luck!

What if you have a trendy "fat footer" with a bunch of links and other information in it? Well, if it's a whole chunk of content, it should be a section, so you'd use one of the sectioning elements—`<nav>`, `<section>`, or even `<aside>`.

But, just to keep things interesting, you *can* wrap that sectioning element in `<footer>` tags. So, `<footer>` can both demarcate content *within* a section in a document outline *and* wrap other sections in the document outline and yet still not create a section in its own right.

Clear as mud, huh? I don't understand why it's that way, and I doubt most web designers will either. I've seen Japanese game shows that make more sense than these elements.

Can I 'ave a Footer, Guv'na?

Proposals for a `<footer>` element have been around for a long time. When it was discussed in 2002—about a decade ago—in regard to XHTML 2.0 on the W3C public mailing list, people soon began criticizing it (see http://lists.w3.org/Archives/Public/www-html/2002Aug/0257.html) saying it wouldn't provide any tangible benefit. A decade later that criticism still seems valid.

ARIA Alternative: contentinfo

Again, as far as accessibility goes, ARIA to the rescue. Its contentinfo landmark reflects the content of traditional footers (in other words, the bit at the bottom of the page with a few links and some fine print) without a presentational name. The ARIA spec describes it as follows (www.w3.org/TR/wai-aria/roles#contentinfo):

A large perceivable region that contains information about the parent document.

Examples of information included in this region of the page are copyrights and links to privacy statements.

Unlike `<footer>`, it should be used only once per document.

Recommendation

We can use `<div role="contentinfo">` once for the page footer. We can also keep using `<div id="footer">` (or whatever you like) with `role="navigation"` if there's substantial navigation elements there.

<main>

As we saw in Chapter 3, the `<main>` tag took some work to get added to the spec. Hickson thought it wasn't necessary, probably because it represented the only real cowpath that anyone wanted him to pave and because it made sense to ordinary web developers. He thought you only needed to mark up things that *weren't* content, and then the rest would, obviously, be content by default.

Luckily, saner heads prevailed. The W3C added `<main>` to its spec for HTML5.1 and then back to HTML5. Hickson begrudgingly took it into the WHATWG spec but decided he'd define it differently. That's right: the only element that ought to be simple and self-explanatory is the one that can't be agreed upon.

Here's how the W3C defines `<main>` (`www.w3.org/html/wg/drafts/html/master/grouping-content.html#the-main-element`):

> The main element represents the **main content** of the body of a document or application. The main content area consists of content that is directly related to or expands upon the central topic of a document or central functionality of an application.

> The main element is not sectioning content and has no effect on the document outline.

> The main content area of a document includes content that is unique to that document and excludes content that is repeated across a set of documents such as site navigation links, copyright information, site logos and banners and search forms (unless the document or applications main function is that of a search form).

> User agents that support keyboard navigation of content are strongly encouraged to provide a method to navigate to the main element and once navigated to, ensure the next element in the focus order is the first focusable element within the main element. This will provide a simple method for keyboard users to bypass blocks of content such as navigation links.

> Authors must not include more than one main element in a document.

> Authors must not include the main element as a descendant of an article, aside, footer, header or nav element.

> The main element is not suitable for use to identify the main content areas of sub sections of a document or application. The simplest solution is to not mark up the main content of a sub section at all, and just leave it as implicit, but an author could use a grouping content or sectioning content element as appropriate.

> Authors are advised to use ARIA role="main" attribute on the main element until user agents implement the required role mapping.

That seems pretty straightforward, right? `<main>` represents the main content area. You can have only one. It's not part of the outline madness, and it should be properly mapped to the ARIA role main. That seems pretty great, right?

Here's the WHATWG definition of `<main>`:

The main element can be used as a container for the dominant contents of another element. It represents its children.

The main element is distinct from the section and article elements in that the main element does not contribute to the document outline.

That's right—`<main>` "represents its children." Note also everything Hickson leaves out: according to the WHATWG spec, you can have more than one `<main>` element (defying the semantic definition of the word *main* in English), you can nest "main" elements ("you're the main of the main of the main of the main!"), and at the end of the day it doesn't actually mean anything; it just "represents its children."

At least the specifications do agree on two things: first, that `<main>` isn't part of the outlining mess that makes the other structural elements so confusing, and second, it's the dominant content area. That's nice, but these differences in browser standards are starting to make HTML5 feel a lot more like the fractured controversial world of competing standards and noncompliant browsers it was supposed to save us from.

Mainly Useless Controversy

As you can see, there's some disagreement about the way that `<main>` should be implemented, but the best part is none of that matters because `<main>` fails for the same base set of reasons the other sectional elements do: it's not supported by older browsers, and it's bad for accessibility.

Beyond that, Opera, Safari, and IE have all yet to implement `<main>` at the time of this writing. Even if accessibility or older browser support isn't high on your list, a large portion of the Internet can't make use of the `<main>` tag.

Remember that both the W3C and WHATWG always seem to agree on one central tenant for HTML5: the browser manufacturers ultimately decide what's really real. Right now, `<main>` is still mostly a work of fiction.

ARIA Alternative: main

Fortunately there's yet another ARIA landmark we can use instead, which is simply `main`. It does what we want it to do and serves the people we're trying to help—blind users.

Here's how the ARIA spec defines `main` (www.w3.org/TR/wai-aria/roles#main):

This marks the content that is directly related to or expands upon the central topic of the document. The main role is a non-obtrusive alternative for "skip to main content" links, where the navigation option to go to the main content (or other landmarks) is provided by the user agent through a dialog or by assistive technologies.

Recommendation

Use `<div role="main">` once for the main content area of your page.

Other ARIA Landmarks

Here are a few more ARIA landmarks that may prove useful when marking up your pages:

- `application` for software widgets on a page
- `form` for forms, except search, which gets…
- `search` for the search form on the page

And they go along with the others we've looked at:

- banner for the overall header

- navigation for, you guessed it, navigation

- complementary for sidebars

- contentinfo for the footer

- main for the main content area

(Note that banner, main, and contentinfo should be used only once per document.)

For more about these landmarks, see Steve Faulkner's excellent comparison to HTML5 elements: www.paciellogroup.com/blog/2010/10/using-wai-aria-landmark-roles/.

For more on ARIA in general, see Mozilla's ARIA documentation: https://developer.mozilla.org/en/aria.

A Funny Thing Happened…Graceful Degradation Died and JavaScript Became Mandatory

In the past couple of chapters I've made several references to the harm these elements can inflict on another small subset of users. For some users, these tags will blow up your page in IE6, 7, or 8 with JavaScript off (which, because of personal choice and over-zealous security concerns, is more common than you may think).

The problem is how IE 6–8 handle "generic" elements. To IE6–8, a generic tag is *anything* it doesn't recognize, whether it's a completely made-up element like <mymadeuptag> or HTML5's <nav>. Given that IE6–8 doesn't recognize generic elements at all, we can't style them without using a sprinkling of JavaScript to tell IE6–8 they exist.

This clever JavaScript workaround was discovered by Sjoerd Visscher and popularized by Remy Sharp in 2009 (see http://html5doctor.com/how-to-get-html5-working-in-ie-and-firefox-2/). Now that we can use a tiny bit of JavaScript to tell IE6–8 that particular elements *do* exist, we can happily style away…or can we?

No, we can't.

But could we?

No.

(For the record, the JavaScript in question is available here: http://code.google.com/p/html5shiv/. You also need to tell other browsers to treat the new elements as block-level elements with CSS, as we touched on in Chapter 2.)

Now we hit the big snag, specifically, the IE 6–8 users with JavaScript off who don't get the HTML5 fix.

Hang on. Does anyone actually turn JavaScript off these days? Is there any data available that could give us some insight here?

Yes, there is.

Yahoo's JavaScript Research

In 2010, Yahoo published the results of research it did into this very question—how many visitors *do* have JavaScript disabled? It turns out that 2.06 percent of visitors hitting Yahoo's U.S. websites (which includes significant non-U.S. traffic) had JavaScript disabled, as did 1.29 percent in the United Kingdom, 1.46 percent in France, and 1.28 percent in Spain. (Brazil was an outlier with just 0.26 percent.)

So, unless you're designing for Brazilian users, you still need to consider users who've disabled JavaScript.

You can read about the research at http://developer.yahoo.com/blogs/ydn/posts/2010/10/how-many-users-have-javascript-disabled/ and about the methodology at http://developer.yahoo.com/blogs/ydn/posts/2010/10/followup-how-many-users-havejavascript-disabled/ on Yahoo's YDN blog.

Let's assume the high end of 2 percent for traffic to the major U.S. sites and that IE 6-8 users make up about 50 percent of your audience. That's at least one in every hundred users with IE6-8 and JavaScript off. Even if it were one in a *thousand*, that's still at least one person every day for a moderately busy site.

So, what happens to these visitors if you use HTML5 structural tags?

If you use `<section>` tags (or any other tags) around existing markup and *don't* style them, nothing. You can still create outlines that way if you really want, as long as you remember that blind users still rely on headings to get around your page.

But if you use `<header>`, `<footer>`, `<nav>`, `<aside>`, or `<article>` (or `<section>` for that matter) where you *are* likely to style them, Bad Things™ happen.

Specifically, users with JavaScript disabled will see your site styled normally, *except* for the parts of the design that use the HTML5 elements. When those elements wrap our navigation, header(s), sidebar(s), or article(s), we have problems. The elements—unlike the rest of the page—won't have our CSS styling applied and so may break in some pretty serious ways.

Here's What Happens...

For example, Figure 4-1 shows the main navigation of one of my client's sites, firstly with `<div id="nav">` wrapping a normal `<ul>` list of links.

Figure 4-1. *The site's navigation with JavaScript disabled and no HTML5 elements*

And Figure 4-2 shows it with a `<nav>` element instead in IE7 with JavaScript disabled.

Figure 4-2. *The same navigation using HTML5's <nav> element with JavaScript disabled*

Not cool, right? And that's just one element. Imagine if the header and sidebar broke down in similar ways, while the body, wrapper, and content areas were all still being styled. Not pretty.

What to Do? Oh, XP...

The safest thing would be to not give IE6-8 users with JavaScript disabled styles at all (which you could do with conditional statements and writing the style element with JavaScript). But I don't advocate this—you're still unnecessarily ruining their experience.

What about IE9 and beyond? Thankfully, IE9 recognizes most HTML5 elements and has improved how it handles generic elements.

Maybe IE9 will replace IE6, 7, and 8 sooner rather than later, and we can forget about these non-JavaScript users. Ah, what a world that would be. Unfortunately, Windows XP users will never get IE9—IE8 is the end of the road for them. As long as XP is around, we'll have IE8 visitors whose experience is unnecessarily ruined because of these elements.

And no one should have to put up with that.

Elements such as <nav> are supposed to (theoretically) help the visually impaired. But when we *do* use <nav> (for example) as intended in the spec and as taught by HTML5 advocates as a replacement for existing structural markup, we unnecessarily hurt another minority in a very real way.

Uh…Web Design Community, What Happened?

One of the most unfortunate parts of the HTML5 hype in web design circles is how quickly we've forgotten the tradition of graceful degradation. Sure, we don't want to be limited to the lowest common denominator. But IE8 is a long way from that, and there's a big difference between giving those with JavaScript disabled something simpler and giving them something that's just plain broken.

Let me make it clear I don't have a problem if *your specific web site* requires JavaScript (and will break in varying ways for IE6–8 with JavaScript off); that's the informed choice you've made. But I do have a problem with this issue being almost entirely ignored in the web design community and the unnecessary pain unwitting designers and developers are inflicting on a small group of users.

This issue alone sinks the usefulness of these new elements, so I recommend sticking to <div>s for structure and ARIA roles for accessibility. ARIA roles can at least help solve accessibility problems for one minority without blowing up the site for another.

Hickson himself says this (http://lists.whatwg.org/pipermail/whatwg-whatwg.org/2012-January/034506.html):

> *Naturally, if you are happy with* <div class="..."> *for everything, you are welcome to continue doing that.*

Conclusion: R.I.P. HTML5 Structural Elements

Perhaps the strangest thing about all this is I'm not sure Ian Hickson—the spec editor—is clear about what these new elements are for or what other experts think they'll be used for.

In a conversation with Opera's Bruce Lawson (coauthor of *Introducing HTML5* [New Riders, 2010]) on the WHATWG list in 2009 (http://lists.whatwg.org/htdig.cgi/whatwg-whatwg.org/2009-March/018888.html), Lawson said this (emphasis added):

> *After all, I know of no user agents that can use time, section, footer, datagrid etc **but we mostly expect there to be soon**.*

> *And here's what Hickson said in reply:*

> *I don't. Most of the new elements are just meant to make styling easier, so that we don't have to use classes.*

That's Hickson's offhand rationale—not having to use classes—which we touched on earlier. But it's interesting he has no expectation that user agents will do anything with them. Has he given up on sectioning and outlining? Isn't that why these elements were added in the first place (remember they predated any research), and isn't that how Hickson described them in the specification he edits?

These elements are a lost cause. If people *do* just use these elements instead of classes (which they already are), they won't be considering the outline they'll be creating. They may assume <header> creates a section (it doesn't), or they may use <aside> for a pull quote (and in doing so create a new section), which will mean a lot of broken HTML5 outlines.

So, user agents (screen readers in particular) will have very little incentive to ever use HTML5 outlines—the main point of most of these elements—as a means of navigation, given they'll be (and already are) an utter mess.

It's sad, isn't it? Tim Berners-Lee's 1991 wish for sectioning finally makes it into a shipping HTML spec (after the aborted XHTML 2.0 project), only to be misunderstood and abused two decades later.

And that's *before* we take into account the ambiguities in the spec, the fact they blow up styling in IE6–8, and how much they complicate *marking up a basic HTML page,* of all things.

Here's John Allsopp, author of *Developing with Web Standards* (New Riders, 2009), commenting on the new elements on Jeffrey Zeldman's blog (`www.zeldman.com/2009/07/13/html-5-nav-ambiguityresolved/#comment-44699`):

> *As I waded deeply through the specification, narrowing my focus largely to the new "semantic" elements like section, article, header, footer, and so on I discovered many ambiguities, poorly explained features, and baffling containment rules [as well as] near byzantine complexities.*
>
> *[…]many of the legitimate criticisms of XHTML2 can also be laid at the door of HTML 5. And many others, particular to the specification itself can also be leveled. It's time to address these.*

We have the solution for marking up our pages:

- Use `<div>`s with classes (and/or a single `id` that occurs once on the page if you want).
- Use appropriate heading elements.
- Add ARIA landmarks as appropriate, and you're done.

That's how easy it is to describe structural markup now.

That simplicity has been lost in HTML5.

That's the bad news. The good news is, all is not lost. We can take this opportunity to try using headings in a better structural way to make blind and sight-impaired users' lives a bit easier (and start using ARIA landmarks for the same reason). And we can be happy knowing that our existing HTML structural markup techniques will serve us just fine for many years to come.

Let me finish by saying that despite my criticism of this particular part of the HTML5 spec (and the web design community's advocacy for it), if it weren't for Ian Hickson and the WHATWG, there wouldn't *be* an "HTML5" as we know it today—we could still be waiting for the W3C to get its act together. It's not my aim to bite the hand that feeds…just nibble on its fingers a little bit.

Next, let's talk about the *S* word: semantics.

CHAPTER 5

The Truth About HTML5 Micro-semantics and Schema.org

A common claim made about the new HTML5 structural elements is that they are "more semantic."

In my view, the new elements are "more semantic" in the same way fruit-flavored candy bars are "more nutritious"—not at all.

Nevertheless, the question of semantics in HTML5 gives us an excellent excuse to take a quick trip through the big picture of "semantic" markup. We'll look at where semantic markup came from and what semantic markup promised to deliver but never quite did, and we'll finish with a quick look at something you can use right now—new schemas put forward by the major search engine companies (Google, Microsoft, and Yahoo) that will ideally improve the display of your search results.

By the end of this chapter, your markup nerd-dar will be so finely tuned you'll be able to separate the markup poseurs using *semantic* as a mere buzzword from the hard-core markup wonks who are still waiting for the Semantic Web to arrive, any day now...

Semantics in a Nutshell

When it comes to the Web, there are actually two kinds of "semantics:" the nitty-gritty markup of a given web page and the so-called Semantic Web. Let's start with the semantic markup we practice every day as web designers.

"Semantic markup" was one of the cornerstones of the web standards movement. In 2003 Jeffrey Zeldman, perhaps the best-known advocate for semantic markup and web standards, wrote this on his blog (www.zeldman.com/daily/0303a.shtml):

> *CSS combined with lean semantic markup makes sites faster, more portable, and more accessible. The combination helps sites work in more existing environments and is the best hope of preparing them for environments that have not yet been developed.*

This was a major change in both theory and practice for web designers. We'd keep all the styling information about a page in a separate CSS file and describe the content with "lean, semantic markup," as Zeldman put it.

Here's a (slightly reworked) example of semantic markup Zeldman used in a 2002 Digital Web article (www.digital-web.com/articles/999_of_websites_are_obsolete/). First, Zeldman borrowed some "unsemantic" markup from an e-commerce site to show what we were moving away from (try not to shudder when you read it):

```
<td width="100%"><font face="verdana,helvetica,arial" size="+1" color="#CCCC66"><span
class="header"><b>Join now! </b></span></font></td>
```

And then, with CSS handling the styling, the markup simply became this:

```
<h2>Join now!</h2>
```

And lo and behold, there it was: lean, semantic markup that we pretty much take for granted now. It was a big, and extremely worthwhile, shift in practice.

But what makes this example "semantic" and not the first one? *Semantic* is just a fancy way of saying "meaningful," and by using heading tags (<h2>), it now means something to browsers (and screen readers): "This is a heading." Screen readers can (and do) use these headings to navigate around a document, and browsers can give these elements default styling (for example, making it a block-level element).

It also makes it easy for us humans to read. When we scan the markup, there's no doubt about what this text is—it's a heading. Simple, right?

This highlights the two key groups that matter in "semantic markup": humans and machines (browsers, screen readers, search engines, and so on). It should be both "human readable" and "machine readable"—Semantic Markup 101.

"Machine readable" semantic markup has other benefits. Search engines can scan, index, and search our content in a way that's much harder (if not impossible) with Flash sites or web sites consisting purely of images (as print designers are occasionally wont to churn out).

That said, Google doesn't care much about what markup you use.

These Problems Have Been Solved

Here's the thing: the solution to these problems has been around for more than a decade, no matter what flavor of HTML you are using. Search engines can index our content, screen readers can understand it, and our lean, semantic markup makes it easy to read and maintain.

Then the pedants took over.

The people in web design circles began to think "Well, if *semantic* is good, then *more semantic* must be better, right?" Not really.

Beyond the point of human readability and basic machine readability, "more semantic" doesn't mean anything (irony ahoy!). But this hasn't stopped people debating which elements are more semantic or more appropriate, which nine times out of ten is about as useful as debating whether it's "splade" (or, more correctly, "splayd" for you sticklers out there) or "spork." (Splade, obviously).

There's No Such Thing As "More" Semantic

I humbly propose that the unqualified use of "more semantic" be banned from web design discussions about HTML elements posthaste.

Whenever you hear someone going on about something being "more semantic," ask them this simple question: "For who?"

If all they can come back with is "But it's ... MORE SEMANTIC!" they're just making a vague claim about nothing. But if they say something like "More semantic for screen readers," *that's* a valid claim we can evaluate.

Do screen readers *really* do anything different for these "more semantic" elements? Are they supported at all? Or do they cause bugs like the HTML5 elements did when they were first used? (See www.accessibleculture.org/blog/2010/11/html5-plus-aria-sanity-check/.)

(Remember: because of the no-JavaScript IE6–8 issues, using HTML5 elements for accessibility is about as useful as dieting on doghnuts.)

Likewise, if they say "But it's more semantic *for search engines*," we can evaluate that specific claim. What does Google's developer guidelines say? What does the SEO community think? And so on.

But please, no more unqualified claims of "But it's *more semantic*" when discussing HTML5. These dubious assumptions have been attaching themselves like barnacles to the good ship Web Standards for years, and it's time we revved up the high-pressure hose and cleaned them off (assuming that's how barnacles are, in fact, removed).

OK, mini-rant over. The human readability and basic machine readability problems have been solved, this is where we're at, and we may hope that HTML5 will take us forward. But before we get to HTML5's approach, let's talk about the Big Idea™ behind semantic markup.

Big Ideas in Semantic Markup: The Semantic Web

What if we could take the "machine-readable" part of semantic markup further? What if the machines (and browsers in particular) could read our markup and know not just what content appeared but what given blocks of content actually meant?

That's the big idea behind semantic markup. If we can describe the content of our pages *accurately* and *specifically*, then machines can do cool stuff with the data.

This is (or perhaps was) partly the idea behind the Semantic Web—a big, broad concept that would be driven by the XML-ified Web. (Read more about it here: http://en.wikipedia.org/wiki/Semantic_Web.) The Web would be a perfectly described library of documents, marked up in excruciating detail with XML. An XML-based future was something many influential people believed in. In fact, in the earlier markup example from 2002 and the use of <h2>, Zeldman described web standards as a way we can "transition from HTML, the language of the Web's past, to XML, the language of its future."

However, as we saw in Chapter 1, the move to XML died, and with it the dream of a true Semantic Web. Instead, the Web became a wonderful platform for applications, went social, and kept on being the Web we know and love. But it wasn't the capital-*S* Semantic Web people had hoped for.

We need to keep this history in mind when people talk about "semantic" elements in any situation, whether it's HTML5 or whatever future HTML evolves. What kind of "semantics" are they referring to—basic human- and machine-readable semantics we all use every day or the dead-end dream of the XML-powered Semantic Web?

Semantics: Not Dead Yet (Or: Google & Co Drop a Micro-Semantic Bombshell)

There's actually a third option that sits between the lean, semantic markup we use now and the pie-in-the-sky Semantic Web, called microdata (and microformats), which adds a layer of metadata to our markup.

(A variety of approaches compete here, particularly microformats, microdata, and RDFa. But I'll just be referring to the overall concept as *micro-semantics*, which is also known as "structured data.")

With micro-semantics, we simply embed semantic data into our existing HTML document. Let's look at how micro-semantics could help daily life on the Web.

E-commerce with Real (Micro) Semantics

Let's use online shopping as an example. Here, truly semantic markup could *theoretically* help desktop browsers (in other words, all of us), the visually impaired using screen readers, and search engines.

- *Desktop browsers*: Let's say we're shopping online for a new TV and doing our research by visiting a bunch of web sites to compare features and prices for specific models. In most cases (well, if you're as obsessive about research as I am), this means copying and pasting the relevant information from each site into a separate document—which is both tedious and prone to error.

- Now, imagine if these e-commerce sites all marked up their pages with a `<productdetail>` tag and nested `<price>` and `<specs>` tags. Our browser could easily find the product detail part of the page, and with a single click we could add the price and specs into a comparison shopping list. With specific, meaningful tags, your browser—a machine—can find, compile, and sort certain information for you very quickly. After all, that's what they do best.

- *Screen readers*: It could also help the blind or vision-impaired. Imagine a blind person doing the same research for a new sound system. If the e-commerce pages were marked up with these `<price>` and `<specs>` tags, their screen reader could theoretically read out *just* the price and product specs. They could then save those details to their comparison shopping list and move on. But until it happens, they have to try to navigate around highly complex pages by having headings and content read to them.

- *Search engines*: With the prices and specs marked up correctly, Google, Bing, and other search engines could display the price of a product fairly reliably in their search results and improve the whole search experience. (This is actually possible right now, which we'll get to).

Those are just a few examples of what's possible when we have truly semantic markup. Machines—browsers, screen readers, and search engines—can easily pick out useful information and do cool things with it (such as create a comparison shopping list).

The problem is, to use different tags to describe this data, the HTML spec would need a squillion different tags. Every kind of content—from poems to products to policy documents—would need its own tags so the machines knew what the content was. The list of HTML tags would literally be a small dictionary or, rather, a very *large* dictionary as more and more tags were added to the spec. Authors writing about HTML would quite likely lose their minds.

The good news is we *can* mark up our content and make this comparison shopping possible (especially the search engine example) without needing any more HTML tags. We simply annotate our existing HTML with attributes and values that machines can read. (I'll talk more about this soon).

Adding a handful of new elements HTML5-style, however, is not a path to "more semantic" documents. They don't help machines do much with the data, and our markup becomes more cluttered—hardly a way to make it more readable.

Instead, we need a new mechanism to describe this data. Ideally that's where HTML5 will lead us.

Can the Real Semantics Please Stand Up?

I know what you're thinking. "If only we had a way of adding tags that didn't pollute the entire spec. Some sort of eXtensible Markup Language." But as we saw in Chapter 1, we tried that, and it failed.

Clearly we need a way to extend HTML that doesn't involve adding a dictionary's worth of elements to the spec or trying to XML-ify the Web.

There is a third option, and a bunch of people have been working on various solutions for quite a few years.

Here's the idea in a nutshell: just attach attributes with values from an agreed bunch of terms to our existing HTML. Here's an example (I've made up the attribute and value):

```
<div class="myclass" semanticdata="mysemanticvalue"> ... content ...</div>
```

As you can see, it's pretty simple. But it's worth teasing out the terminology because the different terms and implementations can make a simple idea seem far more complex than it actually is.

We need to distinguish between several pieces of the micro-semantics pie:

- *The infrastructure*: We can take different technical approaches when *adding* semantic data to a document (that is, what HTML infrastructure we use). It boils down to which attributes we use—the existing `class` attribute (microformats), the new HTML5 attributes such as `itemprop` (microdata), or attributes such as `property` and `content` (RDFa). Not surprisingly, people interested in the nitty-gritty get all worked up over which is best. But it's *what* we say, not *how* we say it, that's much more interesting.

- *The vocabularies*: What we say—the *kind* of data that we stick in these attributes—is where the rubber hits the road. And we need to work together to make it work. The people implementing the data (web designers) and the companies that might do something with it (for example, search engines) need to agree on a stable set of terms—a vocabulary—to describe a review, person, or event so everyone is on the same page.

- *The concept*: And then there are the communities built around different ways to implement this infrastructure and vocabularies and do cool things with it.

One group that has been doing cool things with micro-semantic data is the microformats community. They have an active community (`http://microformats.org/`), a microformats way to use HTML as infrastructure (the `class` attribute), and specific microformat vocabularies. These are the various parts of the micro-semantics pie and demonstrate how communities have been able to come together to do semantics in a meaningful way on the Web.

You may have heard of and perhaps implemented microformats in the past. Unfortunately, as I write, its future has been more or less killed off by the search giants that have proposed a new way forward for micro-semantics or "structured data."

Why Should We Care About Micro-semantics?

In 2011 Google, Microsoft, and Yahoo launched what may be the biggest effort to get real semantics into HTML documents in the history of the Web.

And how did they launch it? With a blog post and a web site that had all the pizzazz of a "My First HTML Page" template knocked out during a hurried lunch break (see Figure 5-1). And they also managed to single-handedly annoy everyone already invested in the process who've been evangelizing micro-semantics for years. Not a good start.

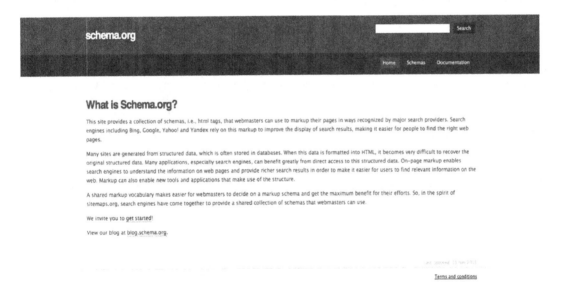

Figure 5-1. `Schema.org`. *Who said semantics weren't sexy? Oh ... everyone. Right*

Schema.org: The Future of Semantics?

In mid-2011 a handful of engineers from Google, Microsoft, and Yahoo decided they didn't like the current, community-driven approaches and announced they were picking HTML5's microdata as the winning *infrastructure* (that is, the HTML attributes we should use to add micro-semantic data). And so they released Schema.org (http://schema.org/)—a list of vocabularies, or "schemas," that the major search engines would use to display richer search results.

In this way, all three parts of the micro-semantic pie were changed. The infrastructure (HTML5's microdata), the vocabularies (Schema.org), and the drivers (corporations, not communities) were all new.

(You can read Google's announcement at http://googlewebmastercentral.blogspot.com/2011/06/ introducing-schemaorg-search-engines.html, Microsoft's announcement at www.bing.com/community/site_ blogs/b/search/archive/2011/06/02/bing-google-and-yahoo-unite-to-build-the-web-of-objects.aspx, and Yahoo's at http://developer.yahoo.com/blogs/ydn/introducing-schema-org-collaboration-structured-data-44741.html).

Figure 5-2 shows an example of a richer search result.

reviews.cnet.com › Reviews › Tablets ▾
Nov 12, 2013 - ★★★★✦ Rating: 4.5 - Review by Scott Stein -
Price range: $399.00 to $459.00
Imagine the **iPad** Air shrunken down to an even smaller size:
that's the new **Mini** in a nutshell. Read our full ...

Figure 5-2. *Google iPhone review, and you'll get results similar to this one. Note how much metadata is included—rating, reviewer, date, and breadcrumbs are all present here*

Couldn't We Do This Before?

This is similar to the Rich Snippets micro-semantics initiative Google launched in 2009, which you may have heard about (or even implemented). But Rich Snippets supported only a handful of existing vocabularies and let authors choose between microdata, microformats, and RDFa. (Plus, it was supported only by Google.)

Now we have one "approved" infrastructure for implementation (microdata), one set of vocabularies at a central location, and a big reason for implementing them: support in Google, Bing, and Yahoo.

That's a big deal.

(Keep in mind this is purely for search result *display*, not search *ranking*. It's important our clients know the difference).

What's remarkable isn't the search giants choosing one infrastructure but rather the 300-odd vocabularies that will potentially define semantics on the Web for years to come. And it was all done behind closed doors with no standards process (or community involvement) whatsoever.

The Semantic Web We've Been Waiting For?

Make no mistake, this is the biggest, actually-supported thing to happen for semantics on the Web since, well, pretty much forever.

Way back in Chapter 1 we looked at how XML was supposed to transform semantics on the Web but didn't. (It was just Architecture Astronauts at work.) We've also looked at how HTML5 adds a few semantic elements that either are harmful or add up to very little. (Adding more elements to HTML proper isn't a solution for semantics.)

This approach of micro-semantics promises a middle way interested communities have been exploring for some time. Let's run through the existing approaches before we look at the Schema.org launch (and everything that was so horribly wrong with it).

Microformats

The microformats community has been developing and advocating micro-semantics with reasonable success for years, after kicking off in 2004 (see `http://microformats.org/wiki/history-of-microformats`). This is from `http://microformats.org/about`:

> *Designed for humans first and machines second, microformats are a set of simple, open data formats built upon existing and widely adopted standards. Instead of throwing away what works today, microformats intend to solve simpler problems first by adapting to current behaviors and usage patterns (e.g. XHTML, blogging).*

For example, in February 2011, all of Facebook's events were published using microformats (see `http://microformats.org/2011/02/17/facebook-adds-hcalendar-hcard`). And with the appropriate browser extension (such as the Google Calendar extension for Chrome), a button would appear next to an event, which you could click to add the details to your calendar. Pretty neat, eh?

How did Tantek Çelik, one of the founders of Microformats.org, react to the Google and Microsoft Schema.org announcement (`http://twitter.com/#!/t/status/77083481494142976`)?

> *#schemaorg spits in the eyes of every person and company that worked on open vocabularies like vCard, iCalendar, etc.*

Ouch.

RDFa

Microformats was a simple, straightforward, limited-by-design approach to micro-semantics.

RDFa (or Resource Description Framework—in—attributes) was the W3C's much more complex (but more flexible) approach to machine-readable data that's been kicking around since 1997 as just "RDF." (RDFa was started in 2004.) It never really captured developer interest in any significant way, but it's still hanging around.

As debate raged about the Schema.org announcement mid-June, Mark Pilgrim quipped the following (`http://twitter.com/#!/diveintomark/status/80980932957450240`—link now 404s; this was before Pilgrim's Internet disappearing act):

> *The W3C: failing to make RDF palatable since 1997*

Zing.

But there have been some interesting real-world uses, such as the GoodRelations vocabulary for e-commerce (`www.heppnetz.de/projects/goodrelations/`) that could drive the e-commerce example we looked at earlier.

Web designers generally prefer the simplicity of microformats to the flexibility and complexity of RDFa. Nevertheless, a community interested in micro-semantics had grown around RDFa.

How did Manu Sporny, the current chair of the W3C's RDF Working Group, react to Google and Microsoft's Schema.org announcement? In "The False Choice of Schema.org" (`http://manu.sporny.org/2011/false-choice/`), he said this:

> *Schema.org is the work of only a handful of people under the guise of three very large companies. It is not the community of thousands of Web Developers that RDFa and Microformats relied upon to build truly open standards. This is not how we do things on the Web.*

Yikes.

Microdata

Finally we have microdata, the new format used in Schema.org.

Nothing compels web authors to add esoteric metadata to their pages like several competing, slightly different metadata formats. So, Ian Hickson, the HTML5 editor, decided microformats was too cold and RDFa was too hot, so he invented a third approach—microdata—that he felt was *just right* (so to speak). (Here's Hickson's lengthy WHATWG post introducing the feature: `http://lists.whatwg.org/htdig.cgi/whatwg-whatwg.org/2009-May/019681.html`.)

Note that microdata, as far as the HTML5 spec is concerned, is about providing the *infrastructure* (with new, valid attributes) for adding micro-semantics. It doesn't specify what those vocabularies should be or who should invent or maintain them. It is completely separate from the actual vocabularies on Schema.org (for example).

And this is the format that won, in a blessed-by-the-tech-giants sense.

(For a lengthier discussion of the various formats and the implications of Schema.org, see Henri Sivonen's excellent "Schema.org and Pre-Existing Communities" at `http://hsivonen.iki.fi/schema-org-and-communities/`.)

Microdata and Schema.org

Now Google, Microsoft, and Yahoo are pushing not only a single format (microdata) but also a single set of vocabularies for real semantics on the Web.

Everything has a specific vocabulary (or "schema"): books, movies, events, organizations, places, people, restaurants, products, reviews … you name it. (See the full list here: `http://schema.org/docs/full.html`.)

There are even schemas for identifying parts of web pages themselves, including the header, footer, sidebar, and navigation. I guess ARIA, HTML5, and so on, weren't enough.

If this takes off, and that's a *big* "if," it will be a huge revolution in how we mark up our pages—bigger than XHTML, HTML5, and whatever flavor of HTML comes next.

Has the Semantic Web finally arrived?

How Not to Launch an Initiative

> *"schema.org … there's just nothing quite like throwing away years of vocabulary/ ontology work"*
>
> —Jay Myers, *June 3, 2011;* `http://twitter.com/#!/jaymyers/status/76344419867037696`

Well, not if the tepid launch of this new initiative is anything to go by. It was pretty much a textbook case of what *not* to do.

Here are a few things they could have handled *slightly* better:

- *Consultation*: The Schema.org announcement came from nowhere—no consultation with the community, no heads up, just a desire to "get something out there."

- *Outreach*: It's generally not a great idea to piss off the people who've spent years advocating something similar to what you're launching. Instead of getting the microformats and/or RDFa communities on board (or at least encouraging a migration path), Google, Microsoft, and Yahoo completely ignored them. And that made them very unhappy campers.

- *Human face*: Schema.org launched as an utterly generic site with almost no human aspect, just a "feedback" button. Who edits it? Who thought it up? Who do we talk to? What's the process? *Is* there a process? It's a complete mystery as far as the web site goes. Indeed, the FAQ asks "Who is managing schema.org on an ongoing basis?" and answers "Google, Bing, and Yahoo are managing schema.org on an ongoing basis." Right, well, I guess we can always just contact Google, Bing, and Yahoo then. (To be fair, they eventually got a Schema.org blog up here: `http://blog.schema.org/`.)

- *Newbie friendly*: For most web site designers, micro-semantics is a pretty "out there" concept. And while Schema.org does have a "Getting started" guide (`http://schema.org/docs/gs.html`), it needs a much friendlier explanation of the how, why, and what of micro-semantics (including schema examples) if they want anyone besides the in-the-know über nerds to pick it up.

- *A not-comically-bad web site*: The list of schemas was originally presented in an ASCII art–style list, with dire markup like this (`http://schema.org/docs/full.html`):

```
<br>     |          
;|    <a name=Movie><a href=../Movie>Movie</a>: <span
class="slot">duration</span>, <span class="slot">director</span>, <span
class="slot">actors</span>, <span class="slot">producer</span>, <span
class="slot">trailer</span> <br>     |    
     |          &nb
sp;     <span class="slot">productionCompany</span>, <span
class="slot">musicBy</span><br>
```

(That describes movies, by the way.) How are we supposed to take these micro-semantics seriously when they can't even use basic HTML semantics on their own web site? *(Update: In 2012 this markup was improved by changing the list to … a giant table, complete with nested tables and spacer cells. Go figure.)*

And let's not mention the huge number of schemas listed (more than 300!), the fact microdata hasn't been implemented correctly (see `http://jenitennison.com/blog/node/156`), or the issues about patents (see `www.seobythesea.com/?p=5608` halfway down). What a mess.

All this for potentially the biggest change to web semantics since the Web kicked off.

What Do the People Behind Schema.org Think?

Kavi Goel, a product manager at Google, participated in a session at SemTech 2011 (the "Semantic Technology Conference") that discussed Schema.org. And some of the responses don't exactly inspire confidence. (See the W3C's official transcript here: `www.w3.org/2011/06/semtech-bof-notes-smaller.html`.)

Here's an example (slightly abridged):

Ivan Herman: Schema.org is out there, … how do you envisage the process for the future whereby schema.org might be a place where new vocabs are developed. I [sic] place to make it a more open social process?

Kavi Goel: I don't have a great answer right now. I don't think any one company wants to own this in its entirety. By going with 3, we showed we [Google] weren't just doing it. […]

Then it leaves the question of where is the completely open discussion … We don't have an answer yet, but this is important. We'll need to sort out the stuff that's out there.

Kevin Marks: Ours [microformats] has an edit button, yours has a feedback button. The CORE of microformats is we reach agreement. YOU said "we did it in a closed room". You haven't shown your work, your evidence, how others can get involved. This is the most worrying thing.

Kavi Goel: That's a totally valid point. Microformats did a great job creating an open community.

There's no good answer for why we didn't do that.

Coming to microformats with a whole bunch of new things could have been an option. We did want to get something out there.

Earlier in the discussion, Goel said this:

The achievement was to get something out there. We know it's not perfect. We can make it better. We hope this can be a step toward great adoption.

Here's hoping. The rush to "get something out there" seems to have done more harm than good at this stage, but they can redeem themselves. We now have one format and one set of vocabularies to use for micro-semantics on the Web. If Google (and/or Microsoft) actually throws some resources at it and someone at either company actually takes ownership of the project, it could be a very big deal indeed.

To the credit of those involved in Schema.org, consultation is finally taking place, and interested parties are discussing a way forward. See, for example, "Schema.org Workshop—A Path Forward" at `http://semanticweb.com/schema-org-workshop-a-path-forward/`.

Also see the sporadically updated Schema.org blog for further outreach efforts: `http://blog.schema.org/`.

Wrapping Up: Semantics and HTML

The waves from the Schema.org announcement are still rippling out across the Web as I write. But even so, we can still say a few things about semantics, HTML, and what we should do:

- *The semantic problem*: True semantics that describe *meaning*, and not just *structure,* happen in a layer *on top of* HTML. This seems to be the solution to the longstanding problem of semantics on the Web. XML won't bring us true semantics, nor will more HTML tags. It's a layer of micro-semantics on top of our existing HTML that will.

- *Microformats and RDFa are probably dead ends*: Microformats has done really well over the years, and I love its simple format. But the decision by Google and Microsoft makes these formats look like dead ends, and the micro-semantics ecosystem (including browser add-ons and validators) will presumably move to microdata and Schema.org vocabularies. Of course, Schema.org could flop hopelessly too, and the microformats community (for one) could keep plugging away. (Google is not *dropping* any support, in any case).

- *Get involved*: It's worth reading up on and experimenting with microformats tools that already exist (such as browser extensions and bookmarklets) to get a taste for what's possible with micro-semantics. But the fact Schema.org appears to be the future means we as a community need to study the various schemas and provide feedback.

- *Questions remain*: Many questions about the process (will there be one?) and future of Schema.org remain unanswered—questions even the instigators can't answer, as Kavi Goel demonstrated. And there are bigger questions about its widespread use. Will mainstream adoption lead to attempts to spam search engines? (People will certainly try.) Will it all turn to "metacrap" (`www.well.com/~doctorow/metacrap.htm`)? We will see.

- *It's ready to go*: Google and Microsoft's "It's better to ask for forgiveness than permission" attitude with Schema.org means the standards process won't be going on for years—it's good to go right now. And if it is widely adopted, our online shopping example may eventually become a reality. At the time of this writing, Schema.org continues to be the dominant player in the semantic markup-adjusting-things arena, though adoption is slow and primarily restrained to web gurus who know enough to implement it (like you, gentle reader). For now, here's the February 2012 announcement of using Schema.org micro-semantics to describe videos, which is "now the recommended way to describe videos on the Web": `http://googlewebmastercentral.blogspot.com/2012/02/using-schemaorg-markup-for-videos.html`. And here's a 2013 article by Searchengineland.com describing the importance of Schema.org's microdata in Google's Hummingbird search algorithm: `http://searchengineland.com/schema-org-7-things-for-seos-to-consider-post-hummingbird-172163`.

- *It's being used right now*: Companies such as eBay, IMDB, Rotten Tomatoes, and others have implemented Schema.org's semantics and are benefiting from improved display of their search engine results right now, as this article demonstrates: `www.seomoz.org/blog/schema-examples`.

Ultimately, Schema.org is a case of glass half-full/glass half-empty. We now have a well-supported, standard set of semantic schemas we can easily add to any HTML structure. And if we search with Google, Bing, or Yahoo, we can get tangible results. The chicken-and-egg problem of adding semantic data has been solved, the format has been chosen, and the schemas have been released.

But rushing the launch (which was underwhelming, to say the least), abandoning any standards process whatsoever for the vocabularies, and trampling years of existing work are heavy prices to pay.

CHAPTER 6

■ ■ ■

The Truth About HTML5 and SEO

One odd myth that keeps perpetuating in books and blogs is that new (or even old) HTML elements will help with search engine optimization (SEO). Let's put this one to bed right now (with phasers set to "rant") and consider the broader question of markup and SEO.

SEO is all about ranking well for given search terms in a search engine's index (usually Google, but it could be Bing or even China's Baidu). For example, I might hope this book ranks well for *HTML5 book* (hey, I can dream). But this ranking has little to do with markup—semantic or otherwise. (I'm simplifying greatly here; industry web sites like `http://searchengineland.com` and `http://searchenginewatch.com` demonstrate how vast the world of modern SEO is, but we'll keep it simple here and focus on the issue of markup and rankings.)

SEO in the Dark Ages

A million years ago, search engines ranked your page by just looking at the content of your page—what keywords were used, where they were used, and how frequently they appeared. To this day people still think they need the `keywords` meta tag (`<meta name="keywords" content="redundant, page, keywords">`) because Google uses it in its rankings.

It doesn't. Google has been ignoring it for years because people abused the hell out of it. (See `http://googlewebmastercentral.blogspot.com/2009/09/google-does-not-use-kewords-meta-tag.html`) Today the `keywords` meta tag serves only as a useful indicator to see which SEO "experts" are still stuck in the '90s.

Stuff Your Keywords

Remember the old joke "How many SEO experts does it take to change a light bulb, lightbulb, light, bulb, lamp, lighting, lightswitch, switch, energy"?

Google doesn't care as much as we'd like to think about the keywords on our sites because people lie, fudge, and cheat when it comes to the data they control. (For a broader look at this phenomenon with metadata, see "metacrap": `http://en.wikipedia.org/wiki/Metacrap`.)

Google's breakthrough innovation was to look at what *other* web sites said about a given site by looking at the quality, quantity, and content of links pointing back to it. That is, "off-page" factors determine how your web site ranks for a given search term far more than the "on-page" metadata. (It's also why comment spam took off—people tried to game Google's rankings by posting spammy links everywhere, thinking more links would result in better rankings.)

HTML and SEO

The new HTML5 elements are a form of metadata—data about data—and Google couldn't really care less whether you use an `<article>`, a `<footer>`, a `<div>`, or even a `<table>` to structure your page.

(No, really, Google doesn't care if you use tables for layout. That isn't to say you should, but it gives you an idea of what Google is dealing with. See Matt Cutts' explanation here: `www.youtube.com/watch?v=fL_GZwoC2uQ`.)

Google has to make sense of the Web as it is—the glorious, hideous mess of invalid tag soup—to get the best information possible back to its users. To put it another way, the burden is on Google (and Bing, and Baidu) to rank the Web, rather than on every single web author (including those wielding Front Page) to provide perfectly marked up pages to be blessed by the ranking fairy.

The 0.000001 percent of pages that use valid HTML5 are largely immaterial. Google won't crawl your page and say "Wow, there's an `<article>` tag; I'm definitely going to rank this page higher than the next guy!" (But if you believe that, please see my next book, *30 Incredible HTML5 SEO Secrets Guaranteed To Super-Charge Your Rankings!*)

But What If It Helped … Somehow?

SEO can be a ferociously competitive business, where the basic strategy is usually getting more and better links than your competitors (see this article and discussion on a modern approach to "link building": `www.seomoz.org/blog/strategic-link-building-why-you-dont-need-to-outrun-lions`).

If we're serious about SEO, this is the sort of thing we need to focus on. Yet despite the huge significance of a site's link profile, some people still insist that maybe, just maybe, using the new HTML5 elements will "help" search engines parse your content and therefore improve your search ranking. But that's like saying Kobe Bryant could be "helped" with some suggestions on how to play basketball. You can assume they've got it sussed over at the Googleplex by now.

Again, this doesn't mean we should write sloppy markup—far from it. We still have to maintain it, after all. It's just that new, fancy markup and search engine rankings have little to do with each other.

And we should provide the search engines with more metadata for search result *display* when they ask for it. (Schema. org proves helpful in this regard, as we saw in the previous chapter.) Metadata for search result *display* is far less likely to be abused, and therefore it should remain useful. We just shouldn't believe more metadata means better rankings.

As of this writing, Google hasn't shown any inclination for respecting the semantic nature of HTML5 tags, and HTML5 has "been out" for a few years now (though the W3C isn't on target to "release" it until 2014). Google's Hummingbird search algorithm, released in September 2013, represents its biggest (public) shift since launching the company, and it completely ignores HTML5 tags in favor of microdata. If HTML5 is going to impact SEO, it's not going to do it any time soon.

But let's say I'm wrong and Google does someday look favorably on HTML5 tags. Guess what would happen? People would abuse the hell out of them to try to get an advantage, and Google would remove whatever benefit it gave those tags to begin with. Such is the arms race between the army of engineers working on good-quality search results and the many site owners and SEO consultants dedicated to manipulating them.

(That "manipulation" isn't always bad, mind you—it is both possible and preferable to add value by producing great content that people link to and by raising your search rankings the good ol' fashion way, as described by Matt Gemmell in "SEO for Non-dicks" at `http://mattgemmell.com/2011/09/20/seo-for-non-dicks/`.)

Zombie Myths Must Die … Eventually

When web standards first took off, we *could* argue that web standards were good for SEO, insofar as they were better than a Flash page that made it impossible for a search bot to "see" the links and content buried in a Flash file. Similarly, print designers who exported their entire sites as images weren't doing themselves any SEO favors because text in images is nigh on useless. But as far as Google is concerned, if enough good links come back to a site, then that's highly relevant to its ranking—even if it's a pure Flash site.

This myth about SEO and markup probably grew from these beginnings. If basic text and markup help search engines, then *better* markup must help them *even more*, right?

No. It's time to put this myth to bed: HTML5 does not help SEO. The difference in ranking between you and the next guy is not because of the tags you use on a given page. HTML5 brings a lot of interesting things to the table (particularly as we'll see in the coming chapters), but improved search engine rankings is not one of them. HTML5 for SEO is about as effective as homeopathy.

■ ■ ■

The Truth About HTML5's Other New Elements

We've covered structural markup in some depth; now let's get down to the nitty-gritty. HTML5 redefines several inline and block-level elements and introduces a few more. We'll run through some of the changes and additions and then consider the broader philosophy behind these elements.

Be Bold or Die Trying

Let's start our look at these elements with something as seemingly innocuous as the `<b>`, `<i>`, `<strong>`, and `<em>` tags and what's changed in HTML5.

Only in web standards land can we turn something as straightforward as **bold** and *italic* into a complicated mix of dogmatism, high-level theory, and broken pragmatic reality.

When web standards took off, we all endeavored to separate *presentation* from *content*. No longer would font tags and tables clutter our markup. Instead, we'd style our pages with CSS and describe our content in a meaningful (in other words, semantic) way with appropriate tags.

This put the poor old `<b>` and `<i>` tags in a tough spot. They were ostensibly *presentational*—they described how text should look, not what it meant—and we were running away from presentational tags as fast as our fingers would carry us. So, we all embraced the `<em>` tag instead of `<i>` (for "emphasis"), and the `<strong>` tag instead of `<b>` (for "strong emphasis"). These new tags now described the meaning of the text—it was *emphasized*, and how "emphasized" text looked (or sounded) was (theoretically) up to the browser or screen reader. We could then use `<b>` and `<i>` for purely stylistic reasons and `<strong>` and `<em>` for semantic purposes—a subtle difference but a difference nevertheless.

I embraced the change (you may have, too), thinking that mattered. But it didn't. Yes, it helped draw a line in the sand between presentational and semantic markup, but this was splitting rather narrow hairs. There was no pragmatic benefit. Here are some examples:

- *We just swapped one for the other*: Given `<strong>` still bolded text and `<em>` still italicized text, we all just swapped `<b>` for `<strong>` and `<i>` for `<em>`, and that was that. The difference between what was "emphasized" and what was just bold or italicized styling *without* any particular emphasis was lost, given we kept using them for presentational purposes anyway. WYSIWYG editors were particularly guilty of this. The difference was just too subtle.

- *Screen readers ignored them altogether*: The main benefit of these "semantic" tags (supposedly) was that screen readers could read the text with "emphasis" or "strong emphasis." In fact, screen readers, by and large, ignore them altogether. (See www.paciellogroup.com/blog/2008/02/screen-readers-lack-emphasis/ for further discussion.)

- *Search engines don't care*: Google treats `<strong>` and `<b>` and `<em>` and `<i>` *exactly* the same. (See Matt Cutts' video here: http://www.youtube.com/watch?v=awto_wCeOJ4.)

So, for all the dogmatism about these elements, the reality is pretty simple—use whatever you want. The humans who read it won't care, and the machines that read it (screen readers and search engines) don't care either.

But where do these elements fit in HTML5?

I guess if you're writing a spec, you have to *try* to make some sense of how these elements are used, with some emphasis (pun intended) on how they *should* be used. Here's what the spec says (emphasis added):

*<i>—The i element represents a span of text in an **alternate voice or** mood, or otherwise offset from the normal prose.*

*<em>—The em element represents **stress emphasis** of its contents.*

*<b>—The b element represents a span of text to be **stylistically offset** from the normal prose without conveying any extra importance.*

*<strong>—The strong element represents **strong importance** for its contents.*

HTML5doctor.com has an entire article on how this might work in theory (see http://html5doctor.com/i-b-em-strong-element/), but it's really pure fiction. If you think people will actually mark up their documents in this way, I have 15 billion web pages I'd like to show you. And Ian Hickson himself likes to say this (www.webstandards.org/2009/05/13/interview-with-ian-hickson-editor-of-the-html-5-specification/):

[I]f they [browser vendors] don't implement it, the spec is nothing but a work of fiction. [...] I don't want to be writing fiction.

If the HTML5 spec documented actual behavior (that is, "paving cowpaths"), the spec would just say <b> and <strong> make text bold, <i> and <em> make text italic, and screen readers tend to ignore them altogether. That's the reality. Everything else is fiction.

This may seem like small fry, but we've touched on a bigger philosophical question: how much of marking up a document in HTML is word processor–like formatting, and how much is marking up the *meaning* of the text? For most web authors—usually our clients using the content management systems we set up for them—it's about word processor–like formatting, *and that's OK*. We'll return to this shortly.

Wrap Your Anchor Around This, and Other Bits and Pieces

Let's do a quick roundup of some other features and elements available in HTML5.

Wrap Anchors Around Block-Level Elements

We can now do things like wrap a link around an <h1> heading and paragraph, which could be useful for items such as blog posts. We need to set the wrapping <a> element to display:block; or there could be unexpected behavior. There were issues with this in early versions of Firefox (3.5), but they've since been fixed. I still recommend testing thoroughly when wrapping links around block-level elements.

<mark>

There's a new <mark> element we can use to highlight text (with appropriate CSS) instead of, say, <span class="mark">keyword</span>. This could highlight search keywords in search results, for example.

<figure> and <figcaption>

The <figure> and <figcaption> elements let us mark up a photo, chart, table, code snippet, or any other self-contained content that's referenced from "the main flow of the document," as the spec says. So, we might have this:

```
<figure><img src="myphoto.jpg"><figcaption>Yup, this is my photo.</figcaption></figure>
```

(See the spec for more examples: www.whatwg.org/specs/web-apps/current-work/multipage/grouping-content.html#the-figure-element.)

These elements may be mildly helpful for accessibility (that is, screen readers could read out the figure and its caption), but it's a complex issue. See this extensive write-up by Steve Faulkner for more: www.paciellogroup.com/blog/2011/08/html5-accessibility-chops-the-figure-and-figcaption-elements/.

These elements also suffer from the same IE6–8 no-JavaScript styling problem we discussed earlier.

<time>

The new <time> element was included mostly for microformats (well before Schema.org was born) but should be useful for future micro-semantic initiatives. Beyond that, <time> is deceivingly complex. It's the drama queen of HTML5 elements, and if <time> were a TV show, it would be *The Bold and the Beautiful*.

In 2011 alone it was killed off by Ian Hickson, then half-revived in the W3C HTML5 spec, and then re-added by Hickson in an improved way to the HTML5-but-we-just-call-it-HTML WHATWG spec. Bruce Lawson blogged about <time>'s removal and reappearance at www.brucelawson.co.uk/2011/goodbye-html5-time-hello-data/ and at www.brucelawson.co.uk/2011/the-return-of-time/.

And it has been subject to a great deal of debate on the WHATWG mailing list before all the 2011 drama (Ian Hickson summed up one debate in 2009 here: http://lists.whatwg.org/htdig.cgi/whatwg-whatwg.org/2009-March/018888.html).

It's worth pondering how the HTML5 editor can arbitrarily kill off an element on a whim, add a new one (<data>), and then reinvent the previously dead element in the face of a backlash, in what is supposed to be a specification that browser makers can implement.

(If you're a sucker for punishment or are coming off some kind of Charlie Sheen-esque bender and *really* need some sleep, there's also a 8,000+ word WHATWG wiki entry on <time> here: http://wiki.whatwg.org/wiki/Time.)

So, how do we use this new, risen-from-the-grave version of <time>?

In its current incarnation, the <time> element allows a variety of strings such as a year string (2011), a month string (2011-11), a date string (2011-11-12), a time string (14:54) with or without seconds and microseconds, combinations of date and time strings (2011-11-12T14:54:39.92922), and more complex strings with timezone offsets (2011-11-12T06:54:39.92922-08:00).

For example, you could use it like this:

```
<p>The Y2K bug destroyed civilization on <time>2000-01-01</time>.</p>
```

This is more liberal than the original incarnation of the <time> element, and for a full list of valid strings, see the spec: www.whatwg.org/specs/web-apps/current-work/#the-time-element.

The <time> element also allows a machine-readable date/time value that can be stuck in the datetime attribute, with something more human-friendly in the <time> tags (or indeed, nothing at all), such as this:

```
<p>The Y2K bug destroyed civilization at the <time datetime="2010-01-01"> beginning of this
year</time>.</p>
```

This is handy for micro-semantics, such as Schema.org microdata.

You can also add a boolean pubdate attribute to indicate when an <article> (or the overall document if it's not within an <article>) was published:

```
<p>This Y2k article published on <time pubdate datetime="2000-01-01T01:42">Dec 31, 1999</time>.</p>
```

(Remember, a *boolean* attribute simply means "yes" by including it, in other words,"this is the publication date," or "no" by excluding it, in other words, it doesn't accept values.)

<details> and <summary>

The new <details> element functions as a show/hide box without having to use JavaScript. It has a boolean attribute (that is, stand-alone, with no value) of open, which tells the browser to display the box as open by default. But if the attribute is absent, it will be collapsed, with the <summary> element describing what appears when collapsed.

Here's an example:

```
<details>
    <summary>Show/hide me</summary>
    <p>You can see this when expanded<p>
</details>
```

This would give the result shown in Figure 7-1.

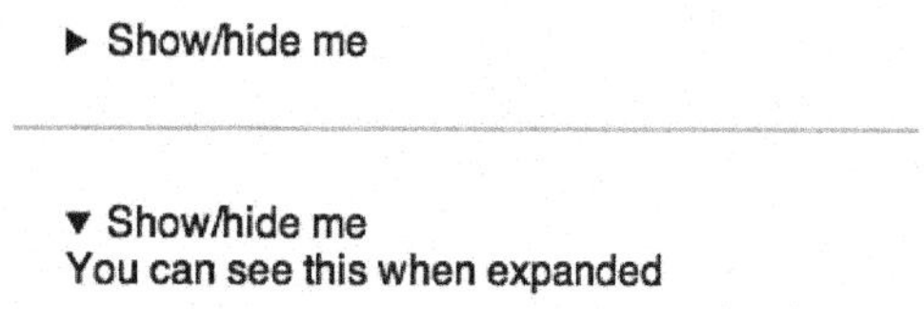

▶ Show/hide me

▼ Show/hide me
You can see this when expanded

Figure 7-1. *The <details> element closed (above) and open (below)*

The spec suggests it could be used in complex forms (and uses OS X's file info window as an example) where you want show or hide certain settings or form inputs. Browser vendors are still working out how they should style this by default. Currently, only Chrome, Safari, and Opera support it.

This is a strange addition to the spec and is one of the WHATWG's curious little innovations. Common patterns of JavaScript- or CSS-powered behavior have become quite prevalent in recent years (think tabs, drop-down menus, pop-overs, lightboxes, and so on), and yet there's no desire to have that functionality replicated in pure HTML. A show/hide triangle control was, however, deemed worthy of being included in the spec. Such are the little mysteries of the WHATWG's HTML5.

<small>

Some existing HTML4 elements have also been redefined.

For example, the <small> element now means "fine print," not "visually small." I find the idea of redefining an element this late in the game weird, but there you go.

<address>

I didn't even know there *was* an <address> element. It's a block-level element that, in HTML5, is for contact information for a given section (for example, an <article>, perhaps in the <article>'s <footer>) or the document itself. The spec says it's explicitly *not* for arbitrary postal addresses, which should just be in <p> tags. If someone from the WHATWG finds out you've used it for an arbitrary postal address, expect to have a finger shaken *very* firmly in your direction.

<cite>

In HTML5, <cite> has been redefined to *exclude* the previously acceptable use of citing people's names. It's now only for works. This really annoyed Jeremy Keith, who wrote about it on 24 Ways (see http://24ways.org/2009/incite-a-riot). Again, it's weird the HTML editor can just redefine elements on a whim. It raises the question of whether we should bother with these elements for "inline semantics" at all, which brings us to...

Should We Even Use These Obscure Little Tags?

If and when new *functionality* arrives in browsers or other agents (and not just the bowels of the HTML5 specification), sure, some of these elements may prove handy from time to time.

But let's step back and consider the bigger picture of the purely "semantic" text-level elements. We've already touched on the question of simple word processor–style formatting versus marking up meaning when discussing <b> versus <strong> and <i> versus <em>. Now let's consider the <address> element, for example. In November 2009, Jack Osborne wrote the following on HTML5doctor.com (http://html5doctor.com/the-address-element/):

> *The address element has been around since the HTML3 spec was drafted in 1995, and it continues to survive in the latest drafts of HTML5. But nearly fifteen years after its creation, it's still causing confusion among developers. So how should we be using address in our documents?*

Perhaps, after *15 years*, it's time for a rethink. What's our aim here? Are we going to give it another 15 years? After 30 years, will the Web finally be using <address> correctly? And if it is, so what?

Fifteen years ago we may have assumed that "one day" someone will do something useful with our carefully marked-up pages. We now know better. It's time to reevaluate. We've spent 15 years experimenting with HTML to see what works in terms of semantics and functionality. It's time to take stock of the results.

If HTML5 were truly paving cowpaths here, it would open up the definition (instead of tightening it) for elements such as <address> and <cite> or, better still, make them obsolete altogether. We don't need them. They don't do anything. Micro-semantics *on top of HTML* make them obsolete. The search engines have demonstrated through Schema.org (and earlier initiatives such as Rich Snippets) that they want micro-semantics, not redefined HTML elements. Authors have little use for them. So, why keep them?

This is the truth we need to acknowledge when it comes to these finer aspects of markup. HTML for documents has proven to be pretty lousy for anything but basic semantics that are explicitly tied to formatting (header, paragraph, list, link, and so on) and providing generic page structure (using <div>s, now with some ARIA roles sprinkled liberally), but that's its beauty; it's what makes it so universal and accessible.

Digging into the details of HTML5's markup reveals yet another mixed bag, containing some interesting inclusions, some baffling ones, a lot of squabbling over some incredibly minor issues, and a lack of a coherent vision to really take markup, and the Web, forward.

Then again, criticism of HTML in this regard is hardly new. Here's Clay Shirky in his piece "In Praise of Evolvable Systems" (www.shirky.com/writings/evolve.html) from—wait for it—1996:

> *HTTP and HTML are the Whoopee Cushion and Joy Buzzer of Internet protocols, only comprehensible as elaborate practical jokes. For anyone who has tried to accomplish anything serious on the Web, it's pretty obvious that of the various implementations of a worldwide hypertext protocol, we have the worst one possible.*

> *Except, of course, for all the others.*

And it was ever thus.

■ ■ ■

The Truth About HTML5 Forms

HTML5 forms are a neat example of HTML5's history. The Architecture Astronauts at the W3C developed an XML-based replacement for HTML 4's forms called XForms (http://en.wikipedia.org/wiki/XForms), which was a W3C candidate recommendation back in 2003. It was powerful but completely useless for the Web.

In late 2003 an alternative was proposed to extend, rather than replace, HTML 4's forms (http://hixie.ch/specs/html/forms/xforms-basic-1). This became known as Web Forms 2.0 from the WHATWG and was eventually integrated into HTML5.

Note the timeframe: 2003.

The work the WHATWG was doing in the early- to mid-'00s was meant to extend basic HTML forms and solve the headaches that routinely popped up when using JavaScript to handle complex form interactions.

But in 2005 the idea of JavaScript libraries was gathering steam, with Prototype.js hitting 1.0 (http://en.wikipedia.org/wiki/Prototype_JavaScript_Framework) and jQuery hitting 1.0 in 2006 (http://blog.jquery.com/2006/08/26/jquery-10/).

Web apps were taking off in a big way, and the need for reliable, cross-browser JavaScript libraries was becoming acute. Libraries such as Prototype.js, jQuery (and the many others that were developed through that period, such as MooTools) met the pressing need and continued being developed, with jQuery's UI library appearing in late 2007 (http://blog.jquery.com/2007/09/17/jquery-ui-interactions-and-widgets/). Other fully fledged, web app–focused JavaScript frameworks have since emerged including Twitter Bootstrap, Node.js, Google's Angular, Moustache.js, Batman. js, Backbone, and the list goes on and on (see a comparison here: http://en.wikipedia.org/wiki/Comparison_of_ JavaScript_frameworks).

In many ways, these libraries provided all the functionality the WHATWG wanted to build into HTML, and far sooner.

Going Native Slowly

Native HTML5 form functionality is nevertheless starting to appear in modern browsers, including IE10+ (there's no HTML5 forms support in IE9 and older). While the browsers might seem modern, the functionality isn't. By the time IE10 shipped it was almost a decade since Web Forms 2.0 was proposed, and it will be several more years before HTML5 forms functionality becomes mainstream (that is, when IE10+ usage becomes widespread).

That said, more advanced HTML5 form functionality is also starting to appear in mobile. For example, in iOS5, a simple HTML5 element gave us access to the native iOS date picker widget. This highlighted the best of web standards—we drop in a simple HTML element, and the browser then provides the appropriate widget. In this case, it's a touch-based widget that would have been unimaginable in the early '00s.

However, then in iOS7, Apple removed this feature from Safari, and it once again gave the user a simple text input. There was no real explanation for the change, and no one liked it. This represents the worst part of web standards—by relying on the browser implementer to provide the input mechanism, you offload the experience of using your site to a browser implementer who may not really do it well and might change it later on a whim with no explanation.

In any case, on the desktop we'll still be using JavaScript for our forms for a while, if only to support IE9 and older. The modern JavaScript libraries will become faster, will be more feature rich, and will offer even more functionality (and styling options)—all before the WHATWG's 2003 ideas for forms ever get widespread adoption.

Still, there are some handy features we can use today (especially for mobile), and we'll cast a critical eye over the other new functionality to see what can be used now (and whether it *should* be).

Forms Can Make or Break a Site

Designers have mixed feelings about forms, ranging from a vague distaste to outright loathing. (Then again, you may be a *form connoisseur* and the exception to the rule.)

Nevertheless, we all need to start loving forms—or at least hating them a little less—because the success of our sites may depend on it. Whether people are trying to sign up, register, check out, or even contact us, it could all come down to the quality of the form.

Bad forms are bad business, and oh boy, are there some bad forms out there (see just about every small-time e-commerce site ever). The last thing you want is people willing to give you money falling at the last hurdle because your form wasn't up to scratch.

Designing thoughtful, humane forms (and testing them thoroughly), on the other hand, is good business. Sometimes it's $300 million of good business: www.uie.com/articles/three_hund_million_button.

I mention this simply because forms appear to be so under-appreciated in the web design world, despite being so crucial to a site's success. People have written entire books dedicated to form design (see http://rosenfeldmedia.com/books/webforms/).

But for now let's focus on HTML5's form features.

Good News, Bad News

Let's do this "good news, bad news" style.

The good news is HTML5 has some new form features that will make forms less reliant on JavaScript for common functionality such as client-side validation, range selectors, date widgets, and even color pickers.

The bad news is IE9 (and older) doesn't support any of them.

The good news is scripts, including jQuery libraries will let us use HTML5 form features where supported and provide fallback where browsers lack support.

The bad news is some native browser UIs for these form widgets are *worse* than the JavaScript alternatives they'll replace—harder to use and harder (if not impossible) to style.

The good news is some additions to forms are backward compatible and provide some nice touches for iOS and Android devices, so you can use some of *those* features now.

The bad news is, as I write this, large chunks of major HTML5 forms functionality are implemented unevenly, even in non-IE browsers. So, we need to tread carefully when implementing them.

Despite all this, we can implement some small things today. So, shortly we'll look at HTML5 form features in terms of the "no-brainers": the kinda/sorta/maybe features and the features that are interesting but not quite ready for prime time.

HTML5 Forms Resources

As of writing, tracking down which browser supports which forms feature (and how well they implement it) is a bit of a nightmare. With major browsers on rapid release schedules (Chrome and Firefox, particularly) it doesn't make much sense to document who-supports-what in depth here, so in this chapter we'll just take a run through the major features and the major browser support issues. Check out the following resources, though, if you really want to get your teeth stuck into HTML5 forms, and, as always, test any new features on your site thoroughly before going live with them.

If you're after authoritative detail on current browser support and browser implementation details for HTML5 form features, see Wufoo's excellent resource: `http://wufoo.com/html5/`. I'll be dropping links to specific pages on Wufoo's HTML5 forms site as we go. The site has the following:

- Full demos compatibility charts

- Screenshots of supported/unsupported behavior

- Descriptions of browser quirks

- JavaScript fallbacks and more

It's definitely worth checking out. Other useful resources include the following:

- The always-handy `http://caniuse.com/` has great information on browser support, with links to more information for a given feature.

- Mark Pilgrim's *Dive Into HTML5* book has a useful chapter covering some of what's new in HTML5's forms: `http://diveintohtml5.info/forms.html`.

- Peter-Paul Koch has a handy compatibility table of the new HTML5 inputs and form attributes: `www.quirksmode.org/html5/inputs.html`.

- There's an extensive (if not particularly reader-friendly) browser compatibility chart on Wikipedia that classes browsers by rendering engine: `http://en.wikipedia.org/wiki/Comparison_of_layout_engines_(HTML5)#Form_elements_and_attributes`.

- Opera's developer site has a brief rundown on the new HTML5 form features: `http://dev.opera.com/articles/view/new-form-features-in-html5/`.

- IE10+ has relatively sound forms support, but as we noted before, earlier versions of IE do not. Check Microsoft's documentation for up-to-date information on support for this feature: `http://msdn.microsoft.com/en-us/library/ hh673546.aspx#HTML5_Forms`.

HTML5 Forms: The No-Brainers

HTML5 introduces a few things we *can* start using right away, particularly input fields for e-mail addresses, URLs, and search terms. These are alternatives to the familiar `<input type="text">`. The good news is browsers that *don't* recognize these new input types just behave as if the field was just `type="text"`.

HTML5 also introduces a variety of new *attributes* for our input fields (such as `autofocus` and `autocomplete`), some of which we'll look at here, and others we'll touch on in the following sections. The attributes here we can generally start using straightaway because browser support is reasonably good and a *lack* of browser is not particularly consequential.

New Input Types: E-mail, URL, Telephone Number, and Search

HTML5 introduces a bunch of new input types, which iOS and Android devices currently use to display a keyboard appropriate for the input type. Sometimes these touches are subtle (the `email` input type includes the @ key, the `url` input type gets a `.com` key, and so on), and sometimes they are more obvious (for example, the telephone number input `tel` type gets a numeric keypad).

The new input types with useful mobile keyboard variations (for iOS and Android at least) include the following:

- *E-mail*: `<input type="email">`

- *URL*: `<input type="url">`

- *Telephone number*: `<input type="tel">`

- *Search*: `<input type="search">`

These input types aren't just useful in mobile contexts—they are (search notwithstanding) supposed to provide client-side validation too. So, in Firefox Chrome, Opera, and IE10+, if you use `type="url"`, for example, and a user doesn't provide a valid URL, you would get an error bubble something like you see in Figure 8-1 (each browser has its own variation).

Figure 8-1. *Using the new input types also provides some input validation in supported browsers*

Validation is implemented unevenly for the various input types and across the various browsers (for example, `tel` has no specified default validation at all), so tread carefully. (Of course, client-side validation is merely a convenience for the user.)

Styling these validation errors is currently highly experimental. There are some experimental CSS3 pseudo-elements in WebKit (for example) that allow you to style the error bubble. You can see the syntax and result at the end of this document: `http://trac.webkit.org/wiki/Styling%20Form%20Controls`.

The search input field is a bit different from the other three we've discussed; the spec doesn't require browsers to do anything special, but some browsers (particularly Safari) round the corners of the search field and may provide a list of previous searches and a clear button (a circle with an *x* in it) when you've entered something.

Older browsers just treat these field as `type="text"`, as mentioned, so there's no harm in using these input types now.

For more, see the Wufoo documentation:

- *E-mail*: `http://wufoo.com/html5/types/1-email.html`

- *URL*: `http://wufoo.com/html5/types/3-url.html`

- *Telephone number*: `http://wufoo.com/html5/types/2-tel.html`

- *Search*: `http://wufoo.com/html5/types/5-search.html`

(There are other new HTML5 input types, such as `range`, `number`, and `date`, which we'll deal with separately in the "HTML5 Forms: The "I Wouldn't Yet But You Can If You Really Want" section.)

Attributes: Autocomplete, Autofocus, Readonly, and Spellcheck

In addition to changing the way that different form items are rendered in HTML5, the new standard also adds a few new attributes to our form item controls. Let's take a look.

Autocomplete

```
<input type="text" autocomplete="off">
```

HTML5 specifies an `autocomplete` attribute that is particularly helpful for turning browser autocomplete *off* (autocomplete is on by default). You may want to do this when a browser's autocomplete suggestions would be inappropriate (for example, a one-time authorization key, as the spec suggests) or confusing (for example, autocomplete suggests the user's name when the user should be entering another name). All major browsers support it.

Autofocus

```
<input type="text" autofocus>
```

The boolean `autofocus` attribute automatically assigns focus to a given input when the page loads. The quickest way to see this in action is to go to `http://google.com`; the search box is automatically focused, and you can start typing right away. This is typically done with JavaScript, but it can be a nuisance to some users. For example, with my focus now in Google's search box, I can't use the Delete key to go back a page in my history; it thinks I want to delete text in the search field instead.

To deal with this (rather mild) problem, HTML5 moves this autofocus functionality into markup, instead of relying on JavaScript, so your browser can (theoretically) disable it with a preference or extension.

All modern browsers support Autofocus. Support in IE began with version 10but Mark Pilgrim details a fallback script here for IE9 and below: `http://diveintohtml5.info/forms.html#autofocus`.

Readonly

```
<input type="text" value="You can't touch this" readonly>
```

HTML5 specifies a widely supported (and self-explanatory) boolean `readonly` attribute. All major browsers support it.

Spellcheck

```
<input type="text" name="captcha" spellcheck="false">
```

With the `spellcheck` attribute, we can, as per the `autocomplete` attribute, exert some control over default browser behavior. For example, we can turn it off for inappropriate fields, such as CAPTCHAS. You have to specify whether `spellcheck` should be `true` or `false`. All major browsers support it (including IE10+, but not 9 or below.)

HTML5 Forms: The Kinda Maybes

Here are a couple of HTML5 forms features that may help in some contexts, or at least let you experiment on your blog. Browser support here may be mixed, implementations may differ, and fallbacks should be considered.

Attribute: Placeholder

HTML5 introduces placeholder text for form fields, which is a welcome addition. Designers like it because it lets us put the field labels (or support text) in the field itself and design more compact forms (see Figure 8-2). It's well supported in all major modern browsers.

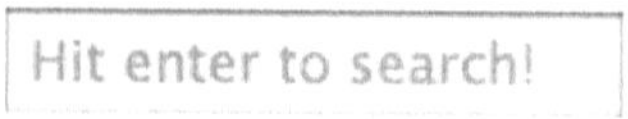

Hit enter to search!

Figure 8-2. *The placeholder attribute in action*

The syntax for this placeholder text is dead simple too. Just add `placeholder="My placeholder text"` to the given field:

```
<input type="search" placeholder="Hit enter to search!">
```

Neat, right? So, why is this in the "kinda, maybe" section?

- *No styling*: Support for styling placeholder text is currently experimental (see this discussion: `http://stackoverflow.com/questions/2610497/change-an-inputs-html5-placeholder-color-with-css`).

- *No IE9 (and older) support*: The lack of support in IE9 and older is a shame because this is otherwise well supported. The lack of IE9 support means we'll have to provide alternatives for some time, which can raise a few tricky issues. Thankfully, the Modernizr feature detection script (`www.modernizr.com/`) can help in providing a fallback where appropriate.

- *Fallbacks are tricky*: Fallbacks aren't always appropriate. We could fall back to JavaScript, but JavaScript placeholders for some details (for example, username and password) can interfere with the browser's built-in autocomplete functionality, which gets ugly.

- *Consistency for conversion rates*: This is the fallbacks-are-better-than-native problem. If (if!) modern JavaScript-based placeholder text improves a form's usability (and therefore its conversion rate, which you can discover through A/B testing if you're really determined), then it should be used for *all* browsers, regardless of their HTML5 support. In fact, if the JavaScript option gives us more design flexibility, why use the native functionality at all? This is true—for the time being—of most HTML5 forms functionality.

HTML5's simple placeholder text may be fine in simple situations (when support is there), but when conversion rates (and design flexibility) are all important, JavaScript solutions are generally going to offer more flexibility (and look a lot nicer to boot).

That's a lot to consider for what is otherwise a simple feature. Ideally, placeholder text support will mature to the point where these issues are moot, but we'll be waiting for IE9 and below to dwindle before it can be used without a fallback.

For more, see `http://wufoo.com/html5/attributes/01-placeholder.html`.

<progress>

```
<progress value="77" max="100">77% complete</progress>
```

HTML5 introduces a `<progress>` element in the forms section of the spec, and it's intended to represent the "completion progress of a task." It's intended for (surprise) progress bars and would be commonly (but not exclusively) used in web apps and updated via JavaScript as the task progresses. It could indicate upload progress, or when no value is given, it could indicate that the client is waiting for a response from the server.

We can use the optional attributes `value` and `max` to show progress made so far. We're encouraged to indicate progress inline as text for browsers that don't support `<progress>`.

The idea here is the browser should style this element natively so it looks like a typical OS progress bar (similar to when you copy a file, for example). As of this writing, all modern browsers support `<progress>` excluding Safari but including IE10+ (IE9 and older do not).

Figure 8-3 shows a few examples from Chrome on OS X; these are from Peter Beverloo's demonstration that you can try for yourself (`http://peter.sh/examples/?/html/meterprogress.html`).

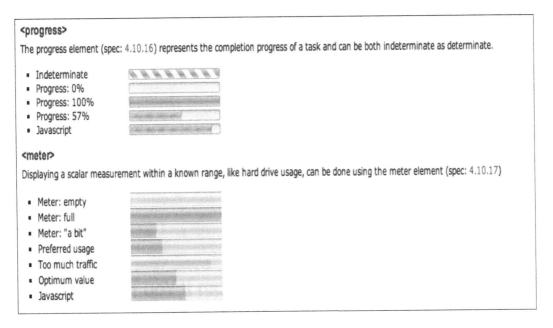

Figure 8-3. *Examples of the <progress> and <meter> elements*

Other browsers just ignore the tags and show the text (for example, "77% complete"). For the latest on browser compatibility, see Wufoo's handy chart: `http://wufoo.com/html5/elements/2-progress.html`.

This seems like an odd addition on its own, but when you consider the web applications heritage of HTML5, it makes much more sense.

For more, see `http://wufoo.com/html5/elements/2-progress.html`.

<meter>

```
<meter min="0" max="100" value="50">50 of 100 people "liked" this</meter>
```

While `<progress>` is a "kinda, maybe," `<meter>` should really fall under "I wouldn't yet," but they make sense together, so we'll keep `<meter>` here.

The `<progress>` and `<meter>` elements sound similar, but they have different use cases and serve different purposes. The `<meter>` element is for gauges, such as a donation gauge indicating $5,000 progress toward a $10,000 goal. It could also be used to indicate the percentage of people who voted a certain way or "liked" something, to indicate the number of tickets sold for an event (as the spec suggests), or even to represent disk space on a hard drive. It's explicitly *not* for sole values such as, say, $5,000 on its own or for height and weight.

Hickson says he added it to the spec mostly to stop people from abusing `<progress>`.

There are six attributes to describe the gauge: value, min, low, high, max, and optimum (only value is mandatory, and we'll touch on some of these attributes in the following sections).

Then things get weird.

The `<meter>` element seems simple enough, but things get funky with the way this element is styled. Let's look at Chrome, for example. Chrome applies native styling, so you get nice meter bars like that shown in Figure 8-4.

Figure 8-4. *The <meter> element in Chrome*

However, trying to make things easy and native (drop the element in; the browser does the rest) takes us down a strange path. What if we want to style the `<meter>` element completely differently? Well, we have to undo all the default browser styling and then apply a lot of experimental CSS3, which has almost no support in modern browsers, as Steve Workman found (see `www.steveworkman.com/web-design/html-5-web-design/2009/my-problem-with-html-5-styling-meter/`).

How crazy does it get? WebKit includes some experimental CSS pseudoclasses for `<meter>` styling, including `meter::-webkit-meter-even-less-good-value`, and even a built-in *star rating system* with `-webkit-appearance: rating-level-indicator;` (see `http://trac.webkit.org/wiki/ Styling%20Form%20Controls` for more).

On the one hand, it's nice to see browsers actually doing something with HTML5 elements—a pragmatic reason to use them is welcome. On the other hand, treating `<meter>` like a natively styled form control takes us down a pretty strange path with lots of bizarro CSS3. Do we really need native star rating systems in WebKit?

Meter is currently supported in Firefox, Opera, Chrome and Safari – at the time of this writing there is no IE support at all, so you're safest just treating it like an experimental novelty rather than a full blown usable tag.

For more, see `http://wufoo.com/html5/elements/1-meter.html`.

HTML5 Forms: The "I Wouldn't Yet But You Can If You Really Want"

Let's look at the `required` and `pattern` attributes and then several other input types that fall back to `type="text"`, including `number`, `range`, `date`, and `color`.

Attribute: Required

```
<input type="text" name="musthaveaname" required>
```

The boolean `required` attribute does exactly what you think—it tells the browser that a given `input` (or `textarea`) must have a value before it can be submitted. Note that fields must have a `name` attribute for `required` to take effect.

Safari's half-hearted implementation of this feature (see `http://css-tricks.com/forums/discussion/11524/modernizr-giving-a-semi-false-positive-with-safari-input-attribute/`) currently puts this feature in the "I wouldn't yet..." basket because it reports to feature-sniffing tools that it *does* support the feature when it doesn't really, creating a false positive. This makes it difficult to create a general fallback without resorting to browser sniffing. IE9 and older do not support the `required` attribute.

Browsers vary in the way they warn a user when they try to submit a form with an empty value for a required field. The ability to style these warnings is experimental too—it's the same situation we touched for the validation warnings given by the new input types (for example, if you enter a non-URL value into a URL input field). WebKit, as mentioned, offers CSS3 pseudo-elements that let us style the error bubbles: `http://trac.webkit.org/wiki/ Styling%20Form%20Controls`.

The other big caveat with this attribute is (as the Wufoo page points out) that you get an error only when you submit the entire form. Modern JavaScript techniques check for a value on blur (in other words, as you work through the form) and are therefore more user friendly.

For more, see `http://wufoo.com/html5/attributes/09-required.html`.

Attribute: Pattern

```
<input pattern="[0-9][A-Z]{3}">
```

The `pattern` attribute allows us to specify a regular expression that a given field's value must match. (The previous regex matches a number followed by three uppercase letters, for example, 1ABC.) This might be used for ensuring that a user's post code (or ZIP code) matches an appropriate format or a submitted URL matches a particular domain (for example, it contains `facebook.com` if providing a Facebook profile URL). Regular expressions are not for the faint of heart.

Unfortunately, the `pattern` attribute suffers from the same false positive problem in Safari that we looked at for `required`. It also suffers from the same usability issues we discussed for `required`.

Remember, client-side validation should only ever be used as a convenience for the user, while server-side validation should do the heavy lifting. This sort of validation is trivial to circumvent and should obviously never be used for security purposes or input sanitation.

There are also plenty of solid, modern JavaScript validation scripts out there that we're going to be relying on for some time, and they offer more user-friendly features (such as validating while you type, or at least as you move through the form).

For more, see `http://wufoo.com/html5/attributes/10-pattern.html`.

Input Type: Number (Spinner)

```
<input type="number" name="itemquantity" min="2" max="12" step="2">
```

Earlier we looked at input types for e-mail addresses, URLs, and telephone numbers. HTML5 also introduces an input type for plain old numbers. Desktop browsers generally use this input type to provide a UI for incrementing a field's numerical value (for example, the quantity of an item in a shopping cart).

As of writing, only IE10, Safari 5+, Chrome, and Opera support this input type. iOS Safari just gives you a numerical keyboard, and Opera 11 lets you type any character. The `number` input type accepts attributes `min` and `max` to constrain the range of possible values, and it accepts `step` to increment in certain amounts (for example, by two if you're buying things that come only as a pair).

Browser validation for this field is quite a mixed bag (see the Wufoo page for more). The real problem, though, is the UI. In WebKit browsers, for example, it's pretty diabolical. They give you the measly "number spinner" shown in Figure 8-5, and I don't see how older people (at the very least) would cope with such tiny buttons.

Figure 8-5. *The number input type usually gives a number spinner*

This is a case of the browser makers letting the side down with lousy native interface widgets. There are better JavaScript methods for giving users up/down arrows to increment a value, and any widget you design yourself is going to be more usable than the WebKit implementation.

The UI problems, poor browser support, and inconsistent implementation make it too early to implement.

For more, see `http://wufoo.com/html5/types/7-number.html`.

Input Type: Range (Slider)

```
<input type="range" name="myslider" min="0" max="10" step="2">
```

The `type="range"` input gives us a slider (see Figure 8-6), which is fine. Support is absent in Firefox but has been present in Opera and WebKit (in other words, Chrome and Safari) for a long time, and is now in IE10+ as well. It's also supported in Safari on iOS5 and newer. You can also use the attributes `min`, `max`, and `step` to constrain the possible values and the increments the slider can move in.

Figure 8-6. Chrome's range slider on a Mac (it's different again on PC)

Browser implementation and styling, however, is a bit all over the place. In my view, better jQuery options exist that provide cross-browser support, more features, and a better, more consistent UI.

You could fall back to the native range widget where browsers support it, but why would you bother? It makes sense to use native widgets only if they're actually better (that is, demonstrably more people actually complete the form), which is something you shouldn't assume without the conversion rate data to back it up. For now (and the foreseeable future), use JavaScript.

For more, see `http://wufoo.com/html5/types/8-range.html`.

Input Type: Date (Time/Calendar Widgets)

```
<input type="date">
<input type="month">
<input type="week">
<input type="time">
<input type="datetime">
<input type="datetime-local">
```

HTML5 specifies several date- and time-related inputs (`date`, `month`, `week`, `time`, `datetime`, `datetime-local`) that should bring up either a date picker (for date, month, and week) or a number spinner (for time values).

Unfortunately, browser support for these is worse than any other input type we've looked at so far. Currently, Chrome, Safari, and Opera are the only browsers to implement a date picker with, shall we say, a *functional* look about it (see Figure 8-7 for Opera's styling).

Figure 8-7. Opera's rather functional date widget

iOS5 Safari introduced support for some of these date inputs, giving users the native date picker control to use for these fields, which was really very handy. Then Apple yanked them in iOS7, returning the user to the default text input field, for no real reason. This kind of flaky standards support in mobile is the a great example of why I take a "Just use JavaScript" stance in this chapter.

As mentioned, this is web standards at their best—an HTML feature conceived long ago is implemented in a clever way on a platform that didn't exist when the feature was dreamt up.

Should you use the native functionality where possible? For mobile users? If they ever implement it (or implement it again, in iOS's case). On the desktop? In several years a universally supported date picker widget will be handy in noncritical situations. But when the forms are crucial to a site's business, it's a lot of control to give up in terms of styling and custom functionality.

In comparison, jQuery UI (for example) already provides customizable, themeable date picker widgets that offer multiple months, inline display, keyboard shortcuts, and more (see Figure 8-8).

Date:

◀	**March 2012**							**April 2012**							**May 2012**					▶
Su	Mo	Tu	We	Th	Fr	Sa	Su	Mo	Tu	We	Th	Fr	Sa	Su	Mo	Tu	We	Th	Fr	Sa
				1	2	3	1	2	3	4	5	6	7			1	2	3	4	5
4	5	6	7	8	9	10	8	9	10	11	12	13	14	6	7	8	9	10	11	12
11	12	13	14	15	16	17	15	16	17	18	19	20	21	13	14	15	16	17	18	19
18	19	20	21	22	23	24	22	23	24	25	26	27	28	20	21	22	23	24	25	26
25	26	27	28	29	30	31	29	30						27	28	29	30	31		

| Today | | | | | | | | | | | | | | | | | | | Done |

Figure 8-8. *The jQuery UI date widget is a much more flexible option*

The overwhelming lack of browser support means it's JavaScript or bust for date widgets for the foreseeable future, and there's nothing wrong with that.

For more, see `http://wufoo.com/html5/types/4-date.html`.

Input Type: Color (Color Picker)

`<input type="color">`

For some reason, HTML5 also specifies a color picker, as shown in Figure 8-9.

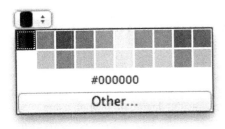

Figure 8-9. *Opera's color picker widget*

As of this writing, only Chrome, Opera and (oddly enough) the BlackBerry browser support it. There are many better JavaScript alternatives.

For more, see `http://wufoo.com/html5/types/6-color.html`.

Input Type and Element: Datalist

```
<input list="mydatalist" name="phonelist">
<datalist id= "mydatalist">
   <option value="iPhone">
   <option value="Android">
   <option value="Blackberry">
   <option value="Windows Phone">
</datalist>
```

HTML5 introduces a `<datalist>` element that's used in conjunction with the `list` input attribute to provide a set list of suggestions in a drop-down menu as you type. See Figure 8-10 for an example. (As you can see in the previous code, the `list` attribute on the `<input>` element matches the `id` on the `<datalist>` element.) These are just suggestions—users can still enter whatever they want. It's essentially just a simple autosuggest feature and could be useful for, say, choosing your country when you're filling out your details on an e-commerce site. (The usual alternative—a giant `<select>` list—generally proves pretty unwieldy.)

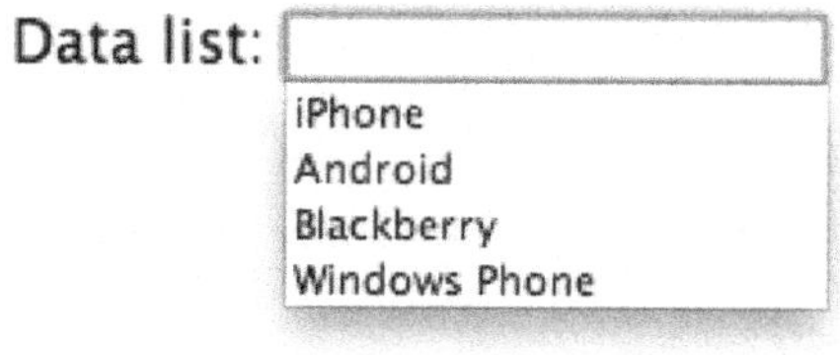

Figure 8-10. *Opera's datalist implementation is pretty good*

Chrome, Firefox 4+, Opera 9+ and IE10 support it, but Safari does not (oddly enough.)

There's also much better JavaScript approaches for this kind of functionality. See, for instance, the very cool Chosen from Harvest: `http://harvesthq.github.com/chosen/`. It offers a variety of `<select>` list replacements, with a very clean UI, solid compatibility for all modern browsers and graceful degradation for older browsers.

You Hypocrite. I Thought Requiring JavaScript Was the Worst Thing Ever

It may seem strange that I'm advocating JavaScript for forms when I was chastising HTML5 advocates earlier in Chapter 4 for making JavaScript mandatory for basic layout for IE6–8 users. The difference here is that it's still possible to gracefully degrade your form for users with JavaScript disabled—there is no graceful degradation when using HTML5 elements for those users.

What About Accessibility?

If we're going to use JavaScript for forms, we should still try to ensure our forms are accessible. There's a myth that screen readers can ignore modern, unobtrusive JavaScript and proceed as if JavaScript was disabled. Not true. Here's Roger Johansson (`www.456bereastreet.com/archive/201011/accessibility_myths_in_2010/`):

> *If screen readers really did not support JavaScript, or screen reader users in general had JavaScript disabled, [then using unobtrusive JavaScript and not thinking much about accessibility would] be a reasonable approach. However, screen readers run on top of web browsers that support JavaScript and, as I mention in "Unobtrusive JavaScript is not necessarily accessible JavaScript", most screen reader users do have JavaScript enabled.*

For screen readers to access forms, they need appropriate labeling, descriptions, and structure. But they still see our JavaScript, so we need to make it accessible to blind users.

And that wraps it up for HTML5 forms!

CHAPTER 9

▩ ▩ ▩

The Truth About HTML5's Canvas, Gaming, and Flash

Canvas lets us draw programmatically on a specific area of a web page. And it can do some pretty cool things: design enhancements, visualizations, drawing/painting applications, image manipulation, and games (the visual side, at least).

Later we'll get into the nuts and bolts of Canvas. But first let's look at some big-picture stuff and the inevitable comparisons to Flash.

Canvas is not Flash, and comparing a single piece of web technology for (primarily) 2D graphics to a feature-rich, broadly supported client environment *and* a mature ecosystem of development tools is a bit apples and oranges. Canvas alongside HTML5 (and related) technologies, however, *is* being touted as a serious Flash competitor. But exploring Canvas (and HTML5 on the whole) made me wish I could do some of the amazing things being done with Flash. This isn't a popular opinion—I'm writing about web standards, so shouldn't I hate Flash? It's also not one I thought I'd have; I haven't used Flash for a decade, and as a stereotypical designer/Apple fan (tautology?) I regularly experience the memory-hogging, crash-tastic, resource-consuming, pain in the ass that Flash is on the Mac (and apply Flashblock liberally).

And while HTML5 has come a long way, Canvas and WebGL still haven't replaced Flash. Support for <video> is letting many sites integrate interesting animated backgrounds and the popularity of scroll effects is making them feel more interactive, but for something truly immersive Flash still feels like the only game in town. Don't believe me? Go to any modern video game or movie site. Nine of out ten of them are still built in, you guessed it, Adobe Flash. That's not to say things aren't changing, though, and Adobe themselves have started to build Canvas export features into Flash Professional. We'll consider some examples and pit these technologies head to head in the rest of the chapter.

Flash Is Dying, and HTML5 Is All We've Got

Nevertheless, it's hard to escape the fact that Flash is dying.

As you know, there's no Flash on iOS devices, as has been widely discussed. (See the April 2010 piece "Thoughts on Flash" by the late Steve Jobs for *why* Apple chose not to support Flash: www.apple.com/hotnews/thoughts-on-flash/.)

But there won't be any Flash plug-in on future Android devices, either. In November 2011, Adobe announced it was discontinuing support for the Flash plug-in on mobile devices altogether (see http://blogs.adobe.com/conversations/2011/11/flash-focus.html), shifting its focus to Flash-driven native apps through Adobe AIR and, ultimately, HTML5.

Windows Phone has also never supported the Flash plug-in.

The absence of Flash on iOS devices (at a minimum) made offering a mobile, HTML-only version of a site a necessity for most sites. And if you are going to build an HTML version of your site anyway, you need a pretty good reason to build an additional Flash-based desktop site. But the justification could still be made in some cases—a simple HTML site for mobile and a rich Flash site for desktop, perhaps.

Then Microsoft dropped a bombshell.

In September 2011, Microsoft announced that for Windows 8, the nonlegacy version of IE10 would not support *any* plug-ins (http://blogs.msdn.com/b/b8/archive/2011/09/14/metro-style-browsing-and-plug-in-free-html5.aspx). No Flash, no Silverlight, nothing. Flash for mobile browsers was a nonstarter, but this announcement from Microsoft signaled the beginning of the end of Flash on the desktop, too.

The writing for Flash was on the wall. The default experience of the flagship operating system that will run on hundreds of millions of the world's desktops wouldn't support Flash (or any other plug-in technology).

Shortly after making the announcement, Microsoft reversed its decision and decided to keep on supporting Flash, but the damage was done. Like many "dying" and "dead" technologies before it, Flash continues to exist comfortably long after passing from vogue, and a company as large and widespread as Microsoft can't stop supporting it so quickly. At the same time, Adobe has drastically reduced the size of the Flash development team, moved it all off-shore, and doesn't seem to be investing resources in extending the platform. Flash, the plug-in, is still dying, though it may be a while before it's finally dead.

Can Canvas and HTML5 Fill the Gap?

At some point in the future, advanced graphics and audio won't be delivered through a plug-in like Flash. Already each new year reveals more and more people who connect to the Web primarily or exclusively through post-PC devices such as phones and tablets, where Flash doesn't exist. Consider the implications:

- *Advertising*: Site owners and advertisers can't sit idly by as their ad revenue and click-through rates fall, and they're not going to go back to animated GIFs. There's going to be a huge shift to HTML5-powered (and mobile-viewable) banner ads, and Canvas will have a big role to play there.

- *Media delivery*: Audio and video content will need to be delivered using HTML5, but as we'll see in the next chapter, that's not as straightforward as it sounds.

- *Games*: HTML5 games will also rely heavily on Canvas, as we'll explore later in this chapter.

- *Sites*: Finally, there's going to be a massive number of legacy Flash sites that simply can't continue to work in their current Flash-powered form. Restaurant sites, I'm looking at you. (There's a niche in converting Flash-based restaurant sites waiting there for someone!) Sadly, this also means great interactive sites like the Lego Star Wars III site will need to be rebuilt, but ideally this encourages enterprising designers and developers to push web standards to their absolute limits to enable the kind of incredible experiences Flash has been delivering for years to a post-Flash world.

Flash Authoring for HTML5?

For a while, Adobe played with the idea of using its Flash authoring platform as a way to generate HTML5 content. Adobe introduced this idea in 2009, when it demoed such functionality at the MAX conference (see the demo at http://youtu.be/v69S22ZBBqA), and again in early 2012 with an announcement of an extension Adobe was working on called "The Adobe Flash Professional Toolkit for CreateJS" (see the announcement and a video of it in action here: http://blogs.adobe.com/creativelayer/html5-flash-professional/). (Erroneous reports made the rounds in mid-2010 that Flash CS5 would export to Canvas, based on the MAX 2009 video resurfacing, but that was not the case.) The latest demo shows a simple animation making the jump from Flash to Canvas and playing smoothly on a PC and iPad, but whether this tool will be sophisticated enough for most web professionals (when it's eventually released) remains to be seen.

Just a year later, however, Flash as an HTML5 IDE started looking less and less like a real part of Adobe's plans. In 2010 Adobe also released an experimental FLA-to-HTML tool called Wallaby [http://labs.adobe.com/technologies/wallaby/] that relies heavily on SVG and WebKit-only CSS3. Wallaby was then rolled into a new JavaScript creation platform called "CreateJS", sold as a "suite of JavaScript libraries and tools for building rich, interactive experiences in HTML5", which Adobe still supports and promotes at the time of this writing (http://www.createjs.com/).

Then in 2011 Adobe released a preview of new product they were calling "Edge" (http://labs.adobe.com/technologies/edge/), a simple HTML animation tool that relied mostly on JavaScript, despite "HTML5" claims. It allowed users to make complex animations and tweens, similar to those from Flash, but using 100% "open web" technology. At the time of this writing, Edge is now a full product line from lAdobe, and includes things such as an animation application (the original "Edge", now Edge Animate, and still no Canvas support), a coding environment, a design tool (Reflow), typography tools, and PhoneGap, which Adobe acquired in October 2011.

At the time of this writing, Adobe have just announced an update to their Flash Professional CC line, which adds support for exporting animations to Canvas. This is a big step, and something that has stirred up quite a bit of interest. Could this be the Canvas animation tool that designers and developers have been clamoring for? At this point, we'll just have to wait and see.

And Then Apps Happened

Because of the immaturity of some important HTML5 features (especially audio and video, as we'll see in the next chapter) and the lack of mature design tools for things such as Canvas, some site owners may have no choice but to stick with Flash over the next few years, especially as a legacy technology. Or, they'll start pushing apps.

We're entering a strange period for the Web.

On the one hand, as far as technology goes, web standards have won, and won handsomely. They have persevered in the face of numerous challenges from proprietary technology (Flash, Silverlight, and many others that have fallen by the wayside), implementer apathy (for example, Microsoft letting IE stagnate in the '00s), and specification dead ends (the W3C's XHTML 2 debacle). For web purists, this is an incredible victory that seemed anything but certain several years ago. After all, Microsoft—*Microsoft!*— tried releasing a desktop version of its browser that *only* supported web standards and has not only joined the party in implementing cutting-edge web technology but is doing it particularly well.

On the other hand, the web standards we've got with HTML5, and the associated development tools, are still not very good. Canvas, as we'll see, has its uses, but Canvas, and HTML5 in the broadest sense, still has a long way to go in development, adoption, and tool set before it can rival what can be done with Flash today. So, what will happen when developers want to do something cool but they can't do it in the browser?

They'll create apps.

iOS apps. Android apps. Windows apps. Mac apps. Platform-specific apps that, ironically, take us away from the true promise of the Web—that it's available to all, from any platform. We saw an explosion in platform-specific software in the '90s as desktop PCs became common, and then web apps started to emerge in the '00s—software that was liberated from any specific platform vendor. Now we have a fierce competitive environment where major platform vendors (that is, Apple, Google, and Microsoft) see having the best apps as a competitive advantage, *and* two of those vendors are doing their bit to "sunset" Flash as a relevant web technology platform.

This leaves us in the curious situation where there is an exploding market for apps and a rapidly maturing web standards environment but some gaping holes in the web technology platform that gets broadly labeled as "HTML5."

It's an interesting time for the Web—web standards won but so far without the technology for the Web to go all the way as a ubiquitous platform for all. We've instead seen a '90s-esque explosion of platform-specific apps and the threat that vendor-specific "walled gardens" will make the Web a second-class citizen.

All is not lost, though. For one, many of those "native" apps are powered in large part by web standards under the surface. And Adobe, for its part, is also investing in HTML5 development tools and getting involved in the web standards process. The browser makers are improving their browsers at a breakneck speed, and new specifications to bridge the gulf between web standards and native app development are appearing all the time. We'll explore this more in Chapter 12 when we look at HTML5 and web apps.

Let's Bury Flash-isms with Flash

If Flash is dying on the Web, we should aim to bury some Flash-isms with it. Let's make sure we remember the lessons of the Flash era, especially when it comes to splash pages, loading screens, pointless animation, annoying widgets, and over-engineered, over-designed "experiences." They were mostly terrible ideas. Some things simply don't bear repeating, whether it's done in Flash, mountains of JavaScript, advanced CSS3, Canvas, or some ungodly combination of these technologies.

Let's also be careful of judging a technology too quickly. Canvas is going through its awkward adolescence at the moment—full of potential, embarrassing mistakes, experimentation, monosyllabic grunts, and finally (ideally!) maturity. Whenever new technology enters the web scene, it's generally shown off in a bunch of experimental or inappropriate ways as a gimmick before settling into its groove and being used moderately and appropriately. I hope Canvas finds its groove quickly.

We're Not in Canvas Anymore

That's the background. Now let's look at what the Canvas element actually does.

The `<canvas>` element defines a bitmap area—or "canvas," if you will—that you can program and draw on with Canvas' JavaScript API. The Canvas element has been kicking around since 2004 and was rolled into HTML5. All modern browsers support it natively (including IE9, although IE6–8 need to use emulation), as do modern mobile browsers.

The actual element looks like this:

```
<canvas id="mycanvas" width="500" height="200">
    Sorry, your browser doesn't support canvas.
</canvas>
```

Like other things in HTML5, browsers that don't understand `<canvas>` tags just see them as a generic element (like `<mymadeupelement>`) and ignore them, exposing the text between them.

That's it as far as the HTML goes. Everything else happens through the JavaScript API, which lets us do the following:

- Draw shapes, gradients, and shadows

- Manipulate images and text

- Create animations (by redrawing the canvas enough times per second)

Working with Canvas is like drawing on a single layer in Photoshop. You have only one layer of pixels to work with, and once you draw over them, they're gone. So, to do animation (in games, for instance), we need to redraw the canvas for every frame. Canvas has no sense of managing and manipulating objects (that's more SVG's thing, which we'll look at in Chapter 11), but a variety of libraries (for visualizations and games, in particular) have sprung up to help deal with this.

Given Canvas is manipulated through its JavaScript API, the extent you'll want to get your hands dirty will depend on your interest in JavaScript and drawing graphics programmatically. Here's an example of how we would draw a basic square (using the earlier `<canvas>` element and `<body onload="draw();">`):

```
function draw() {
    var canvas = document.getElementById('mycanvas');
    var context = canvas.getContext('2d');
    context.fillStyle = "rgb(200,0,0)";
    context.fillRect (10, 10, 100, 100);
}
```

This function gets our mycanvas Canvas element (using the 500 x 200px example we looked at earlier), sets the fill color to red, and then draws a solid red rectangle using the fillRect(x, y, width, height) function. As you can see in Figure 9-1, we've drawn a red square that is offset 10px on the *x*-axis, is offset 10px on the *y*-axis, and is 100px wide and 100px high. (I've added a 1px border around our <canvas> with CSS so you can see the size of the element itself.)

Generic Canvas

Figure 9-1. *Our simple Canvas example*

We won't delve into the workings of the Canvas API because there's plenty of solid resources online, including the following:

- Mozilla's Developer Network Canvas tutorial is a great place to start because it covers the basics and has a bunch of links in each section to other resources:
  https://developer.mozilla.org/en-US/docs/Web/Guide/HTML/Canvas_tutorial

- Opera has a short introduction to the basics of Canvas here:
  http://dev.opera.com/articles/view/html-5-canvas-the-basics/.

- Mark Pilgrim's *Dive Into HTML5* has a lengthy chapter on getting started with Canvas:
  http://diveintohtml5.info/canvas.html.

- There's a tutorial for creating a breakout clone with Canvas here:
  http://billmill.org/static/canvastutorial/.

- There's a whole site dedicated to Canvas tutorials here: www.html5canvastutorials.com/.

- The HTML5 spec for web developers (without all the implementer detail for browser vendors) has a concise run-through of Canvas's features here:
  http://developers.whatwg.org/the-canvas-element.html.

Canvas has great potential for gaming and visualizations, along with more mundane uses such as creating charts and even tooltips. But perhaps the most exciting use for Canvas is bringing 3D to the web in a roundabout way with WebGL.

We'll look at that in a moment. First, let's look at some examples of Canvas in action.

Cool Things with Canvas

You can do a bunch of cool things with Canvas, from animations to full-blown games. Let's start with something a bit more modest, though: tooltips.

Tooltips

Can the humble tooltip demonstrate that Canvas can be a better supported option than cutting-edge CSS3? I think so. Tipped (Figure 9-2, http://projects.nickstakenburg.com/tipped) is a great example of using Canvas to enhance a page. By drawing tooltips programmatically through the JavaScript API, there are no images to worry about. Check it out:

Figure 9-2. *Tipped examples*

Tipped

Tupped makes it easy to create new skins and themes, as well as effects such as rounded corners, shadows, and gradients, all on the fly with Canvas and its JavaScript API. Plus, with IE6–8 compatibility provided through ExCanvas (which we'll look at shortly), we get all the CSS3-style effects with full IE support.

Charts

Later we'll touch on some SVG-based charting tools (including gRaphaël and the excellent Highcharts). But there's no shortage of Canvas-based charting options either. Here's a small selection.

RGraph

Figure 9-3 shows a Canvas chart built with the powerful-if-not-all-that-pretty RGraph (www.rgraph.net/). The beauty of Canvas-based charts is the solid support in iOS (and Android), where Flash isn't an option. (The paid www.zingchart.com/ does Canvas, Flash, and SVG if you need better cross-platform support. If you're after something simpler, Flot is a popular, free, jQuery- and Canvas-based charting tool: http://www.flotcharts.org/

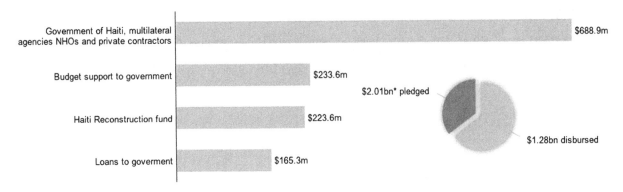

Figure 9-3. *An RGraph chart*

Visualize

Filament Group also has an accessible Canvas charting solution with its Visualize plug-in, which gives results like those shown in Figure 9-4. Visualize is discussed in detail at www.filamentgroup.com/lab/ update_to_jquery_ visualize_accessible_charts_with_html5_from_designing_with/.

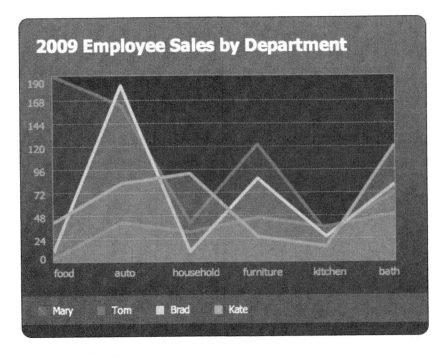

Figure 9-4. *Visualize in action*

HumbleFinance

HumbleFinance (www.humblesoftware.com/finance/index) is an HTML5-driven demonstration of Google Finance–style charting. Figure 9-5 shows an example of how clean the interface is. Because Canvas is just another HTML element, you can easily position other <div>s (or any other DOM object) on top of it, which HumbleFinance has done in Figure 9-5 for the chart labels and other text.

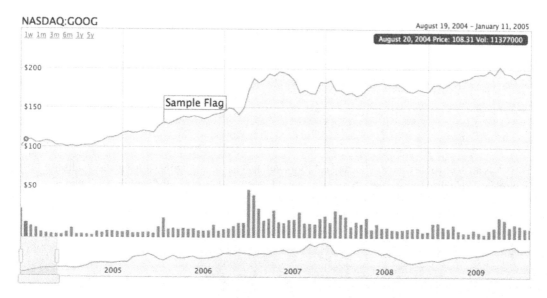

Figure 9-5. *HumbleFinance's sophisticated Canvas-powered chart*

Peity

Peity (http://benpickles.github.com/peity/) is a jQuery plug-in that turns an element's content into a mini pie, bar, or line chart. It takes the values in an element like <span class="line">5,3,9,6,5,9,7,3,5,2</span> and converts it into a <canvas> element that renders the appropriate chart (see Figure 9-6).

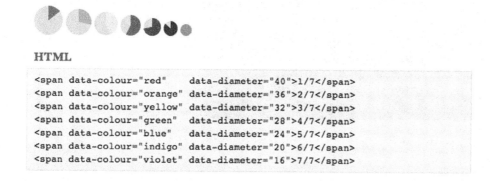

```
HTML
<span data-colour="red"    data-diameter="40">1/7</span>
<span data-colour="orange" data-diameter="36">2/7</span>
<span data-colour="yellow" data-diameter="32">3/7</span>
<span data-colour="green"  data-diameter="28">4/7</span>
<span data-colour="blue"   data-diameter="24">5/7</span>
<span data-colour="indigo" data-diameter="20">6/7</span>
<span data-colour="violet" data-diameter="16">7/7</span>
```

Figure 9-6. *Peity examples*

Similar to Peity, jQuery Sparklines (`http://omnipotent.net/jquery.sparkline/`) takes a similar Canvas-based approach and has even more options.

Visualizations

Canvas is a great tool for creating dynamic visualizations of data, and there are many great implementations of it. We'll highlight a few here.

Processing.js

Some of the best Canvas examples use Processing.js (`http://processingjs.org/`), the JavaScript port of the Processing visual programming language. Examples range from simple games to abstract digital art to visualizations (as shown in Figure 9-7).

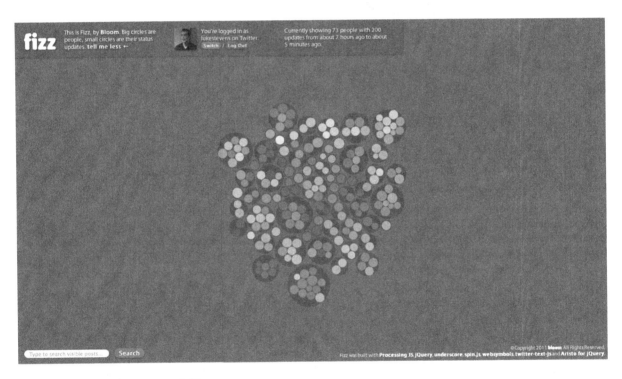

Figure 9-7. *Processing.js example Fizz*

"Evolution of Privacy on Facebook"

One of the most practical examples of a Canvas-based visualization using Processing.js is the interactive "Evolution of Privacy on Facebook" visualization (Figure 9-8; see `http://mattmckeon.com/facebook-privacy/`). Because it's implemented in Canvas, it will work on iOS devices, but we still have to worry about compatibility with the (currently) larger IE6–8 group.

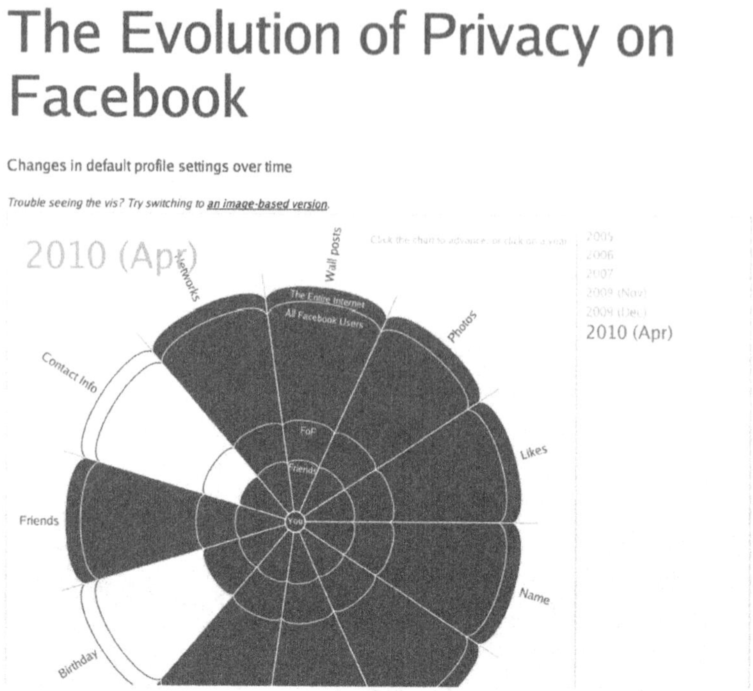

The Evolution of Privacy on Facebook

Changes in default profile settings over time

Trouble seeing the vis? Try switching to __an image-based version__.

Figure 9-8. *The "Evolution of Privacy on Facebook" visualization*

Canvas, Twitter, and Audio Mashup

From the practical to the … well, pretty. The HTML5 Canvas experiment shown in Figure 9-9 uses Processing.js for particle rendering and uses the `<audio>` element to play music (but it's not an audio visualizer). See it for yourself: `http://9elements.com/io/projects/html5/canvas/`. The particles are actually 100 HTML5-related tweets, with their contents rendered as normal HTML in the document. (See the write-up here: `http://9elements.com/io/?p=153`.)

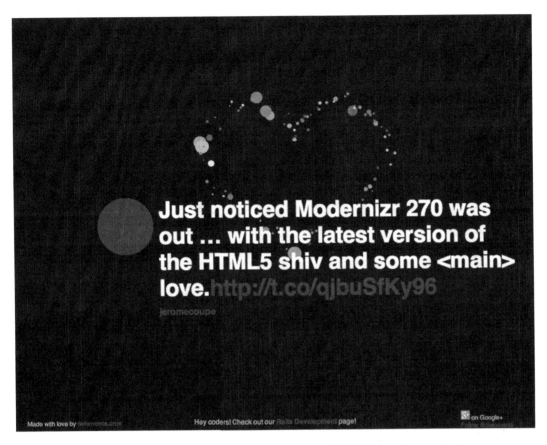

Figure 9-9. *This mashup pulls in HTML5-related tweets, some of which are quite appropriate*

Paper.js

Processing.js isn't the only game in town. Paper.js (Figure 9-10; see `http://paperjs.org`) dubs itself as "The Swiss Army Knife of Vector Graphics Scripting" and demonstrates how the bitmap-based Canvas element can be used for advanced vector graphics scripting, complete with a "Document Object Model for vector graphics" and keyboard and mouse interaction. See their examples for more: `http://paperjs.org/examples/`.

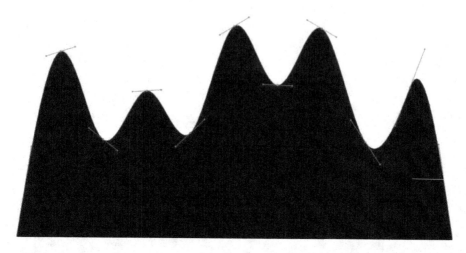

Figure 9-10. Paper.js looks great in motion—be sure to check out the examples on the site

(Smashing Magazine also published an extensive comparison of Processing.js, Paper.js, and the SVG-based Raphaël: `http://coding.smashingmagazine.com/2012/02/22/web-drawing-throwdown-paper-processing-raphael/`.)

Games

A variety of (mostly retro) games have been built with Canvas. We'll take a look at a handful here and then look at some amazing WebGL-powered games.

Google Chrome Racer

Speaking of Paper.js, Google Chrome added a game called "Racer" (see Figure 9-11) to their impressive HTML5 experiments that uses Paper.js, Canvas, and websockets to create a multiplayer game that runs in Chrome on iOS or Android. Racer shows off a major advantage of HTML5 games: they can run in on platform without having to be ported across devices. It relies on cutting edge HTML5 featurs and only claims to support Chrome, but works well in other modern mobile browsers as well. See more about it on the Racer website: `http://www.chrome.com/racer`.

Figure 9-11. *Google Chrome Racer shows off the power of Canvas on mobile devices*

Biolab Disaster

Biolab Disaster (Figure 9-12; see `http://playbiolab.com`) by Dominic Szablewski is a neat example of retro gaming using `<canvas>` for the visuals. It's a fun little platform game where you run, jump, and shoot your way through the levels.

Figure 9-12. *Biolab Disaster is a fun little platformer*

Canvas Rider

Canvas Rider (Figure 9-13; see http://canvasrider.com/) is another example of the fun (and hard!) browser games that can be built with Canvas. (Warning: it's highly addictive.)

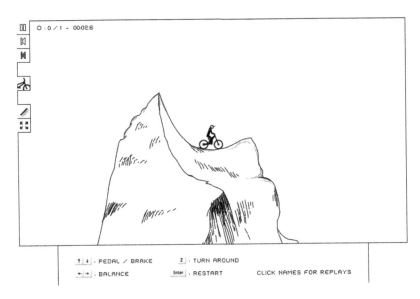

Figure 9-13. *Canvas Rider is addictive*

Cut the Rope

From small gaming experiments to huge international hits. The extraordinarily popular mobile game Cut the Rope (see Figure 9-14) was ported from the original iOS code to HTML5 and released in early 2012. The project was sponsored by Microsoft to show off the HTML5 capabilities of IE9, including its hardware-accelerated Canvas implementation. You can play it in your browser right now: www.cuttherope.ie/.

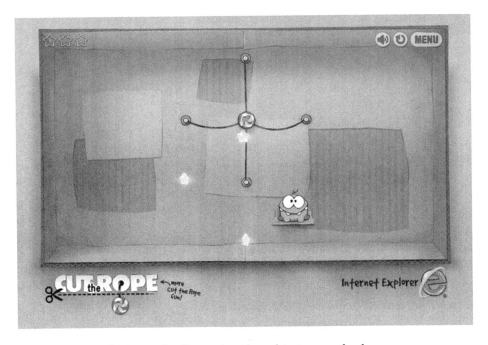

Figure 9-14. *Cut the Rope takes Canvas-based graphics to a new level*

This project demonstrates the potential of web standards for gaming: develop with tools like Canvas and then easily implement your game in modern browsers and bundle it up as a native app for any platform where HTML5 is well supported. We'll take a closer look at gaming and Canvas later in this chapter.

Image Manipulation

Online image manipulation is another category of web page that used to be possible only through Adobe Flash. Since it requires loading a file's raw bytes into memory, rendering the resulting image, and allowing the user to manipulate that image, you can imagine how difficult this was without a full blown image editing engine like Flash. However, recent advances in the ability to store and manipulate memory through JavaScript in Canvas have allowed similar sites to appear in HTML5 as well. Let's look at a few.

PaintbrushJS

With Canvas we can do some pretty impressive image manipulation, as Dave Shea's PaintbrushJS library ably demonstrates (http://mezzoblue.github.com/PaintbrushJS/demo/). PaintbrushJS lets us apply Gaussian blurs (see Figure 9-15), add noise, fade to grayscale (or sepia), and more. And it's all done on the client side with Canvas and JavaScript.

Figure 9-15. *PaintbrushJS can perform some impressive Photoshop-like effects*

Canvas-Driven Web Apps

Some real, honest-to-goodness web apps use Canvas, which show what's possible in the browser right now. They're mostly painting- or drawing-related (this is Canvas, after all), and none better illustrates this than deviantART's Muro—a free, HTML5-powered drawing/painting app (see Figure 9-16). Try it at `http://muro.deviantart.com/` or read more about it at `http://news.deviantart.com/article/125373/`.

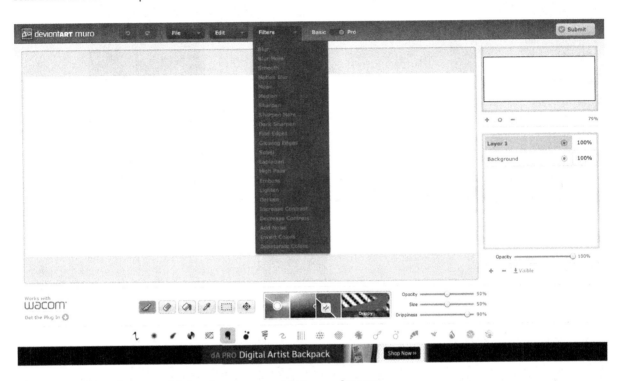

Figure 9-16. *Muro is a powerful drawing program, right in your browser*

Sketchpad

Sketchpad, as shown in Figure 9-17, is another great HTML5-powered painting app that you can play with here: `http://mugtug.com/sketchpad/`.

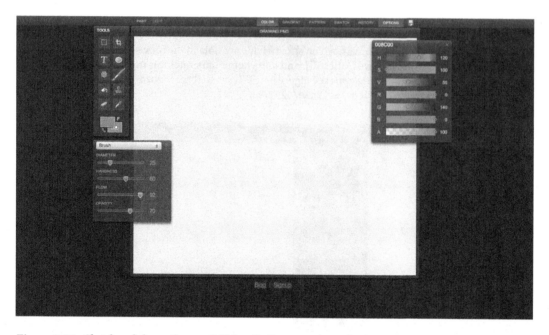

Figure 9-17. *Sketchpad shows the possibilities of a Canvas-powered painting program*

Endless Mural

The Endless Mural (Figure 9-18; see `www.endlessmural.com/`) is "an interactive, collaborative art web site," powered by Canvas and sponsored by Microsoft for its IE9 launch. The project is the work of Automata Studios and Joshua Davis Studios (Joshua Davis was an early Flash and digital art pioneer). The code has been released as Okapi, an "open-source framework for building digital, generative art in HTML5," and is available here: `http://www.okapijs.org/`.

Figure 9-18. *The Endless Mural site lets you create variations of this artwork*

LucidChart

It's not all arty painting, though. Some fully fledged diagramming (paid) web apps also use Canvas, such as LucidChart (shown in Figure 9-19), which you can test here: `www.lucidchart.com/`.

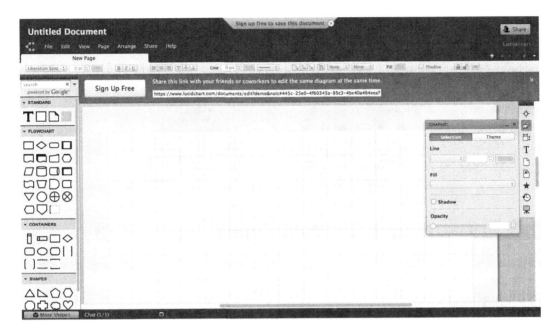

Figure 9-19. *LucidChart lets you dive right in with a couple of clicks, so give it a go*

Drawing Interface Elements

The prior examples all show Canvas being used to do some pretty wild stuff. What about employing it in a more normal context? In this section we'll look at ways Canvas is being used to augment regular interface elements to provide a more interesting experience.

Flash-Style Interface Effects

Rally Interactive pulled off an impressive animated triangle-to-circle effect to show off its work (see Figure 9-20), with screenshots and statistics pulled from Dribbble. I initially assumed it was a bunch of fancy CSS3 (which would be cool in its own right), but Rally Interactive is in fact using Canvas. See it in action: `http://beta.rallyinteractive.com/` (and view source to see how they did it).

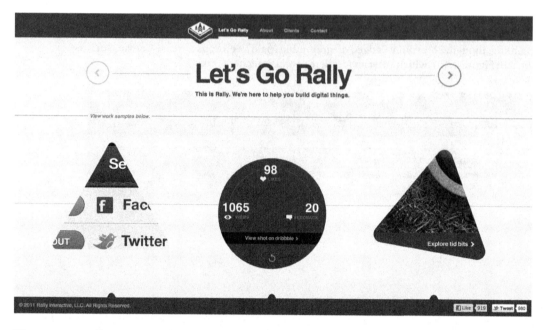

Figure 9-20. *Rally Interactive demonstrates that a clever use of multiple Canvas instances can produce impressive effects*

Background Animations

Google Music's tour page (see Figure 9-21) uses Canvas to render the background animations, which has the thick colored lines scribbling and scrawling as you move from section to section. See it in action: http://music.google.com/about/tour/.

Figure 9-21. *The Canvas-drawn background elements on the Google Music site take you on quite a journey as you browse the site*

Interface Backgrounds with Liquid Canvas

Here's an idea for us web designers: how about using Canvas to draw the *backgrounds* of interface elements? We could position <canvas> elements wherever we like in our markup, even layering them on top of each other as appropriate (using position and the z-index), and then have a small amount of JavaScript render all the graphics—no images required.

This approach could speed up development considerably. No more exporting finicky images from Photoshop to tweak a color scheme for a client. Just change some JavaScript variables and we're done. And with ExplorerCanvas for IE, we might even have better browser compatibility than the current state of CSS3. Plus, hardware acceleration is only making Canvas faster on the mobile and the desktop.

The best (and perhaps only) example of this is the Liquid Canvas JavaScript library (see Figure 9-22) from 2008. (You can read about it at www.ruzee.com/content/liquid-canvas and see it in action at www.ruzee.com/files/liquid-canvas/demo.html.) The demos aren't the prettiest, but the possibilities are certainly intriguing. For example, with Liquid Canvas you can use Canvas to draw backgrounds behind your <div>s with shadows, rounded corners, gradients, and strokes. (There's a tutorial available here: www.caffeinedi.com/2009/11/02/using-jquery-and-liquidcanvas-to-add-drop-shadows-borders-rounded-corners-and-other-effects-to-your-website-even-in-ie6-and-ie7/.)

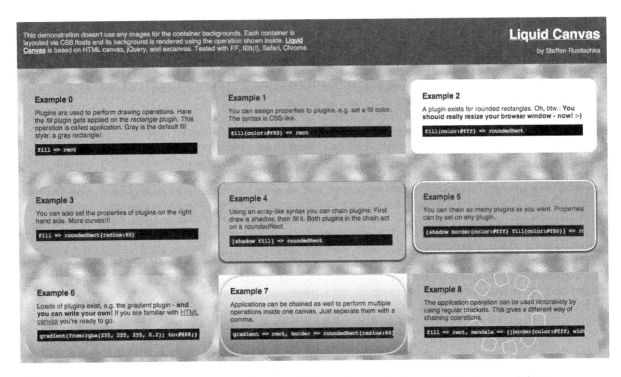

Figure 9-22. *The examples may not be pretty, but Liquid Canvas demonstrates some intriguing possibilities*

With a bit more design love, this could be a great way to A/B test certain aesthetic treatments of a layout, all using JavaScript alone—again, no images to export and maintain in CSS. Of course, there will always be limitations with this approach, and presentation should obviously be CSS's domain long term. (And, realistically, most people are going to stick with CSS3.) But Liquid Canvas certainly gives us a very novel approach to drawing interface elements.

We don't necessarily need to use Liquid Canvas in some (non-IE) situations either. It's been possible to use Canvas elements as CSS backgrounds in WebKit since 2008 (!), as described here: www.webkit.org/blog/176/css-canvas-drawing/. Firefox 4 added similar support in 2011 (http://hacks.mozilla.org/2010/08/mozelement/), and there are workarounds for other browsers (for static Canvas's), as described in the answers here: http://stackoverflow.com/questions/3397334/use-canvas-as-a-css-background. With hardware acceleration arriving and the ability to use Canvas as a CSS background, we have some intriguing options for fast, programmatically generated interface elements.

Consider the possibilities for responsive web design too—we can programmatically redraw CSS backgrounds (in iOS at least) based on the device's resolution. There's no need to download a desktop-sized image and shrink it down or maintain different sets of artwork for different devices; just let a script do the heavy lifting for us. (Let me know if you create such a script!)

While we're floating ideas, I'd love to see something like the Photoshop-esque layer-style panel for CSS3 effects (which is very cool in its own right—see http://layerstyles.org/builder.html) built for Canvas. It could generate the Liquid Canvas–style JavaScript, which you could then drop into your page and have the effects rendered on just about all browsers. Heck, it would be cool if Photoshop itself could export to Canvas.

Canvas may not be a Flash replacement, but these examples show it certainly opens up some interesting doors.

The Sometimes Good and Sometimes Bad Canvas Emulation for IE6–8

While IE6–8 don't support Canvas, all is not lost. Several emulation options can give these browsers at least *some* support using IE's native, legacy Vector Markup Language (VML); Microsoft's Silverlight plug-in; or Flash.

Each approach has its pros and cons. VML is slow and loads elements into the DOM. (Canvas elements get re-created as vector elements, so the more that get loaded, the slower it gets.) But animation is smooth, and the Canvas on the whole remains in the DOM.

While IE6–8 don't support Canvas, all is not lost. Several emulation options can give these browsers at least *some* support using IE's native, legacy Vector Markup Language (VML); Microsoft's Silverlight plug-in; or Flash.

Each approach has its pros and cons. VML is slow and loads elements into the DOM. (Canvas elements get re-created as vector elements, so the more that get loaded, the slower it gets.) But animation is smooth, and the Canvas on the whole remains in the DOM.

Throw in issues with interactivity, mixed support for features in the Canvas API, and performance issues for processor-intensive applications, and you have quite a mixed bag. You can still render some impressive animated effects (albeit slowly) or render static images and have them available in the DOM (which is great for charts and the like). But it may be a case of "so close, so far" if performance isn't up to scratch or a crucial feature isn't supported.

Here are the tools that do the emulation. Check out their demos in IE 6, 7, or 8 to get a feel for how they perform (for example, try these in IE: http://code.google.com/p/flashcanvas/wiki/Examples). In some cases (such as static Canvas renderings), you may never know it's being emulated, while in other cases you may get away with acceptable-if-not-perfect emulation. Just remember that Canvas emulation can be a pretty murky area; it's rarely a get-perfect-support-for-free-IE6–8 card.

Here are some Canvas emulation utilities:

- ExplorerCanvas (a.k.a. ExCanvas) is the most well-known. It uses VML, and there's an unsupported Silverlight option too. Check it out at http://excanvas.sourceforge.net/.

- FlashCanvas, as shown in Figure 9-23, is a Flash-based implementation for Canvas under active development (see http://code.google.com/p/flashcanvas/ and http://flashcanvas.net/). A Pro version is also available.

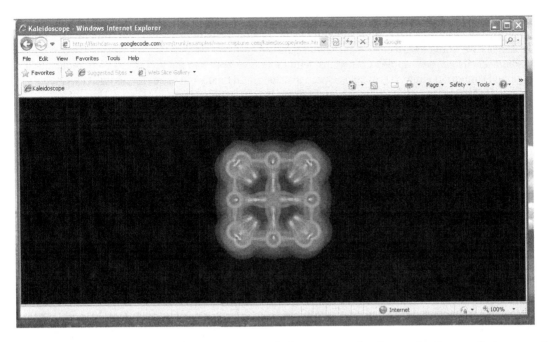

Figure 9-23. *This kaleidoscope FlashCanvas example demonstrates that impressive Canvas effects are possible even in IE7; they're just slow*

- fxCanvas is another Flash-based implementation (albeit less mature) of Canvas for IE and is also under active development: `http://code.google.com/p/fxcanvas/`.

- Finally (and most intriguingly) is the Japanese uuCanvas that claims to offer rendering in either VML, Silverlight, or Flash. Read about it here: `http://uupaa-js-spinoff.googlecode.com/svn/trunk/uuCanvas.js/README.htm`. (Again, Google Translate will help.)

The Haphazard World of Web Standards (Or: How Did We End Up with Canvas?)

Let's touch on the history of Canvas because it illustrates how haphazardly these features can be developed (as was the case with much of HTML5, which is in some ways just a grab-bag of tech that's been around for years).

> *"HTML5" is just a buzzword for 7 years worth of neat stuff.*

> —Dave Balmer, `www.slideshare.net/dbalmer/rockstar-graphics-with-html5-media-uk`

Do you use OS X's Dashboard feature? That's where Canvas originated, back in 2004. Apple wanted Dashboard widgets to be easy to write, so it based them on the good ol' web stack of HTML, CSS, and JavaScript (and native code if you wanted) and used WebKit to render them. (WebKit is the rendering engine behind Safari and Google's Chrome.)

But Apple thought the web stack for rendering Dashboard widgets had limitations, so it added a few features to WebKit, the major one being Canvas. Safari uses WebKit, and so Safari now supported Canvas. And lo, Canvas on the Web was born.

This, in the tradition of new web technology, caused considerable concern.

Vendors adding browser-specific features to HTML, without any standards process, is what the web standards movement was trying to get *away* from. Had Microsoft and Mozilla responded with their own, incompatible attempts at something like Canvas, we would have a great mess on our hands.

So, Ian Hickson *reverse engineered* Apple's Canvas implementation and put it in the WHATWG Web Applications 1.0 spec. Canvas gained support in Firefox 1.5 in 2005, Opera 9 in 2006, and finally IE9 in 2011. The WHATWG Web Apps 1.0 spec became HTML5 as we saw in Chapter 1, and Canvas is now an official part of HTML5. Hats off to Hickson for all his work bringing it into the spec.

(For more on Canvas' history, see `http://peter.sh/2010/06/thank-you-microsoft-html5-canvas-is-a-go/`.)

The Canvas Element and Accessibility

In terms of accessibility, Canvas can be a bit of a nightmare. There's nothing for a screen reader to read—just a black hole and whatever text (if any) the designer has put between the `<canvas>` tags.

Vendors are trying to address this. For example, IE9+ exposes the fallback content between the `<canvas>` tags to assistive technology. The idea here is that when the browser *does* support Canvas but the vision-impaired user can't see it, they can still get something useful in the form of alternate text via their screen reader, for example. (Well, that's the theory. At the moment they'll get a lot of erroneous "Your browser doesn't support canvas" messages, because that's how the fallback content has been used to date.) For more, see accessibility guru Steve Faulkner's discussion of this feature at `www.paciellogroup.com/blog/2010/09/html5-canvas-accessibility-in-internet-explorer-9/` and the right way to make content inside of a canvas accessible at `http://blog.paciellogroup.com/2012/06/html5-canvas-accessibility-in-firefox-13/`.

As for the accessibility of the Canvas element itself, it's a thorny issue that has been discussed for *years*, and it still hasn't been resolved. There's a summary of the last few years of discussions at `www.paciellogroup.com/blog/2011/12/html5-canvas-accessibility-discussions-2009-2011/`, but that's as far as we've come.

Let's not repeat the accessibility mistakes of decades past with `<canvas>`. We could in theory render fancy text, an entire web page, or a web application (which has been done!), with JavaScript in a `<canvas>` area. But it's a terrible idea and about as useful (from an accessibility perspective) as having our design as one giant image.

(You can do some crazy things with text in Canvas, though, as this tutorial illustrates: `www.html5rocks.com/tutorials/canvas/texteffects/`. So, we may still do text replacement with such techniques.)

The Current State of Canvas

Technologies (web or otherwise) don't exist in a vacuum. Their success often depends on having a conducive environment around them. There's certainly plenty of enthusiasm *for* Canvas, but what about the environment *around* it?

Primitive Development Environment

It's worth remembering the environment around Canvas is still quite primitive, so there are few (if any) development tools. (Flash has been successful not just because of Flash Player's ubiquity but also the mature tools available to developers.)

The situation is changing. HTML5 game engines (for example, `http://impactjs.com/`, which was used for the game Biolab Disaster, featured earlier) usually have some support for Canvas, but they're pretty niche- and developer-oriented, not quite what we need for general web design.

In terms of tools for designers, there's an Adobe Illustrator to Canvas plug-in from Microsoft's Mike Swanson (`http://visitmix.com/labs/ai2canvas/`). And Adobe has been working on Canvas animations for some time, as we looked at earlier, first through Flash Authoring and now through Adobe Edge. (Adobe has also been experimenting with more generic "HTML5" export, but it uses the term *HTML5* quite loosely. We'll look more at Adobe's position when we discuss SVG in Chapter 11.)

Performance

One of the exciting things about Canvas is that you can view it on everything from iOS, where Flash isn't an option, to the desktop. In simple, static cases, such as graphs and charts, this is a reality now. But for anything more processor-intensive (such as animation and gaming), recent mobile devices simply haven't been powerful enough to do anything other than simple tasks.

This is changing, though, particularly as mobile devices get faster and Canvas gets hardware acceleration (as Microsoft promised and demonstrated for IE9 mobile: www.gsmarena.com/ internet_explorer_9_on_wp7_aces_ html5_drawing_test-news-2524.php). Apple has also dramatically improved Canvas performance in iOS Safari starting in iOS5. See jsPerf.com for up to date performance statistics across all of the prominent browser, platforms, and devices (http://jsperf.com/canvas-draw-tests).

Sencha also reported dramatic Canvas iOS5 speed improvements: www.sencha.com/blog/apple-ios-5-html5-developer-scorecard/. (Sencha's HTML5 blog posts are excellent for keeping up on feature support, by the way.)

Hardware acceleration is making a big difference. But at the moment anything Canvas-intensive can quickly turn into a relative chug-fest on your not-cutting-edge phone or tablet (as the iOS4 and Android device results earlier demonstrated).

Limited IE Compatibility

As we saw, IE6–8 can support Canvas to varying degrees and in several ways (VML, Flash, Silverlight). If you're set on using Canvas, this may be a godsend. But compared to Flash, it may be a total headache and limit Canvas's uptake until IE9 becomes the new baseline for design and development. (Remember, IE8 is the end of the line for Windows XP users, so we'll need to wait until Windows XP finally disappears before we can assume native Canvas support.)

While simple or static Canvas implementations may be perfectly acceptable with emulation, complex animation and games are probably out of the question. This creates an odd situation when Flash-style interactivity is a necessity—we can either support IE8 and older with a Flash-based experience that won't work on mobile or create something for modern browsers that won't work on IE8 and older. Some poor designers and developers may end up doing both and may ironically end up creating a more advanced Flash experience for the legacy desktop browsers and a simpler Canvas-based version for the modern browsers. Here's to the speedy demise of IE8 and the rapid development, adoption, and maturation of new web standards.

Again with the Glass Metaphor

This is another one of HTML5's "glass half-full, glass half-empty" situations. It's amazing what people are doing with what was once an OS X Dashboard feature from 2004—from nifty design features (such as tooltips) and interactive experiments to games and full-blown web apps. Canvas wasn't designed with these things in mind; it just turned out to be useful in those situations. That's the "glass half-full" perspective. If you're waiting for a mature, "write-once, run-anywhere on the desktop" environment such as Flash, however, it probably looks like the glass is half empty. We're going to be waiting a good while yet.

HTML5 Gaming: Canvas or Not?

Canvas often gets mentioned when discussing HTML5 and games, so let's take a brief look at the state of HTML5 gaming. Could you use your existing web skills to write games using HTML and JavaScript that run in any modern browser? Sure, if you're comfortable developing in JavaScript. Will the game be any good? Well, that depends....

One of the biggest trends in recent years has been casual gaming, both in browsers and on mobile devices such as the iPhone. From FarmVille to AngryBirds to CandyCrush, social games on the web (primarily inside of other services like Facebook) or mobile devices have been a dominant force in the gaming world for recent years and keeps growing as smart phone penetration grows.

So, an open, cross-device platform for creating casual, social games is appealing, from both a hard-nosed business perspective and an idealistic "open platform" perspective, and HTML5 fits the bill quite nicely.

The key is to understand what type of "gaming" we're talking about here. Graphically these are often simple 2D games, similar to what was around in the early '90s. In this sense, it's very much "back to the future"—we're using the latest web tech to create games that look 20 years old in the very modern, mobile world of social networking.

Is It Even Canvas?

For all the HTML5 hype, some of these HTML games and game engines have *explicitly avoided* features such as Canvas for performance reasons, relying on DOM scripting and CSS3 (which is partly hardware-accelerated on iOS devices) to get the job done. Here's what one group of developers found from a quick tech demo that followed an HTML gaming engine approach (http://seb.ly/2011/04/html5javascript-platform-game-optimised-for-ipad/):

> *So what's the answer to getting the performance on iOS? Forget HTML5 canvas, all the moving objects in this game are HTML div elements, we're just moving them around by controlling CSS properties with JavaScript.*

When discussing HTML5, we need to look closely at the technology and techniques people are actually using. What you think is Canvas may well not be. Canvas may be used more widely in web-based gaming as performance improves (and hardware acceleration becomes the norm), but it's worth keeping in mind just how liberally the term *HTML5* gets thrown around.

Don't get me wrong: the demos and ports have shown us the scope of what's possible for HTML5 games on the desktop now and in mobile browsers in the not-too-distant future. Just keep in mind the phenomena of casual gaming in the browser is less about the latest technology and more about big ideas such as social networking, which the traditional web stack can exploit in pretty interesting ways. That said, hardware-accelerated, 3D gaming is also coming to the browser through Canvas thanks to WebGL, which we'll look at shortly.

Getting Started with Canvas Game Development

Nevertheless, if you want to get hands-on with Canvas for gaming, check out the tutorial and overview (just ignore the hype in the article) at www.html5rocks.com/tutorials/casestudies/onslaught.html or the absolute beginners tutorial at www.lostdecadegames.com/how-to-make-a-simple-html5-canvas-game/. And don't forget the game examples we looked at earlier, including Cut the Rope (www.cuttherope.ie).

For a detailed rundown of all the different technologies available for "HTML5" games (in the broader sense) and their delivery and monetization options, check out this excellent article from January 2012: "The Reality of HTML5 Game Development and making money from it" (www.photonstorm.com/archives/2759/the-reality-of-html5-game-development-and-making-money-from-it). For a more up-to-date listing of popular HTML5 games, check out html5games.com.

HTML Gaming: Beyond HTML5

There is also a lot of developer interest in taking the web platform beyond HTML5 and including things like the Joystick API, surround-sound support, and extensions to CSS. It's a bit dated now, but the W3C held a workshop all about html.next and games – see their detailed write-up for more: "Report on the Workshop on HTML.next for Games" (www.w3.org/2011/09/games/). We'll touch on the post-HTML5 web platform in Chapter 12.

Canvas: What's in It for Me?

Now that we've looked at some specific use cases for Canvas on the web, let's consider canvas from a different perspective: what type of people is it relevant to?

Canvas for Web Designers

How much Canvas will matter to you depends on where you work and the projects you do. If you work in a big-budget agency, where Facebook components are mandatory for massive, national, or worldwide marketing campaigns, you may find new gaming capabilities very interesting.

If you're a freelancer doing client work on tight budgets, the off-the-shelf charting tools like we saw may not be *quite* as sexy but extremely useful nevertheless. Canvas emulation for IE6–8 may prove handy as a cross-device solution (as opposed to Flash-based tools) that covers IE6+ *and* iOS devices.

Canvas-based image editing tools for content management systems could start springing up too, and if you like to tinker, there is enormous room for experimentation. You may want to experiment with rendering interface elements with Canvas (as the Liquid Canvas and Tipped libraries demonstrate) or see how far you can push Canvas in the way studios like Rally Interactive have demonstrated.

Canvas for Students and Hobbyists

A free, open, and relatively simple platform such as HTML, JavaScript, and CSS could create a fertile environment for kids who want to cut their teeth on simple game design. With tutorials and development libraries springing up all over the place, they have enough information to start making simple (and not so simple) games. It would be great to see this happen in schools, and it wouldn't need much resourcing—just a half-decent PC (or a $35 Raspberry Pi: `www.raspberrypi.org/`) and a modern-ish browser.

Canvas for Flash Designers

I was all ready to beat down on Flash again here, but then Adobe dropped a bombshell. As of December 2013, Flash Professional CC now includes full native support of Canvas. This is great news for pretty much everyone involved. Canvas has been screaming out for a good authoring tool, and there are an awful lot of designers and developers out there who are familiar with Flash Professional. You now get to design and animate within Flash Professional's mature toolset, and then push it straight out to Canvas. At the time of this writing this is still very fresh news, so nobody's really had much of a chance to put it through its paces, but if it works well then we should see a lot more people switching over to Canvas, and a lot of stunning work appearing. Flash is dead, long live Flash!

Suck It and See

We have enormous scope for weaving the `<canvas>` element into our web pages in subtle (or not-so-subtle) ways. But whether Canvas becomes a staple web design tool or simply the Java applet of our time is up to us. Let's give it a go and see what we can come up with.

2D Canvas's 3D Future: WebGL

I've left the best to last—one of the most exciting developments related to Canvas is WebGL (Web-based Graphics Library). Despite Canvas's ostensibly 2D origins, the new WebGL standard gives Canvas a hardware-accelerated 3D context powered by OpenGL—*if* the browser (and underlying hardware) supports it. This opens the door to modern, 3D gaming in your browser.

(The WebGL spec wasn't developed by the W3C or the WHATWG but instead by nonprofit technology consortium Khronos Group, which sprang from Mozilla and shepards OpenGL as well. So, it's not HTML5 per se, but it's still cool.)

The WebGL working group includes Apple, Google, Mozilla, and Opera. (See the Wikipedia entry for more: http://en.wikipedia.org/wiki/WebGL.) Microsoft was a late adopter of WebGL, citing some legitimate concerns around security that were echoed by others (such as John Carmack, founder of id Software and a highly respected gaming developer: https://twitter.com/#!/ID_AA_Carmack/status/81732190949486592). But with Microsoft on board in IE11, it's looking very likely that WebGL will be the de facto hardware-accelerated 3D content technology provider for the modern Web.

(Here's a techcrunch blog post on Microsoft's adoption of WebGL: http://techcrunch.com/2013/10/21/with-internet-explorer-on-board-webgl-is-ready-for-prime-time/.)

3D on the Web: WebGL Alternatives

WebGL isn't the only game in town, either.

The major players in browser technology were eyeing 3D development years ago. Adobe Flash had a thriving 3D development community years before it introduced hardware accelerated 3D in 2010. Around the same time, Microsoft introduced hardware accelerated 3D in its Silverlight plugin. But with Silverlight all but gone as a browser plugin and Flash quickly disappearing, what options do 3D developers still have?

Interestingly, Unity Technologies, which makes the popular cross-platform (and very mobile-friendly) 3D engine Unity, has been distributing its own browser plug-in, which it claims has seen 225 million downloads. It is also rolling out an export-to-Flash option so users don't need to download the Unity browser plug-in. Microsoft also recently announced a deal with Unitey for creating content for Windows 8 devices, dedicating "porting labs" to help developers, and claims at least 1000 game ports to date (see their announcement here: http://blogs.windows.com/windows_phone/b/wpdev/archive/2013/11/18/1000-unity-apps-across-windows-store-and-windows-phone.aspx).

It's worth noting that Unity's made a lot of headway into all of the areas Flash was tryin to get to extend it's life: games, 3D, and exporting directly to mobile devices. More than Canvas, WebGL, or any other HTML5 technology, Unity may be the player that actually replaces Flash in those contexts.

WebGL also has old-school predecessors. Displaying 3D on the Web isn't new—Virtual Reality Modeling Language (VRML), for example, dates back to 1994 (see http://en.wikipedia.org/wiki/VRML). But with hardware-accelerated 3D now pretty much a given on any platform (including smartphones), the potential for 3D on the Web for gaming and beyond (for example, 3D-modeled product previews, medical models, maps, and more) is infinitely greater.

Who knows? Maybe we'll finally have the technology for that 3D "virtual" shopping mall experience we've all been, uh, craving...

So WebGL isn't the only game in town, but support and popularity are growing fast. Let's look at a few demos and you can make up your own mind about whether you think plugins are a part of the 3D-and-gaming web's future or not.

Show Me the Demos!

When it comes to WebGL, seeing is believing. So, fire up the latest version of your favorite browser and check out these cool demos. And remember, this is all happening in <canvas>—just another element in the DOM (which we can push around with CSS3).

HelloRun

This addictive and immersive game by HelloEnjoy shows off just how far rendering in a browser has come in recent years. The game (Figure 9-24) renders an immersive 3D environment complete with reflections, fog, and a slew of lighting effects, all rather smoothly and without relying on a plugin. You can play it here: `http://hellorun.helloenjoy.com/`.

Figure 9-24. HelloRun shows the full power of WebGL in a simple and addictive browser game

Epic Citadel

In 2013 Epic Games released a demo of the Unreal Engine 3 running in WebGL (Figure 9-25). The company released a small level called the "Epic Citadel" that allowed a player to navigate an immersive, if small, 3D world. It demonstrated that WebGL could be used to deliver console-quality experiences in the browser. Check it out here: `http://www.unrealengine.com/html5/`.

Figure 9-25. *Epic's Unreal Engine 3 running in a browser*

Angry Birds

Yep, Angry Birds in the browser (Figure 9-26, `http://chrome.angrybirds.com`). WebGL delivers hardware-accelerated 2D graphics as well. (Take a moment to consider the implications of 2D, WebGL-powered interfaces for web sites, not just games.) Try Angry Birds on the Web for yourself at `http://chrome.angrybirds.com`. Interestingly, when WebGL isn't available, this falls back to DOM animation (including moving 2D Canvas elements around), so you can compare the performance and how much a 2D game like Angry Birds benefits from hardware acceleration. (You still need Flash for sound because of the poor state of audio for games in browsers.)

Figure 9-26. *The Angry Birds juggernaut hits the Web thanks to WebGL*

Rome "3 Dreams in Black" Interactive Music Video

This incredible music video for Danger Mouse's Rome project (Figure 9-27) is a great example of how interactive WebGL can be. Check it out in Chrome at www.ro.me, though it should be viewable in the latest Firefox versions as well. It's an amazing experience, and there are even user-submitted 3D models in the desert at the end.

Figure 9-27. *The Rome experience is an absolute must-see*

You can watch a video of the team behind the film (though "film" doesn't do it justice) with clips of the experience here: `www.youtube.com/watch?v=ReH7zzj5GPc`.

It will be exciting to see what designers, artists, and engineers can produce with this technology in the future. (I just hope it doesn't turn into too much of a marketing tool. Imagine reading the news on a mainstream news site when suddenly a big Canvas element is overlaid and you're thrust into a 3D "brand experience.")

glfx.js Image Manipulation

Earlier we saw how Canvas can manipulate images in 2D, but WebGL unleashes even more power thanks to its hardware acceleration: `http://evanw.github.com/glfx.js/`. The WebGL-powered glfx.js image effects library lets us apply hardware-accelerated, Photoshop-like filters such as brightness/contrast, curves, denoise, hue/saturation, unsharp mask, lens blur, tilt shift, triangle blur, zoom blur, color halftone, perspective transformations, swirls, and more (Figure 9-28). Check out the demo to see it in action: `http://evanw.github.com/glfx.js/demo/`.

Figure 9-28. *The tilt shift effect in glfx.js is one of many Photoshop-esque effects*

Quake II

Quake II (figure 9-29) has also been ported to WebGL, using "WebGL, the Canvas API, HTML 5 `<audio>` elements, the local storage API, and WebSockets to demonstrate the possibilities of pure web applications in modern browsers such as Safari and Chrome." For more, see `http://code.google.com/p/quake2-gwt-port/`. (You need to download and compile the code to actually play it, but there's a video of it in action here: `www.youtube.com/watch?v=fyfu4OwjUEI`. There's also a Quake 3 demo level in WebGL here: `http://media.tojicode.com/q3bsp/`.)

Figure 9-29. *Quake II running in the browser using only web technologies*

In a response to a tweet that said this:

Not sure if the best endorsement of JS engine speed in 2010 is ports of games from 1997...

Joel Webber, one of the engineers behind the port, wrote the following (http://blog.j15r.com/2010/04/quake-ii-in-html5-what-does-this-really.html):

What's the point? What this code currently proves is that it's feasible to build a "real" game on WebGL, including complex game logic, collision detection, and so forth. It also did an excellent job exposing weak spots in the current specs and implementations, information we can and will use to go improve them. [...]
[O]ne can envision a world where game developers can deploy their games as easily as we currently deploy web pages, and users can play them just as easily. And that's a pretty damned compelling world to imagine.

Send a link. Play the game. That's what WebGL (and the other emerging 3D technologies) will enable. Or, in fact, *is* enabling.

GT Racing: Motor Academy

In December 2011, Gameloft debuted a WebGL-powered version of its game GT Racing: Motor Academy on Google+ (Figure 9-30). This is an interesting look at not just the future of gaming technology in the browser but distribution through social networks too. (Gameloft's Baudouin Corman discussed these issues with Gamasutra here: www.gamasutra.com/view/news/39273/Gameloft_Embraces_HTML5_With_3D_Game_GT_Racing.php.)

GT Racing: Motor Academy `+1` 21k   ⚙ ▾

Figure 9-30. *Playing GT Racing live in the browser on Google+*

Skid Racer

GT Racing isn't the only WebGL-powered racing game. Skid Racer (Figure 9-31) is an original, WebGL-powered "kart racer" that's available online here: `https://skid.gamagio.com/play/`. (The irony of a web-based, Chrome-only game should be noted, but we'll give the developer the benefit of the doubt and put it down to distribution issues.)

Figure 9-31. *The console-like Skid Racer may represent one of the first steps in modern, 3D, web-distributed games*

More WebGL Demos

Here are some more WebGL demos and examples:

- Mozilla's Flight of the Navigator demo (http://videos-cdn.mozilla.net/serv/mozhacks/flight-of-the-navigator/) is an interesting mashup of new web technology. It's mostly a WebGL fly-through with HTML5 audio but with real-time Flickr and Twitter integration. Some of the effects (interlacing on billboards, ticker-tape displays, and audio visualizations) are done with Processing.js and 2D Canvas (which we looked at earlier) and then used to texture the 3D WebGL objects. Crazy. (Read more about it here: http://vocamus.net/dave/?p=1233.)

- Google MapsGL is a WebGL-powered version of its ubiquitous maps service, where WebGL is used to enhance the experience. Read more about it and watch a demo here: http://support.google.com/maps/bin/answer.py?hl=en&answer=1630790.

- CycleBlob is a fun light-cycle game on 3D surfaces: http://cycleblob.com/.

- Tankworld is a great little tank shooter: www.playtankworld.com.

- Süperfad's Mission Control, its "global traffic visualizer," is a beautiful 3D visualization of its Google Analytics traffic. See it live at http://superfad.com/missioncontrol/ and read about it at http://superfad.com/blog/post/mission_control.

For more reading, check out HTML5 Games Most Wanted, which covers CycleBlog in depth, and Beginning WebGL for HTML5, both published by APress and available at après.com. For more WebGL demos, see the experiments at www.chromeexperiments.com/webgl or this list of traditional Canvas as well as WebGL games http://www.creativebloq.com/html5/top-20-html5-games-1122788.

Still Early Days for WebGL

The WebGL games and demos show incredible promise, but it's not all beer and Skittles for WebGL development at present. One developer on Hacker News commented on the hardware incompatibilities, software bugs, and inconsistencies that can make it a difficult development environment for small teams, saying this (https://news.ycombinator.com/item?id=3253016):

> [W]e found so many inconsistencies across different hardware and different browsers that it made it not worth it to work on a WebGL project for the time being, especially for a small team. We wrote a number of runtime checks, but we still could not account for all the bugs, or find ways around every one of them.

Nevertheless, as the earlier demos show, amazing things are possible. And if you're interested in the raw performance details of WebGL, check out the extensive post "HTML5 2D gaming performance analysis" (www.scirra.com/blog/58/html5-2d-gaming-performance-analysis) from Scirra, developers of HTML5 game–making tool Construct 2, which concludes the following:

> Hardware accelerated 2D canvases are fast, but WebGL is still way faster. It is in the realm of native engines, which is frankly amazing considering how inefficiently designed JavaScript is, and is a testament to the amazing job browser makers have done in writing JIT compilers for JavaScript.

WebGL's also made inroads in mobile browsers, gaining support in the mobile versions of Firefox, Opera, Chrome (if enabled), and IE (with a polyfill.) At the time of this writing mobile Safari is the only holdout and Apple hasn't announced any plans to make it available.

That wraps up our discussion of Canvas, Gaming, and the future of immersive experiences without Flash. Next we'll dive into the exciting and misleading world of HTML5 Audio and Video support.

The Truth About Audio and Video in HTML5

Both <audio> and <video> are welcome additions to the HTML spec. We don't use proprietary tools (such as Flash) to display images, so why should we need them to play audio or video?

Don't get me wrong: I'm not here to bash Flash. Without it we wouldn't have YouTube, Vimeo, and the video revolution that has taken place over the past few years. And Flash still provides advanced video features (such as live streaming, full-screen playback, and DRM, as icky as DRM is) that have either no or very preliminary implementations as open standards.

Nevertheless, HTML5 <video> and <audio> have become almost mandatory for media delivery for one reason: iOS. Given Apple's decision not to allow Flash on its mobile devices, the only way to embed video and audio so it's available for iPhone, iPad, and iPod touch users is to use these new HTML5 elements.

But it doesn't stop at iOS. As we saw in the previous chapter, in late 2011 Adobe announced it was abandoning the Flash plug-in on mobile altogether and shifting its focus to native apps and HTML5.(For more on the demise of the Flash plug-in, check out the discussion in the previous chapter.)

We're racing toward a post-Flash future. Unfortunately, our open technologies are just not ready to replace all that Flash offers. Web standards won, and we're going to get caught with our pants down if we're not careful. That leaves apps to fill the gaps, taking us back to the '90s with platform-specific software.

We'll return to the issue of our post-Flash future shortly. For now, let's look at the new HTML5 <audio> and <video> elements as they currently stand. While these elements are specified quite simply, issues outside the spec make their implementation *interesting*, to say the least. First let's look at the basics.

Native <video> and <audio> in Action

So, how do we use these new elements? In theory, it's pretty simple. Let's start with <audio>.

The <audio> Element

For audio, we can use this:

```
<audio controls autoplay loop muted preload="auto">
    <source src="myaudio.ogg" type="audio/ogg">
    <source src="myaudio.mp3" type="audio/mpeg">
    <!-- Fallback content, such as a Flash player, here -->
</audio>
```

This will give us something like the Chrome example shown in Figure 10-1 (note that browsers render the <audio> element however they want, and there can be considerable difference in player size).

Figure 10-1. *The default audio player in Chrome, Safari, and Firefox (from top to bottom)*

Let's run through this. First, you *can* stick the src attribute in the opening <audio> tag if you like, instead of using the <source> element. But because of mind-bogglingly annoying issues with codec support (which we'll delve into shortly), we often need to specify two source files for maximum HTML5 compatibility.

And that's what the <source> element is for. Browsers work through the list of <source> elements until either they find a file format they support or (if we've included one) they get a fallback option—perhaps a link to the file or (more commonly) a Flash media player. (See the following resources for a tutorial on implementing a Flash fallback.)

Both <audio> and <video> are implemented in a backward-compatible way, insofar as older browsers (such as IE8) will ignore the <audio> and <source> elements altogether (IE8 just sees those elements as generic tags, like <mymadeuptag>). This means whatever fallback content we include will be visible to the older browsers but ignored by the modern ones.

We can also use scripting to give a Flash fallback to browsers that support the <audio> (or <video>) elements but *not* the codec we've used. We'll look at media players that do the heavy lifting for us at the end of this chapter.

<audio> Attributes

Back to the <audio> element. The attributes controls, autoplay, loop, and muted are *boolean* attributes—including them makes them true, and excluding them makes them false. (But given that autoplay and loop are tools of the devil, we should probably always leave them out.) The muted attribute makes the browser's player default to mute (though support for this may be patchy), and the controls attribute tells the browser to use its native controls. (The elements can also be controlled through the JavaScript API.)

There's also a preload attribute that's *not* boolean but instead can be none, metadata (preload the metadata for the file only), or auto, which usually means the browser will preload it. But this setting is only a hint—iOS will never preload data because users could be on expensive mobile data networks. (Browser support for preload is relatively new.)

You may have also noticed the type attribute on the <source> elements. Here's an example:

```
<source src="myaudio.mp3" type="audio/mpeg">
```

This attribute tells the browser what container format was used so it can work out whether it supports the file format without having to start downloading it to check. Sadly, audio format support in modern browsers is a bit of a mess, as we'll see shortly.

This is just a brief description of the <audio> element. For *implementation* I suggest you use an HTML5-friendly, JavaScript-based media player. It will help smooth out the implementation issues and save you from reinventing the wheel, which is especially helpful given the immature <audio> implementations in current browsers. We'll look at our media player options at the end of this chapter. (But if you want something simple you can drop in right now, try audio.js: `http://kolber.github.com/audiojs/`.)

However, for audio file *preparation*, you need to understand the issues around codecs that we'll discuss after we look at the `<video>` element. We'll also look at HTML5 audio for games later in the chapter and touch on the flaws and future of `<audio>`.

The WebAudio API

At the time of this writing, the WebAudio API is a working draft and appears to be well on its way to making it into some version of HTML soon (see it live here: `www.w3.org/TR/webaudio/`). It is currently supported by all major browsers except IE.

This is a huge step forward for audio in JavaScript, but lack of support from the world's largest browser means developers should be hesitant to invest too much time and effort or should invest in a fallback along with it. At the time of this writing, Microsoft is considering WebAudio in "a future version of IE," and its development ticket tracking the issue can be seen here: `http://connect.microsoft.com/IE/feedback/details/799529/web-audio-api-support`.

More on how to use the WebAudio API to control audio streams is covered in the following resources and tutorials.

For more `<audio>` resources, see the following:

- For the basics of the `<audio>` and `<video>` JavaScript API, see `https://developer.mozilla.org/en-US/docs/Web/API/HTMLMediaElement`.

- For HTML5 Rocks' "Getting Started with Web Audio API" from Google, see `www.html5rocks.com/en/tutorials/webaudio/intro/`.

- For Mozilla Developer Network's "Using HTML5 Audio and Video," see `https://developer.mozilla.org/en-US/docs/Web/Guide/HTML/Using_HTML5_audio_and_video`

- For Dev.Opera's "An HTML5 `<audio>` radio player," see `http://dev.opera.com/articles/view/html5-audio-radio-player/`.

- For "Building a Custom HTML5 Audio Player with jQuery" by Neutron Creations, see `http://neutroncreations.com/blog/building-a-custom-html5-audio-player-with-jquery/`.

- For the Safari and iOS implementations, see the Safari Developer Library: `http://developer.apple.com/library/safari/#documentation/AudioVideo/Conceptual/Using_HTML5_Audio_Video/Introduction/Introduction.html`.

- SoundJS, part of the CreateJS suite championed by Adobe, Microsoft, and AOL, provides a single API to handle common difficulties in cross-browser audio support: `www.createjs.com/#!/SoundJS`.

- SoundManager 2 is a favorite open source audio library for "reliable cross-platform audio under a single JavaScript API": `www.schillmania.com/projects/soundmanager2/`.

The beauty of having the `<audio>` and `<video>` elements available as ordinary HTML is you can style them with CSS, including advanced CSS3. Check out the beautiful Zen Audio Player (shown in Figure 10-2, playing Girl Talk no less) to see what's possible: `https://github.com/simurai/ZEN-Player`.

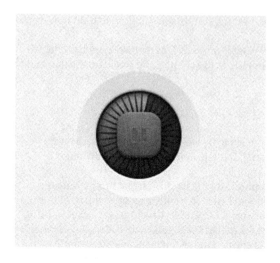

Figure 10-2. *The Zen Audio Player really is a thing of beauty—be sure to see it in action*

The crucial thing to understand with `<audio>` is the codec situation, so keep reading and we'll get delve into it after a brief trip through the `<video>` element.

The `<video>` Element

For video, we can use this:

```
<video controls autoplay loop muted preload="auto"
poster="myvideobackground.jpg" height="250" width="300">
    <source src="myvideo.webm" type="video/webm">
    <source src="myvideo.mp4" type="video/mp4">
    <!-- Fallback content, such as a Flash player, or a link to the file here -->
</video>
```

(If you want to see what's *really* involved with `<video>` implementation, including browser issues, setting MIME types, and more, see Kroc Camen's wonderfully thorough "Video for Everybody" article: `http://camendesign.com/code/video_for_everybody`.)

As you can see, it's a similar setup to the `<audio>` example. In fact, the `controls`, `autoplay`, `loop`, `muted`, and `preload` attributes all behave the same way. But they're not *quite* the devil's tools as they are for audio. Here we could have an autoplay, looping video advertisement that's muted until the user decides otherwise.

And just like `<audio>`, we have to deal with codec support issues by specifying multiple video files for maximum HTML5 compatibility. We use the `<source>` tag to give browsers a list of video files, and they use either the first one they support or the fallback content (such as Flash Player). The `type` attribute gives browsers a hint as to which file they should try to play. We'll discuss this after looking at the codec situation.

The `<video>` element has several of its own unique attributes. The main one is `poster`, which is the static image that's displayed until the first frame of the video is available. This may be only for a second or two in some cases, but on mobile devices (such as iOS) the poster is shown until the user initiates playback.

(At least that's the theory. IE's handling of the `poster` image is quirky for versions 9 and 10, as Ian Devlin found: `www.iandevlin.com/blog/2011/12/html5/the-problem-with-the-poster-attribute`. The bug appears to be fixed in IE11. Older versions of iOS and Android had problems as well, but they're largely unused at this point, while

IE9 and 10 continue to have significant percentages of the market. Speaking of Ian Devlin, he has a great post on how to implement poster in newer browsers here: www.iandevlin.com/blog/2013/03/html5/html5-video-and-background-images.)

The height and width attributes are also specific to the <video> element. But again, because the <video> element is just another bit of HTML, it can be styled and manipulated with CSS, including advanced CSS3. You can transform and animate the video itself, add shadows, and so on. This is one of the coolest things about <video> being just another element in the DOM. You can even use the <canvas> element to manipulate your video source, as discussed here: http://html5doctor.com/video-canvas-magic/.

Video Accessibility

Media accessibility is also being developed. A <track> element has been added to the spec to provide captioning. Or, as the spec puts it: "The track element allows authors to specify explicit external timed text tracks for media elements" (http://dev.w3.org/html5/spec/Overview.html#the-track-element). The <track> element sits between the <video></video> tags and looks like this:

```
<track kind="subtitles" src="moviecaptions.en.vtt" srclang="en" label="English">
```

You can find presentations and discussions on the issues and proposed solutions at http://blog.gingertech.net/2011/03/29/webvtt-explained/ and at www.iandevlin.com/blog/2011/05/html5/webvtt-and-video-subtitles.

Currently only IE10, Opera, and Chrome support <track>. For more, see "Getting started with the HTML5 track element" (www.html5rocks.com/en/tutorials/track/basics/).

API and Resources

The new HTML5 JavaScript API for media also handles video playback, which lets you roll your own controls. It's covered in the following resources and tutorials.

For more <video> resources, see the following:

- "Video for Everybody" is worth a read and/or bookmark: http://camendesign.com/code/video_for_everybody.Google's HTML5 Rocks HTML5 video article covers the basics and some pretty out-there examples, including SVG and video: www.html5rocks.com/en/tutorials/video/basics/.

- Mark Pilgrim's *Dive Into HTML5* chapter on video has all the gory details on codecs (and the difference between codecs and container files), encoding, browser support, server MIME types, and more: http://diveintohtml5.info/video.html.

- Dev.Opera has an extensive guide on HTML5 video, optimistically titled "Everything you need to know about HTML5 video and audio": http://dev.opera.com/articles/view/everything-you-need-to-know-about-html5-video-and-audio/.

- The Safari Developer Library guide to HTML5 audio and video has all the ins and outs for Safari- and iOS-related implementation: http://developer.apple.com/library/safari/#documentation/AudioVideo/Conceptual/Using_HTML5_Audio_Video/Introduction/Introduction.html.

- Mozilla has a great article covering most of the formats and what's going on with support across the major browsers. We'll get to this in a second, but for more reading, check out its take on things: https://developer.mozilla.org/en-US/docs/HTML/Supported_media_formats

The savior for <video> is stand-alone JavaScript players, which let us use one file, HTML5 (and a given codec) where it's supported, and Flash everywhere else.

We'll get to the media players in a moment. In the meantime, grab a fistful of hair, and get ready to pull.

Codecs, You're Killing Me

OK, so HTML5 for modern browsers and Flash as a fallback for older browsers. Got it.

Not so fast. This is HTML, which isn't so much "Anything that can go wrong will go wrong" as "Anything that can cause disagreement will cause disagreement." And the disagreement here is codecs, for both audio and video.

If you use an <image> tag, all browsers can display the image whether it's a JPEG, GIF, or PNG—there's no mandatory format.

The HTML5 spec (reluctantly) takes a similar view with the <audio> and <video> tags by not specifying a specific format (in other words, a codec) for audio or video.

You specify the format you want to use, and it's up to the browser to support it (or not, as we'll see).

Now if browser vendors all agreed on a single format (or several formats), we'd have universal HTML5 audio and video in all modern browsers. Unfortunately, that hasn't happened. Here's what the HTML5 editor Ian Hickson said on the situation in mid-2009 (http://lists.whatwg.org/pipermail/whatwg-whatwg.org/2009-June/020620.html):

> After an inordinate amount of discussions, both in public and privately, on the situation regarding codecs for <video> and <audio> in HTML5, I have reluctantly come to the conclusion that there is no suitable codec that all vendors are willing to implement and ship.
>
> I have therefore removed the two subsections in the HTML5 spec in which codecs would have been required, and have instead left the matter undefined, as has in the past been done with other features like <img> and image formats, <embed> and plug-in APIs, or Web fonts and font formats.

The Patent Problem

The problem with agreeing on a codec comes down to patents. Some media formats—including MP3 for audio (yes, the humble .mp3) and the popular H.264 format for video (usually used in .mp4 and .mkv files)—have patents that make companies cough up licensing fees to use the decoders in their products.

For big companies such as Apple, Microsoft, and Adobe (with Flash), this isn't a problem—they support both MP3 and H.264. But for ideological and financial reasons, Opera and Mozilla didn't want to support H.264 for video. (In early 2011 Google threatened to drop H.264 support from Chrome on the desktop, but as of this writing that has yet to happen. See the post announcing the drop that hasn't happened: http://blog.chromium.org/2011/01/html-video-codec-support-in-chrome.html. Also see where Google agrees that its VP8 format does violate some H.264 patents: www.businesswire.com/news/home/20130307006192/en/Google-MPEG-LA-Announce-Agreement-Covering-VP8.)

In 2013 Cisco offered to solve all of this for video by open sourcing the H.264 codec. Mozilla agreed to support it, but Opera still doesn't, and Google still does but doesn't want to (http://gigaom.com/2013/10/30/google-sticks-with-vp8-opposes-ciscos-push-for-h-264/). All of the browsers have also standardized on MP3 as an audio format, but Mozilla and Opera remain critics of it for its patent restrictions. At the time of this writing, Mozilla doesn't support MP3 in Firefox for Macintosh, but this appears to be coming very soon.

To further complicate things, in 2012, just as it seemed like MP3 would finally win out in audio codecs, Mozilla began championing its Opus codec for audio, adding yet another to the mix. At the time of this writing, Firefox and Chrome support it natively. (Chrome users must activate it through chrome://settings using the enable-opus-playback flag, which everyone does right?) Opera may add support soon, and it's unlikely that IE will get on board.

At the time of this writing, it appears that H.264 and MP3 will still be the winners, but as of yet there's still no single codec in video that all of the major desktop and mobile browsers support.

What are the alternatives? In the audio department, Mozilla and Opera champion the patent-free Ogg format (ditto for video, but it's seen as inferior). And in mid-2010 Google released the theoretically patent-free WebM video format (after buying it for a cool $100 million) to provide a "Can't we all just get along?" solution for video that everyone could use, thereby resolving the deadlock.

So, everyone could just switch to those, right? Not quite. For something to be truly "patent-free," it generally has to be proven in court. So, Microsoft and Apple take a "better the devil you know" approach and pay royalties for the codecs they use, especially with video and H.264. They figure it's better to do that than opt into supposedly "patent-free" technology that may not be so patent-free after all and could make them liable in the future. Indeed, questions are already being raised about potential WebM patent infringement, so these are valid concerns. (That's the condensed version, in any case!)

Perhaps making matters better, in 2013 Cisco decided to offer everyone a patent-free version of H.264 to end the debate and make it the default standard. Mozilla got on board and promised H.264 in Firefox, but Google is still holding out. Cisco and others take the position that H.264 is the de facto and industry standard anyway, so it's time to get on board. Google takes the position that it's dangerous to rely on a technology that's not truly open because Cisco could pull the free license at any time and because it views H.264 as a dated technology impeding innovation.

In Google's view, everyone should adopt the open and innovative WebM and embrace the future. If only things were that simple.

H.264 Is Baked In

Even if everyone *could* use WebM for video, it's not like Apple *or* Google (with Android) could just push out a software update and have everyone running WebM for video (especially on mobile).

Why not?

H.264 uses hardware acceleration in mobile devices (as well as desktop and other devices), which is how we get to watch high-quality video on low-powered devices without destroying battery life.

Throw in additional issues, such as the industry toolchain built around H.264, and the situation gets even murkier. You can see why a wholesale switch from H.264 would be difficult (at least in the short to medium term) even if everyone *did* decide to move in that direction. This is how one Hacker News commenter put it (http://news.ycombinator.com/item?id=2106285):

> *The digital video world runs on H.264, it has deep, complicated, expensive internal toolchains to support it, legacy archives encoded in it, basically entire businesses built around it. The video production world is far larger and more complex than you're picturing it.*

H.264 on mobile is, for all vendors and for the foreseeable future, a fact of life.

Google Threatens to Take Chrome WebM Only…and Then Doesn't

Let's look at who supports what.

Google, as mentioned, announced in 2011 it was going to *remove* H.264 support from Chrome to focus on WebM (see the announcement: http://blog.chromium.org/2011/01/html-video-codec-support-in-chrome.html), but as of this writing in late 2013, that has yet to materialize. Google-owned YouTube transcodes all videos into WebM so it can serve both WebM and H.264. Yep, Google is duplicating its entire YouTube library. But for what purpose? As long as Google continues to provide both codecs, H.264 remains the one codec everyone can use, and WebM continues to look like an interesting technical exercise with no important future.

As for Microsoft, it shares Apple's position and is sticking with H.264 (see: www.fastcompany.com/1723373/microsoft-sides-with-apple-over-google-onh264-video). Microsoft allows native WebM playback in its desktop players *if* a user installs the codec, but there's no shipping support, and Microsoft doesn't support it in its mobile browsers at all.

Google and Microsoft then released tit-for-tat plug-ins. Google released a WebM plug-in for IE9 (`http://tools.google.com/dlpage/webmmf`), though whether it gets any significant adoption remains to be seen. Microsoft has in turn released an H.264 plug-in for Chrome (see `http://blogs.msdn.com/b/interoperability/archive/2011/02/01/greater-interoperability-for-windows-customers-with-html5-video.aspx`) and Firefox (see `http://blogs.msdn.com/b/interoperability/archive/2010/12/15/html5-video-and-interop-firefox-add-on-provides-h-264-support-on-windows.aspx`) for its Windows 7 users who use Firefox.

After Cisco offered H.264 for free, Mozilla agreed to support it, and there was hope for a consensus. Yet Opera still hasn't gotten on board and has had little to say about it, and Google is pushing ahead with WebM anyway.

Finally, though this barely seems to matter anymore, Adobe Flash, once the only reliable option for multibrowser video, also doesn't support WebM. It said it would back in 2011 but still hasn't implemented it as of 2013.

So, let's review: everyone supports H.264, even Google, which said it wouldn't. No one really supports WebM except Google. Which codec do you think is going to win?

For a further breakdown on browser and device compatibility, see the handy chart here: `http://mediaelementjs.com`.

Codecs: What to Do?

Phew! So, where does that leave us?

If you want maximum *native* HTML5 support—including Opera—you need to store two copies of your audio (MP3 and Ogg Vorbis) and potentially three copies of your video files (H.264, WebM, and Ogg Theora for legacy support in Firefox 3.*x*). Having to encode and store so many different versions is a royal pain in the ass, but there you go.

Alternatively, you can do one of the following:

- Use MP3 for audio, which works natively in all of the modern incarnations of major browsers on desktop and mobile (except Firefox for Macintosh, but this is coming soon, and Opera).

- Use H.264 for video, which works natively in iOS, Safari, Firefox, and IE9.

- Use a media player (or script your own) that uses Flash Player for older and non-codec-supporting devices, given Flash can play MP3 and H.264 in any Flash-enabled browser or device.

Given we need H.264 for iOS (and mobile in general), this scenario—which I would wager will be the most common—means Opera (and potentially Chrome someday if it really drops H.264) will end up getting Flash. That's right—those who stood up for free, open software will end up with proprietary, closed Flash. That is more ironic than a hipster's mustache.

(Alternatively, you can, as mentioned, double encode your video and provide a separate WebM file in a secondary `<source>` element for broad native HTML5 support in modern browsers.)

Reality Bites

The reality may be a little different, though. For one, Google has yet to drop H.264 support, and Firefox finally added it after much debate. Can Opera's support really be that far off? It's difficult to imagine Opera holding out indefinitely. The practical implication for this is encoding media in H.264 (with a Flash fallback for older browsers) and MP3 (ditto) will be sufficient in the long term.

Video Types...Oh My

Now that you (ideally) understand the complexity of the codec situation and the way browser support for each codec differs, let's look at how we can tell browsers which codecs we're using so they can make smart decisions about which video they load.

That brings us to the one video attribute we haven't discussed—the type attribute on the <source> element. Here's an example:

```
<source src="myvideo.mp4" type="video/mp4">
```

This attribute tells the browser what *container* and *codec* is used for the video specified in the src attribute. In the previous example, we've specified only what *container* format is used by listing its MIME type (that is, media format type). The MIME type shown earlier tells the browser "This file is a video using the mp4 container format." *Container formats* like mp4 are a little like zip files, in that they are simply a container for the *actual* video and audio files, which are encoded with specific *codecs* and wrapped up to make the final video file. (The type attribute can also be used on the <video> element itself, not just a nested <source> element, if you're using only one file. The same goes for <audio>.)

The information we put in the type attribute is just a hint to the browser, but it's not necessary for browsers to play the video. What *is* necessary is to edit your .htaccess file on Linux or similarly configure IIS to make sure your server sends this file with the right MIME type, as the instructions describe at http://mediaelementjs.com/ or at http://technet.microsoft.com/en-us/library/cc725608(v=ws.10).aspx and are covered elsewhere (for example, the "Video for Everybody" article mentioned earlier).

We can also specify both the container format *and* the codec used. Here's an example:

```
<source src="myvideo.mp4" type='video/mp4; codecs="avc1.42E01E, mp4a.40.2"'>
```

Here we've specified the container format *and* the codecs for both the video and the audio in the source file. (The video codec is a flavor of H.264, along with the AAC audio codec. Note we also have to use single quotes for the type attribute here because the codecs parameter uses double quotes.)

What's the point of all this? Well, specifying the type attribute means the browser doesn't have to start downloading every listed file just to check whether it can play it. It can scan the markup and potentially start preloading the video file it supports. Leaving it out, however, isn't the end of the world. The following is from "The State Of HTML5 Video" by LongTail Video, written in 2012 (www.longtailvideo.com/html5/):

> Every browser supports the <source> tag for loading multiple sources. Our tests show that including the type attribute prevents some preloading, but breaks compatibility with Android 2.2. Setting the codecs in the type attribute has no impact in any browser.

Note the Android 2.2 compatibility issue. The comment about codecs suggests that from LongTail's testing we (by and large) need to specify only the *container* and the browser will have a go at loading it.

Querying Supported Video Types with JavaScript

We can also query the browser using the <video> JavaScript API and its canPlayType() method to see which formats the browser supports. For example, with the codecs we specified earlier (avc1.42E01E, mp4a.40.2), browsers that support these formats (Safari and IE9+) will respond with probably, which is as close to "Yes, we support this file" as we get in HTML5.

If we specify only the container format (`video/mp4`), Safari and IE9+ (for example) respond with `maybe` because they know they can read that container format but don't know what codecs lie inside. Browsers that don't support a given container or codec format just return a null string.

Things get awfully complicated, though. Here are the three variables we have to deal with:

- *Browser response*: Because of the complexities of encoding media (and especially video), browsers only know for sure that they *can't* play formats they don't understand. In those cases, they return a null string (when queried through the `canPlayType()` method). Beyond that, the HTML5 spec says they must return either `maybe` or `probably` depending on the browser's confidence it can play a certain file based on the information we've provided.

- *Containers and codecs*: There are *container* formats such as mp4, and there are the actual codecs or, more accurately, *flavors* of the actual codecs (such as `avc1.42E01E`) that can be queried.

- *Browser support*: Finally, as we've seen, the codec support from the major browsers is a pretty complex situation.

Therefore, we have multiple browsers supporting multiple container/codec varieties (for both audio and video) and giving one of three responses. Thankfully, the WHATWG maintains a table of browser responses so we can see which response for a given container format, or container and codec combination, we *should* get from a given browser: `http://wiki.whatwg.org/wiki/Video_type_parameters#Browser_Support`. Microsoft has a small script demonstrating how this works here: `http://msdn.microsoft.com/de-de/library/hh325437(v=vs.85).aspx`.

Audio and Video Media Players to the Rescue

What a mess.

Fortunately, people have written tools to take the pain out of serving the right video (or audio) to the right browser. These media players hold your hand through the whole codecs mess and legacy support issues, provide plenty of customization options, and generally smooth out the whole implementation process.

Here are a few examples.

MediaElement (Video and Audio, Free)

`http://mediaelementjs.com`

This is a popular audio and video player that lets you use one file (an H.264 video file, for example) and deploy a consistent UI across all devices using Flash (or Silverlight) for playback where H.264 isn't natively supported. It comes with a jQuery plug-in, as well as plug-ins for Drupal and WordPress. See figure 10-3 for an example.

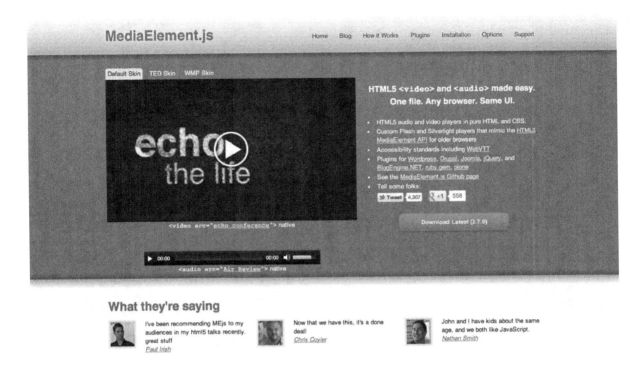

***Figure 10-3.** Mediaelement.js deploys a consistent UI across multiple playback codecs*

VideoJS (Video, Free)

http://videojs.com

VideoJS (figure 10-4) is a slick HTML5 video player that offers some familiar CSS-based skins and similar broad support using Flash fallbacks for HTML5 video. It uses the markup from Video for Everyone (we provided the link to this earlier) and adds JavaScript for broader compatibility and CSS skinning options.

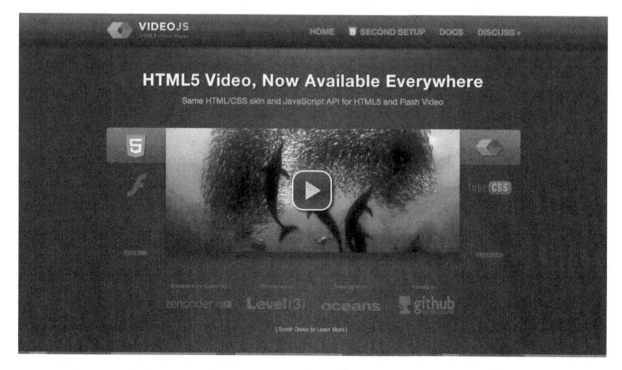

Figure 10-4. *VideoJS is another good framework for providing video with an Adobe Flash fallback*

Flowplayer (Video, Free and Commercial)

http://flowplayer.org

Flowplayer (figure 10-5) is a free, open source player with Flowplayer branding. There's also a commercial offering (with support option) without branding.

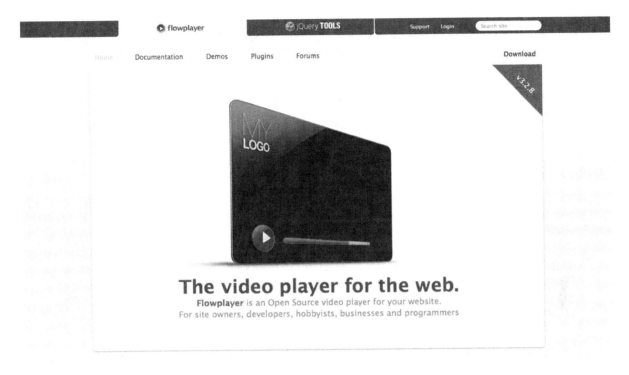

Figure 10-5. Flowplayer is an open source player that has a supported commercial offering

More Media Players

There are a variety of other players out there, including the following:

- jPlayer (`www.jplayer.org`) is a free, open source audio and video player (with handy playlist support).

- Open Standard Media (OSM) Player (`www.mediafront.org/project/osmplayer`) is a free audio and video player written in jQuery that has a visual playlist.

- **JW** Player (`www.longtailvideo.com/players/`) is another option with HTML5 support.

- SublimeVideo (`http://sublimevideo.net/`) is a paid, hosted HTML5 player solution.

- Popcorn.js (`http://popcornjs.org/`) is a "JavaScript event framework" and is part of the Mozilla Popcorn project (`https://popcorn.webmaker.org/`). It's particularly useful if you want to trigger updates of other content on the page in sync with the video.

(Of course, you can always use YouTube or Vimeo and let the native iOS playback take care of itself!)

With these available, there's no need to roll your custom solution. Just grab one off the shelf and skin to your heart's content.

Other Flies in the HTML5 Video Ointment: DRM, Streaming, and Full-Screen Video

We've got basic `<video>` and `<audio>` embedding down, but even with our handy, ready-to-go media players and their Flash fallbacks, there are still some significant missing (or very immature) features that HTML5 video lacks but Flash supports. As codecs continue to mature, there will be pressure on browser makers to support all of the important features of HTML5 video and audio sooner rather than later. When it comes to DRM, that may not be a good thing.

DRM

In February 2012, representatives from Google, Microsoft, and Netflix submitted the Encrypted Media Extensions v0.1 draft proposal (`http://dvcs.w3.org/hg/html-media/raw-file/tip/encrypted-media/encrypted-media.html`) to the W3C's HTML Working Group. The abstract for the proposal said this:

> *This proposal extends HTMLMediaElement to enable playback of protected content. The proposed API supports use cases ranging from simple clear key decryption to high value video (given an appropriate user agent implementation). License/key exchange is controlled by the application, facilitating the development of robust playback applications supporting a range of content decryption and protection technologies. No "DRM" is added to the HTML5 specification, and only simple clear key decryption is required as a common baseline.*

That is, this would provide a mechanism for DRM to happen on top of HTML5, for both `<audio>` and `<video>`, by extending the JavaScript API (the `HTMLMediaElement` interface). The HTML5 editor, Ian Hickson, responded with the following (`http://lists.w3.org/Archives/Public/public-html/2012Feb/0274.html`):

> *I believe this proposal is unethical and that we should not pursue it.*

Hickson also stated "DRM is evil" and then further elaborated on his reasons for rejecting the proposal outright here: `https://www.w3.org/Bugs/Public/show_bug.cgi?id=10902#c24`. Mozilla also expressed concerns, given that DRM and an open source browser are generally mutually exclusive (see this Ars Technica article for more: `http://arstechnica.com/business/news/2012/02/unethical-html-video-copy-protection-proposal-criticized-by-standards-stakeholders.ars`).

> *I mostly agree with Hickson. DRM is evil. Remember PlaysForSure? No? Exactly.*

There is one important difference between DRM for video and DRM for audio, though, and that's streaming. We have a culture of streaming (and renting) video, in a way that we didn't with audio when the music DRM wars were raging. DRM sucked when it was applied to music you bought because if the DRM platform died (and they did), so did your music collection. The temporal nature of streaming media alleviates these concerns, but only to a point. (And if it can be implemented for streaming media, it's not hard to imagine the media majors insisting on DRM for purchased content, too.)

These issues around streaming "protected" content explains Netflix's interest in seeing some sort of DRM available when using web standards. Netflix was keen to use HTML5 (in the broad "web platform" sense) where it can (as it discusses here: `http://techblog.netflix.com/2010/12/why-we-choose-html5-for-user.html`), but Netflix obviously felt it needed some kind of DRM system in place to stream the content it licenses with HTML5. (They also need an actual streaming protocol, as we'll see next.) Some at Google and Microsoft evidently feel this is a necessity too. (Note, though, that Hickson also works for Google, so it's not a company-wide position.)

This may be another case where the post-Flash Web results not in an open standards utopia but in a return to platform-specific apps. That said, given the cost of implementing DRM, that may be a price the standards movement is willing to bear.

Debate raged on the W3C mailing lists, with a summary here: http://lists.w3.org/Archives/Public/public-html/2012Mar/0087.html.

But that debate may have always been moot. In March 2012, Philippe Le Hegaret from the W3C wrote the following (http://lists.w3.org/Archives/Public/public-html/2012Mar/0097.html):

> [L]et's be clear: W3C has many participants interested in finding a solution around media content protection. So, we are definitively interested in the space, independently of whether the HTML Working Group is interested in developing a solution or whether it is done in a separate group. Whatever we choose, we will do our best to get the right balance between producers and consumers.

That is, we're going to implement DRM with or without you because our paid-up members want it. Ominous stuff.

By late 2013 it appears the fight against DRM is over, and DRM won.

First, the Encrypted Media Extensions proposal is in full working draft. It was first publically released in May 2013 with much controversy (www.w3.org/blog/2013/05/perspectives-on-encrypted-medi/), particularly from the Free Software Foundation (you can read the recommendation against EME here: www.fsf.org/news/coalition-against-drm-in-html). The editor's draft can be found here: https://dvcs.w3.org/hg/html-media/raw-file/tip/encrypted-media/encrypted-media.html.

Second and more importantly, Chrome and IE11 already support EME. As everyone should remember by now, the browser makers make the rules. Without them, the spec is a work of fiction. Despite the controversy, it appears like this fight is over, and DRM won this round. It's unlikely to make it into the final W3C spec by 2014 since it's not in revision status yet, but once the browsers are on board, the spec is just a formality.

Third, Netflix is streaming over HTML5 in some cases, using EME. As of late 2013 it's not its mainstream distribution channel, but it's available. Netflix has been a big supporter of EME. When you have browser support and major corporations already using DRM in HTML5, it's hard to imagine a universe in which the spec and other browsers don't get on board very quickly.

Streaming

For a long time, streaming video over HTML5 was one of the largest challenges to moving off of Flash. Flash provided a very stable streaming media solution for decades and was the entrenched solution of choice, and the HTML5 spec wasn't quick in coming up with a better alternative. Ars Technica summed it up well in 2011 through an excellent article titled "The trials and tribulations of HTML video in the post-Flash era" (http://arstechnica.com/business/news/2011/11/the-trials-and-tribulations-of-html-video-in-the-post-flash-era.ars):

> [T]ransitioning video delivery in the browser from Flash to HTML5 will also pose some major challenges for content creators. The standards aren't fully mature yet and there are still a number of features that aren't supported or widely available across browsers.

> For an illustration of how deep the problems run, you need only look at Mozilla's Firefox Live promotional website, which touts the organization's commitment to the open Web and shows live streaming videos of Red Panda cubs from the Knoxville Zoo. The video is streamed with Flash instead of using standards-based open Web technologies.

> In an FAQ attached to the site, Mozilla says that it simply couldn't find a high-volume live streaming solution based on open codecs and open standards. If Mozilla can't figure out how to stream its cuddly mascot with open standards, it means there is still work to do.

A streaming standard has been in the works for some time, called Dynamic Adaptive Streaming over HTTP (DASH), which has the support of Microsoft , the BBC, and others, but there's still a way to go there before support materializes. DASH is also codec agnostic—it doesn't resolve the codec impasse we discussed earlier. (For more, see "What is MPEG DASH?": `www.streamingmedia.com/Articles/ ReadArticle.aspx?ArticleID=79041`.)

Apple currently has its own streaming protocol, HTTP Live Streaming (HLS), which is used to deliver content to its iOS devices. Google added support in Android 3.0+, and it allows encrypted data and works with third-party DRM solutions. See "What is HLS (HTTP Live Streaming)?" for more: `www.streamingmedia.com/Articles/Editorial/ What-Is-…/What-is-HLS-%28HTTPLive-Streaming%29-78221.aspx`.

Regardless of what protocol one uses to stream, by late 2013 the W3C is in working draft for the Media Source Extensions (MSE) API, which allows a page to define support for media streams through JavaScript (`www.w3.org/TR/ media-source/`). The spec currently supports several different types of streams and the ability to define additional through JavaScript libraries (like DASH through `dash.js`). The major players are all planning to support it. Once MSE is in place and fully supported, then streaming is solved, and the provider must simply provide any necessary JavaScript libraries to translate the stream and send the data in a codec supported by the browser to provide real streaming video. IE11 and Chrome already support it, which is how Netflix can stream in HTML5 through extensions on those browsers.

Fullscreen API

Finally, one of the most common things we do with Flash video is make it full-screen. This wasn't possible in HTML5 until recently, when the Fullscreen API spec moved ahead in the W3C (`http://dvcs.w3.org/hg/fullscreen/raw-file/tip/Overview.html`). All of the major desktop browsers are moving ahead in anticipation of the spec. Mobile browsers aren't on board yet, but most of them go full-screen for all video elements by default anyway. Interestingly, the Fullscreen API can make *any* element full-screen, including (for example) the `<canvas>` element, and it could be used for a full-screen reading mode too, for example.

For more on the Fullscreen API, see the following:

- Mozilla's guide to using the Fullscreen API is here: `https://developer.mozilla.org/en-US/ docs/Web/Guide/API/DOM/Using_full_screen_mode`.

- The Mozilla Hacks blog has a tutorial (including styling information) at `http://hacks. mozilla.org/2012/01/using-the-fullscreen-api-in-web-browsers/` and a demo at `http://robnyman.github.com/fullscreen/`.

- Keep an eye on `http://caniuse.com/#feat=fullscreen` for browser support stats and more resources.

Is HTML5 <audio> Ready for Games?

One final note on `<audio>` and its potential for gaming.

Dominic Szablewski posted an epic (and profanity-laced!) rant on the state of HTML5 audio, in relation to developing HTML5 games. It's well worth a read for entertainment value and gives some indication of the (im) maturity of HTML5 audio support, particularly for interactive purposes. Szablewski says this:

Surprisingly, Google's Chrome has the worst HTML5 Audio support of all the good Desktop Browsers - that is every Browser but IE. I'm not an audio engineer, but before Browser vendors took their shot at it, my impression of digital audio was that it is a solved problem. I'm amazed that after so many iterations HTML5 Audio is still that broken.

The Audio support on mobile Browsers (iOS and Android) is laughable at best. It's completely unusable for even the simplest of tasks. You can jump through hoops and ask real nice, but it still sucks ass.

(See the article for more: `www.phoboslab.org/log/2011/03/the-state-of-html5-audio`. I love the Scumbag Steve hat.)

In 2013 the story is mostly still the same. WebAudio is almost ready, the codecs seem to be coalescing, but game developers still run into problems. In late 2013 the game development blog Indiegamr summed it up this way in a post titled "The State of Audio in HTML5 Games" (`http://indiegamr.com/the-state-of-audio-in-html5-games/`):

> *...there is no single codec and format that is supported by all browsers and devices. In addition to this not every device does support the WebAudio-API and some devices only allow audio-playback upon a user-interaction or only allow playing one sound at a time. So what should you do? Setup an audio file for any codec and then check the browser's support before loading and playing the file? While this would be currently the only way to do it right, this not only sounds like a lot of work, but also is. What about browsers that don't support the audio-element at all? – Implementing a flash fallback is no easy task as well.*

The short answer? No, it's not really ready for games.

In the meantime, cross-platform libraries, perhaps with Flash fallbacks built in, are required to get the job done. Here's a short list of libraries to look into:

- SoundJS, part of the CreateJS suite championed by Adobe, Microsoft, and AOL, provides a Flash fallback and handles cross-browser issues gracefully: `www.createjs.com/#!/SoundJS`.

- The HowlerJS framework is open source and freely available under the MIT license. It has no Flash fallback, so it won't support older browsers easily: `https://github.com/goldfire/howler.js/`.

- SoundManager has long been the standard of JavaScript audio. It provides a Flash fallback if required: `www.schillmania.com/projects/soundmanager2/`.

Until IE and others get on board with the WebAudio API, we're stuck with hiding Flash in the background to serve audio. Welcome to the modern Web.

Wrapping Up

Native support for `<audio>` and `<video>` is welcome and necessary for mobile devices in particular. But keep in mind that the technology is still somewhat immature (especially on Android).

The codec issues will not be resolved any time soon, and iOS will still need H.264 for video. So, we need to tread carefully. Don't assume it will work flawlessly just because it's in the spec.

At the time of this writing, we've come a long way. Just a few years ago the codecs were completely fractured and the spec still totally up in the air on basic things such as full-screen video or whether an audio API would ever be included, let alone controversial topics such as DRM. Yet today we have all three included in the working spec, and a majority of the browsers are on board. The codec wars feel like they're winding down, despite Mozilla's push for Opus in audio, and it seems like stability is just around the corner.

But we're not there yet. Until every major browser supports a small set of codecs (let alone a single one) for audio and video, a single API for audio, and consistent streaming and DRM capabilities, audio and video will remain difficult areas for developers. Commitment to the open Web means supporting multiple ways of doing everything. JavaScript frameworks provide some help, and we're still stuck with legacy support through Flash for a good while regardless.

My advice? Find a few good components that do the heavy lifting. Then, keep an eye on what your favorite media player supports, and let it be your guide for which technologies to bet on in the future.

■ ■ ■

The Truth About SVG: The Flash Challenger That Was, Wasn't, and Now...

We touched on the idea of Flash-challenging technology when we looked at Canvas in Chapter 9. But perhaps the most serious challenger to Flash in the past decade has been Scalable Vector Graphics (SVG), an XML format for 2D graphics and animation, which is making yet another mini-comeback. Let's take a very brief look at the dead-again, less-dead-again technology that is SVG.

SVG, SVG...

Oh, SVG (Scalable Vector Graphics)...what can we say about you? You're a separate W3C spec that's been in development since 1998 (on target to be finalized in August 2014!). You're not part of the HTML5 spec, but HTML5 *will* let you appear inline with other markup. You're all about vector shapes, which makes you the Illustrator to Canvas's Photoshop. You've promised so much, for so long—in 2002 people were writing 1,000+ page books about you, such as *SVG Unleashed* (Sams, 2002). Yet you've never made it to the big leagues. What happened?

SVG is both a relic of past web standards and a technology that's finally kinda-sorta-almost arrived (just in time for the development of SVG 2.0). It's an XML format for vector graphics (think of SVG being to graphics as HTML is to text), which means it looks like a bunch of angle-bracketed tags and attributes. Remember when we looked at the history of HTML and how it was going to be all XML? Well, SVG is part of that vision—the vision that didn't work out.

Here's what basic SVG looks like:

```
<svg id="mysvgexample" height="200" width="300" xmlns="http://www.w3.org/2000/svg">
    <rect id="myrectangle" width="200" height="100" fill="red" x="20" y="20" />
</svg>
```

This renders what you see in Figure 11-1.

Generic SVG

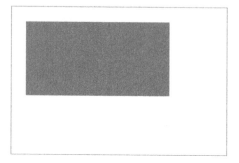

Figure 11-1. *Our exciting SVG demo*

Yep, a red rectangle. I'll give you a moment to recover.

Here's a quick explanation of what's going on here: we've set the `<svg>` element to be 200px high and 300px wide, which acts as a transparent container for the shapes or lines we want to render. (I've given it a border with CSS so you can see its boundaries.) We then create a rectangle with the `<rect />` element, give it a height and width, and give it an x and y offset from the container `<svg>` element. Add a fill (I've used the keyword red, but you could use a hex value too), and we're done.

In HTML5 you can drop this code right into your HTML document, and supporting browsers (IE9+, FF4+, Safari 5.1+, Chrome 7+, Opera 11.6+, iOS 5+, Android 3+) will render it as appropriate.

SVG: Browser Support Arrives at Last

SVG is interesting again because browser support is finally arriving. Currently, all modern and not-so-modern browsers, including IE9 (but excluding, you guessed it, IE6–8) and Android browser 3.0+ (but not 2.*x* or older), support SVG embedded using the `<embed>` or `<object>` element. The IE situation isn't quite as bad as it sounds, though, as we'll see next.

Browsers are also starting to support SVG images in the `<img>` tag and even as CSS backgrounds (specifically IE9+, FF4+, and all recent Safari, iOS, Chrome, and Opera releases).

And there's even great support for applying advanced SVG features such as filters (for example, Gaussian blur), clipping, and transforms to non-SVG objects. Amazingly, at the time of this writing, all of the major browsers on both desktop and mobile now support this; that's a huge improvement from just a year or two ago when support was varied and spotty.

Things get a little less rosy on the more advanced features. At the time of this writing, SVG SMIL animation isn't supported in IE on the desktop or mobile; SVG transform and transition effects aren't supported on any of the mainstream mobile browsers; SVG fonts aren't supported in IE, Firefox, or mobile Opera; CSS filters for SVG are available only in WebKit browsers (including Opera); and SVG Fragment filters are available only in non-WebKitbrowsers (IE and Firefox). For up-to-date information on what is and isn't supported in SVG, check out `http://caniuse.com/#search=svg`.

Support for basic SVG including filters and inline elements has come a long way in the past few years. But in order for SVG to become a major contender and move beyond just drawing static images, it needs full support for advanced animation, CSS transitions, and fragment shaders. Adding to the dilemma, most web designers and developers can't afford to abandon everyone who isn't in the latest browser. A huge portion of the web-browsing population still uses older browsers, and if we rely on dynamic SVG effects out of the box, we'll be abandoning those people to a graphics-less world.

So, what do we do? Is there any way to start using SVG now without having to mess with all this cross- and legacy-browser nonsense? Luckily, there is.

Yes, There Is Real-World SVG We Can Use Right Now

Dmitry Baranovskiy is SVG's hero and savior. He has authored two JavaScript libraries that let designers take advantage of everything SVG can do without having to manage all of the complexities themselves. Both are sponsored by Adobe, who is Baranovskiy's employer at the time of this writing and who has been pushing SVG features to spec through the W3C with a lot of success over the past decade or so.

Baranovskiy's first library is called Raphaël, and it provides SVG compatibility all the way back to IE6. Raphaël lets us do some simple, cool, Flash-like things with SVG. Under active development for several years, it offers browser support right down to IE6 (thanks to VML translation in IE). You can check it out here: `http://raphaeljs.com/`. (And make sure you check out the sister graphing library, gRaphaël, as well: `http://g.raphaeljs.com`.)

His second library is called Snap.svg, and it trades legacy support for more advanced features that work in all modern browsers. Snap was written entirely from scratch and works on SVG elements loaded from anywhere (in the page, downloaded to the page through a file, loaded from text input…whatever). It's free and open source; check it out here: `http://snapsvg.io/`.

We'll look at what SVG can do both by itself and through these libraries in a moment, but for now it's worth keeping in mind that, thanks to Dmitry, simple SVG (including animation) can be used with broad browser support.

Imagine if, all of a sudden, we had to support devices with an extremely wide array of resolution sizes and densities, some of which didn't support Flash. Wouldn't vector graphics—crisp at any resolution and scalable to any size—make life a lot easier? Hold that thought….

The Many Faces of SVG

Let's look at the different faces of SVG.

- SVG, the gigantic spec that's been kicking around (and growing) for a decade

- Advanced SVG as it's being implemented in cutting-edge browsers

- SVG as we can use it today in real-world situations with tools such as Raphaël and jQuery SVG (`http://keith-wood.name/svg.html`)

SVG can be (and is being) used right now for a variety of situations with solid cross-support, including iOS devices, so its time may have finally arrived. And it's just in time, considering Adobe's abandonment of Flash in mobile browsers and its promotion of Snap.svg. (For more on the death of Flash, see the discussion in Chapter 9 where we looked at Canvas and Flash.) And that's not to mention the pressing need for interface elements that can scale up from a phone to an iPad Retina display to a 27" or 30" screen.

SVG in the '00s: The Great Hope That Wasn't

SVG has been on quite a journey. In its full pomp, it's extremely impressive and currently does as much (if not more) than current CSS3 implementations. Full SVG support does everything from animation to the Photoshop-like filter effects we touched on earlier (see this example in Chrome, Opera, or Firefox: `http://svgwow.org/filterEffects/chiseled.svg`) to custom fonts, masking, video, and of course drawing vector shapes. It's all there (in the spec at least—browser support has lagged badly). So, in a way, it's a lot like Flash.

Well, basic SVG is like Flash a decade ago but without the browser support or developer tools. In fact, before Adobe bought Macromedia (which developed Flash), Adobe was championing SVG as an open alternative. And in 2002 some 160 million people were using their SVG viewer plug-in (since discontinued; see `www.xml.com/pub/a/2002/07/03/adobesvg.html`).

To give you a taste of the hype around SVG in the early '00s, here's a quote from a 2002 article on Digital Web titled "SVG: The New Flash" (www.digital-web.com/articles/svg_the_new_flash/):

SVG should soon be widespr ead, and its non-proprietary nature will help to hasten the progress. Flash will continue to be the dominant standard for quite some time because of its large client base. However, SVG is rising quickly. The distribution of the SVG plug-in via browser manufacturers will quickly increase the installed user base, just as it did for Flash. Future versions of various browsers will include SVG viewers as standard, and some already do.

But SVG never really took off. (Let it be said its "nonproprietary nature" hasn't counted for much in the past decade.) It couldn't touch Flash's installed base and never had a development tool as designer-friendly as Flash. And when Adobe bought Macromedia in 2005, as far as vector graphics on the Web went, it was Flash or bust.

Still, SVG never really died either. And with browser support now improving rapidly and the writing on the wall for Flash, perhaps SVG is due for yet another comeback.

SVG Browser Support: Android, What the Hell? Oh, and IE…

One sticking point at the moment is that Android 2.*x* doesn't offer even *basic* SVG browser support, despite Google pushing SVG elsewhere (see http://googlecode.blogspot.com/2009/10/svg-at-google-and-in-internet-explorer.html). That might seem like old news considering that at the time of this writing Android is on version 4 and heading toward 5, but thus is the plight of Android: somewhere around 24 percent of the Android world is still using Android 2 as I type this (for up-to-date stats, see the Android developer dashboard: http://developer.android.com/about/dashboards/index.html). Basic SVG support has been in WebKit, the engine behind Android's browser, for ages; it was just intentionally left out of Android 2.*x* "to save space" (see the comment and discussion here: http://code.google.com/p/android/issues/detail?id=1376#c4). Go figure. Android browsers in 3.*x* and 4.*x* support basic SVG just fine, and most of the advanced features are finally available in 4.4. (aka "KitKat.")

Fortunately for us, there are several libraries available that allow us to translate modern SVG into something IE6-8 (and any other browser) can understand.

Raphaël, the JavaScript library for working with SVG we touched on earlier, falls back to IE's old Vector Markup Language (VML) for compatibility. (It's similar to the Canvas emulation we looked at in Chapter 9 and has similar limitations; in other words, VML is *slow*.)

There's also SVG Web (http://code.google.com/p/svgweb/), which translates SVG to Flash for older browsers that don't support SVG, including IE. (Sadly, this still doesn't help us out with Android 2.*x*. See http://groups.google.com/group/svgweb/browse_thread/thread/77fb6970f5f01e97.)

There's also canvg (http://code.google.com/p/canvg/), which renders SVG in Canvas and provides some SVG support for Android as a stopgap measure until Android 4.0 becomes widespread. This approach is discussed here: www.kendoui.com/blogs/teamblog/posts/12-02-17/using_svg_on_android_2_x_and_kendo_ui_dataviz.aspx. (Fabric.js may also help: http://fabricjs.com/.)

While these tools make basic SVG a reality for just about any browser, remember this is only basic SVG, not the crazy Photoshop-like filters that have become part of the SVG spec.

SVG Demos: What Is It Good For?

Vector graphics are useful in lots of instances, such as maps, charts, illustrations, logos, visualizations, resolution-independent interfaces, and so on. And the success of Flash has certainly demonstrated that the need for animated vector graphics is there. What may otherwise be delivered in Flash can potentially be done in SVG and therefore be available to iOS users.

Let's take a look at some SVG demos to see what it is capable of. We'll look at a few general examples and then a few real-world Snap.SVG and Raphaël examples.

SVG Girl

SVG Girl (Figure 11-2) is an "SVG animated video" that Microsoft commissioned to show off its hardware-accelerated SVG support in IE9 (though it works in any modern browser). It's a brief but incredibly complex and impressive anime clip done with SVG. See it here: `http://jsdo.it/event/svggirl/`.

Figure 11-2. *The animated SVG Girl short is brief but impressive*

SVG performance for this sort of complex animation used to be lackluster, but hardware acceleration makes the world of difference. Hats off to the IE team for hardware-accelerated SVG. (You can read more about it here: `http://blogs.msdn.com/b/ie/archive/2011/03/08/comparing-hardware-accelerated-svg-across-browsers-with-santa-s-workshop.aspx`.)

SVG Edit

SVG Edit (Figure 11-3) shows what can be done with client-side web technologies alone. It's an SVG- and JavaScript-based app for editing SVG. Download it at `http://code.google.com/p/svg-edit/` or try it live at `http://svg-edit.googlecode.com/svn/branches/2.5.1/editor/svg-editor.html`.

Figure 11-3. *SVG Edit is an SVG-powered drawing program that outputs…SVG*

Google Docs

Google Docs' drawing program (Figure 11-4) uses SVG with a VML fallback. (Google also started using SVG for the graphs in Google Analytics in early 2012.)

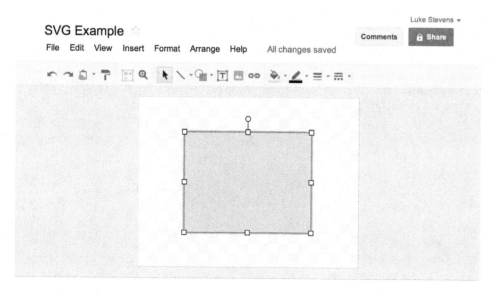

Figure 11-4. *SVG is used in some very high-profile situations, such as the Google Docs drawing program*

SVG Games

You can create games in SVG with JavaScript, but SVG for games hasn't caught on in the same way Canvas has. As part of its IE9 tech demos, Microsoft released a couple of *very* simple retro game examples:

- Asteroids in SVG (Figure 11-5):
  http://ie.microsoft.com/testdrive/Graphics/SVGoids/Default.xhtml.

- A simple Helicopter game with a background that reminds me of the Atari 2600:
  http://ie.microsoft.com/testdrive/Performance/Helicopter/Default.xhtml

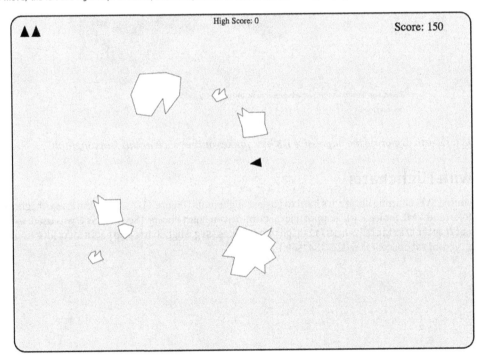

Figure 11-5. SVG-oids may be simple, but it demonstrates the interactive possibilities of SVG

D3.js

D3.js (Figure 11-6 and online at http://mbostock.github.com/d3/) is a "small, free JavaScript library for manipulating documents based on data" that uses SVG for some extremely impressive data visualizations. Check out the examples for more: http://mbostock.github.com/d3/ex/. Also see the 150+ annotated slides from a D3 workshop by D3 creator Mike Bostock: http://bost.ocks.org/mike/d3/workshop/. It starts with a simple introduction of D3 and SVG and finishes with some impressive examples.

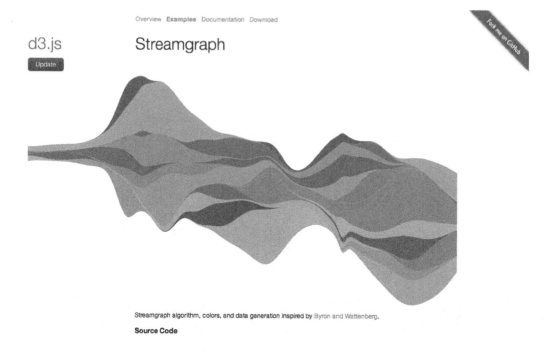

Figure 11-6. *It's worth exploring the impressive D3.js examples online, such as this "streamgraph."*

Charts with Highcharts

For a fully featured SVG charting library, it's hard to go past Highcharts (Figure 11-7 and online at www.highcharts.com/), which is an SVG (and VML for legacy IE support) JavaScript-driven chart library. (See why SVG was used: www.highcharts.com/component/content/article/2-news/12-highcharts-goes-svg. Highcharts also gets a lot of love from developers: http://news.ycombinator.com/item?id=1847569.)

Figure 11-7. *Highcharts has a lot of fans, and its flexible, well-documented API makes it easy to use*

Snap.svg-Powered Demos

Much of the current, real work for advanced browsers is done with the library Snap.svg, which, as we saw earlier, offers a simple and easy way to generate, manipulate, and animate SVG elements.

PBS Kids

PBS Kids uses Snap.svg to power all of the interactive and animated elements on the page, and its home page is full of them: cars carrying major characters drive onto the screen, there's a large interactive dial for selecting a show, and everything clickable has richly animated hover states. The reliance on SVG lets the home page weigh in at just 9.2KB and lets the site focus on images of its characters rather than images for all of the interactive elements. See it in Figure 11-8 and online at http://pbskids.org/.

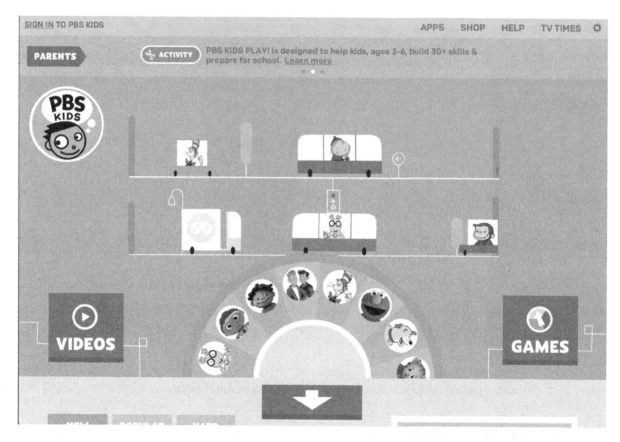

Figure 11-8. *PBS Kids relies on Snap.svg to provide the bold, animated, colorful experience on its home page*

Codrops Animated SVG Icons with Snap.svg

This rich icon set (shown in Figure 11-9) is built entirely with SVG. Each icon has an animation that plays when clicked. The animations are smooth and subtle in modern browsers. View it online here: http://tympanus.net/Development/AnimatedSVGIcons/.

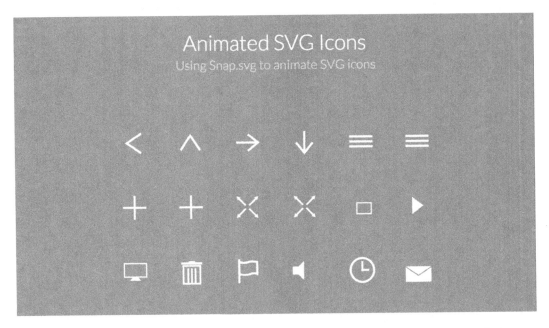

Figure 11-9. *Animated SVG icons built in Snap.svg are a great example of how SVG can provide the same subtle animations that used to be available only through Adobe Flash*

Snap.svg's Demo Page

It shouldn't be hard for a framework to demo itself well, but many provide examples that feel contrived and not really great at showing real-world examples. Snap.svg's demo page isn't anything like that. Shown in Figure 11-10, the animated game example shines particularly well, demonstrating the power of SVG in delivering an animated spinning die and game board. The trees on the game board sway constantly, as if in the wind. It's hard to believe this is all happening natively in the browser, without a plug-in.

Figure 11-10. *Snap.svg's demos page features an interactive, animated game board that does a great job of showing the framework's full potential*

Raphael.js-Powered Demos

Snap.js is amazingly powerful, and many sites are moving in that direction for animation. Yet legacy browsers are still out there, and many of us need to support them. To get the most out of SVG without leaving legacy users behind, Raphaël is the library of choice. Let's look at how it's being used.

thirteen23

thirteen23 (shown in Figure 11-11 and online at `http://thirteen23.com`) is a design consultancy in Austin, Texas, that has done a great job using modern web technologies to pull off an impressive studio site. Its curved, smoothly animated navigation is built using Raphaël. Click around to see the navigation in action (and watch the backgrounds change). Also note the lack of full-page refreshes despite URL changes and without using the /#/ pattern. That's the HTML5 History API in action, which we'll touch on in the next chapter.

Figure 11-11. *The animated, circular navigation for thirteen23 shows what a nice sprinkling of SVG can do*

Markup.io

Markup.io (Figure 11-12 and online at `http://markup.io/`) lets you draw vector lines on (and annotate) any web page with a simple bookmarklet. You can also publish and share your annotated pages. The drawing tools are SVG-powered by Raphaël.

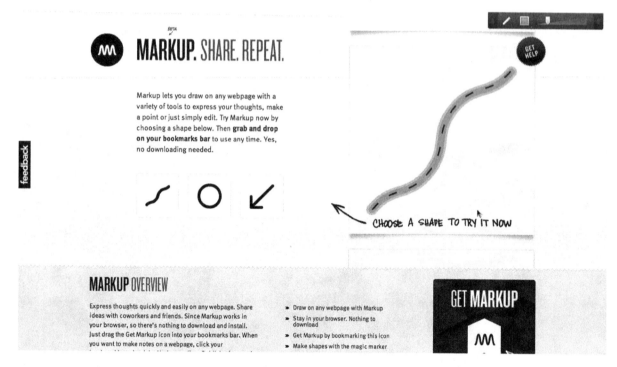

Figure 11-12. Scribble all over your pages with SVG thanks to Markup.io

DrawAStickman.com

The http://DrawAStickman.com agency promo for Hitcents is, in the words of the creator, an "interactive web site where visitors draw a stickman and take part in his animated adventure" that "became a viral success overnight, attracting millions of visitors from every part of the globe and winning numerous awards" (see Figure 11-13 and online at www.hitcents.com/blog/post/making-drawastickmancom-part-1-birth-idea). This brilliantly executed idea has had more than 20 million visits and uses Raphaël for the graphics.

Figure 11-13. *My stickman remained unflappably cheery in the face of a fire-breathing dragon*

Working with SVG

Given browsers now support SVG files in `<img>` tags and even as CSS backgrounds, we can now use SVG files for background gradients, tab backgrounds, and other image elements where a single file can be reused and scaled as needed (see this demo: `http://css-tricks.com/using-svg/`). Combine SVG's flexibility with CSS3's multiple backgrounds, and there are interesting things afoot when it comes to styling visual elements. For example, SVG would be great for styling the controls of a media player for `<video>` and `<audio>` elements.

This isn't just theoretical—designers now use SVG seriously and provide tutorials to get us up to speed. For example, in "A Farewell to CSS3 Gradients," Alex Walker looks at the patchy support for CSS3 gradients, suggests we consider SVG as an alternative, and provides a handy tutorial to do just that: `http://designfestival.com/a-farewell-to-css3-gradients/`.

Responsive Web Design and SVG

Vector graphics may also prove quite helpful in responsive web design situations where we want to display crisp, lightweight interface elements on everything from the mobile to the desktop (and especially on super-high-resolution iOS and Android [3.0+] screens). Again, this isn't theoretical; designers are getting their hands dirty with this right now. In Smashing Magazine's January 2012 article "Resolution Independence With SVG," David Bushell looks at using SVG for interface elements: `http://coding.smashingmagazine.com/2012/01/16/resolution-independence-with-svg/`.

Vector UI elements are not a free responsive lunch, however. While it's tempting to think they can scale up and down effortlessly (they're vectors!), this isn't necessarily true. Large artwork scaled down to very small sizes can become a blurry mess, and small artwork scaled up can look spartan and devoid of detail, as this lengthy article on icons and SVG demonstrates: `www.pushing-pixels.org/2011/11/04/about-those-vector-icons.html`.

(Of course, CSS3's support for gradients, rounded corners, transformations, and animation may place the proverbial pillow on SVG's face just as it comes off of life support for the third time. In fact, SVG filter effects are being ported to CSS and are already in WebKit, as this article explains: www.html5rocks.com/en/tutorials/filters/understanding-css/. Plus, check out these crazy demos of SVG-inspired CSS shaders: www.adobe.com/devnet/html5/articles/css-shaders.html.)

Despite that SVG has been kicking around for more than a decade, the web design community hasn't really given it a thorough workout to see what's possible until recently. So, with the renewed interest in all things web standards, the decline of Flash, the rise of responsive web design, and a reasonable baseline of browser support, it's definitely time to get experimenting again.

SVG Gotchas

There are two key problems, though. The first is performance: complex SVG is slow. Browser makers generally haven't paid much attention to SVG performance because it was always the red-headed stepchild of web standards. Things are starting to change, however. For one, hardware acceleration helps dramatically, as Microsoft has demonstrated with IE9–11. (Yes, *Microsoft* has not only caught up but is now leading the way in some areas of web standards implementation. You're telling me!)

The other problem is tools. No one wants to sit around writing SVG markup by hand. Some drawing tools are available, however, such as the following:

- Inkscape, an open source, cross-platform vector drawing program that uses SVG natively, is here: http://inkscape.org.

- Adobe Illustrator supports SVG, and you can read more about support for SVG here: https://helpx.adobe.com/illustrator/topics.html. See "SVG" halfway down the page.

- Janvas, a framework for interactive graphics in SVG, is at www.janvas.com/.

- Method, an online SVG image editor, is at http://editor.method.ac/ and is open sourced at https://github.com/duopixel/Method-Draw.

- SVG-edit is a "fast, web-based, JavaScript-driven SVG editor" that's free and open source, which we looked at earlier. You can try it live at http://svg-edit.googlecode.com/svn/branches/2.5.1/editor/svg-editor.html, or you can download it at http://code.google.com/p/svg-edit/ (see the links to browser add-ons, too).

- A variety of other tools are listed here: http://en.wikipedia.org/wiki/Scalable_Vector_Graphics#Software_and_support_in_applications.

You can also use JavaScript libraries such as Snap.svg, Raphaël, or jQuery SVG to draw SVG with JavaScript. Nevertheless, most vector drawing and animation for the Web is done in the Flash IDE. What if Flash could export SVG?

SVG: Heir to Flash?

Adobe's dedication to pushing SVG forward, both in the standards community and through support of frameworks such as Snap.svg and Raphaël, is admirable and speaks to its desire for a post-Flash Web. For many, many, many years Flash was the only and preferred solution for bringing animated, interactive elements to the Web. Those elements were locked inside a tiny plug-in element, though, and communicating with them or manipulating them was difficult. Want a dynamic and animated navigation for your site? Well, you might as well build the entire thing in Flash because using it for just the navigation frame was a royal pain.

Yet Flash was (and continues to languish as) much more than simple animations. It was a fully fledged solution for multibitrate-encrypted video streams, a high-powered gaming engine, a 3D engine, and so on and so forth. As we saw in previous chapters, there are many different technologies hiding under banner of "HTML5," and most of them will take a piece of Flash's territory. SVG has been coexisting with Flash for a long time, and now it's finally coming into its own.

The question for SVG isn't whether it can (or should) replace Flash as a solution for constructing interactive and animated page elements but whether it can carve out a niche truly of its own. Snap.svg and Raphaël have certainly helped it carve out that niche, and in the next few years as the browsers mature we'll be able to do more with SVG natively.

Can SVG generate enough interest in the design community after crying wolf in the early '00s? Ironically, it may not be Flash that distracts the web community from SVG but other web standards. With so much activity around web standards development these days, it has a fight for attention on its hands.

Is SVG destined to always be the bridesmaid and never the bride? Or will the folks who wrote the huge tomes on SVG all those years ago get to dust off their work for a belated second edition? Time will tell.

In the meantime, it's easy to get started with Snap.svg or Raphaël, so why not give them a try? Check them out at `http://snapsvg.io` and `http://raphaeljs.com`.

The Truth About HTML5 Web Apps, Mobile, and What Comes Next

This book is primarily about HTML5 for web designers, and what HTML5 delivers for us is, well, mixed.

But it's not fair for that impression to characterize the entire HTML5 spec. Many of the features now in HTML5 began life in the Web Applications 1.0 spec (www.whatwg.org/specs/web-apps/2005-09-01/), and it shows. HTML5 wasn't really written for designers. Instead, it was written more for developers. And from a development point of view, HTML5 looks far more interesting, even for us as designers, as we'll see in a moment.

So, in this chapter, we're going to run through some of the important web app–oriented features of HTML5 that are, in some ways, the real meat of HTML5.

First, though, let's take a quick look at the (rapidly changing) browser landscape for HTML5 web app development.

HTML5 Web App Browser Support

For all the hype, HTML5 browser support for web app features (on the desktop at least) is still a bit of a downer. But we can't blame that on the spec. Ian Hickson and the WHATWG have bent over backward to make HTML5 as implementor-friendly as possible, documenting browser behavior in a way that's never been done before.

Though Microsoft has thankfully embraced auto-updates for IE, legacy IE versions (particularly IE8—the last version of IE for XP) will be with us for years to come. In the business sector, many organizations still have strict policies managed by IT departments regarding updates and adoption lags by several releases. In the consumer market, many are getting the latest versions of IE now without even knowing it, but others on older operating systems won't see that benefit until they bite the bullet and update to a new version of Windows. IE8 is rapidly becoming like (the now thankfully dead) IE6 in the sense that it's the new hard-to-shake, pain-in-our-collective-behinds browser that will hang on as stubbornly as Windows XP does. Microsoft support for Windows XP is over as of April of 2014 and hopefully this will help force at least business users to upgrade. Still, we should expect to support home users for at least a few more years. Here are the worldwide operating system trends, but always check your own analytics data to see what's relevant for your audience: http://gs.statcounter.com/.

But the next decade is actually looking much better than the previous one. Chrome and Firefox are now on release cycles measured in *weeks*. This is what Jeff Atwood said in his post "The Infinite Version" (www.codinghorror.com/blog/2011/05/the-infinite-version.html):

> *Chrome is so fluid that it has transcended software versioning altogether.*

Microsoft, desperate not to be left behind, not only is catching up as fast as it can but is innovating too—from hardware-accelerated Canvas and SVG to a proper CSS layout system in IE10—and it's implementing more standards than most other browsers in IE11. Microsoft is also speeding up its browser releases, aiming for annual version updates (see www.computerworld.com/s/article/9215766/Microsoft_quickens_browser_pace_with_IE10_goes_for_annual_upgrades), and pushing HTML5 hard for its native, installed apps in Windows 8. Updating IE on an annual basis is still slower than Chrome or Firefox, but it's a huge improvement on IE's legacy of slow releases, and pushing auto-updates now means adoption of the latest should go up much more quickly, and we designers/developers can start using cutting-edge features faster.

In the meantime, HTML5 polyfills will keep being refined and enhanced to fill the gaps as best we can until legacy IE (and Windows XP) truly dies out: https://github.com/Modernizr/Modernizr/wiki/HTML5-Cross-browser-Polyfills.

Browser updates and innovation are as important as the spec itself. As Ian Hickson says, a spec that doesn't get implemented exists only as fiction. But this raises other issues: how do you develop for "modern" browsers when they're being updated every couple of months? Part of the answer is feature detection, which we'll look at shortly.

Then there's mobile....

HTML5 on Mobile: WebKit and Beyond

If HTML5 web app development in the here-and-now has one saving grace, it's mobile (specifically iOS and Android) web app development. The support for HTML5 features in WebKit (the saucy minx behind iOS's and Android's browsers) is solid and improving all the time. But we can't assume the mobile web means WebKit even if it dominates, just as we don't develop exclusively for IE on the desktop even when it dominates.

In fact, we can't even assume "WebKit" refers to a consistent platform, either. In A List Apart's "Smartphone Browser Landscape" article from December 2010, Peter-Paul Koch writes the following (www.alistapart.com/articles/smartphone-browser-landscape/):

> *There is no WebKit on mobile. I tested nine mobile WebKit-based browsers and they all behave differently. Not wildly so: Baseline CSS support is good, and JavaScript is definitely workable. Still, each one has its problems and strong points.*
>
> *Because of this variability, it's important to test your websites in as many WebKit-based browsers as you can. Don't assume your website will work on the Android or BlackBerry WebKit-based browsers just because it works in Safari.*

That was as true then as it is now, if not more so. For example, there are two different Android browsers from Google—the stock Browser app and Chrome for Android—and that's not taking into consideration Android OS fragmentation, which is in and of itself a bit of a nightmare and means that every version of "Android Browser" could be different.

Even talking about "mobile" as though it's synonymous for iOS and Android is problematic. The mobile world is so vast—including the "smartphone" market, which has plenty of cheap, under-powered Android devices, legacy iOS devices, and even still legacy BlackBerry devices. It's a mistake to generalize at all. There's also Opera Mobile and Mini and Firefox for Mobile. (In fact, there's a whole Mozilla mobile platform, which we'll discuss in the following section.) And then there's the Windows Phone platform and Internet Explorer Mobile.

Mobile Is a Moving Target: Microsoft's Big Push

The mobile landscape has long been in a state of flux, thanks in no small part to the innovative pushes into this market by lots of different players. Surprisingly, one player who was late to the game was Microsoft, which finally got in seriously in 2010.

Microsoft's modern Windows Phone platform launched as "Windows Phone 7" in late 2010 and shipped with our old friend—and "by friend" I mean sworn enemy—IE7 (well, IE7 and a half). Microsoft thankfully started rolling out IE9 Mobile in late 2011 as part of its Windows Phone 7.5 (a.k.a. "Mango") update. It then updated this to Windows Phone 8 in 2012, which is the current version at the time of this writing and currently uses mobile IE10 as its browser.

The version 8 update vastly matured the Windows Phone platform, and as far as mobile browsers go, IE10 is surprisingly compliant with standards.

Microsoft has unified its desktop and mobile browser code base, and given it is pushing HTML5 hard across the board (especially in IE10) *and* can push out mobile browser upgrades quite efficiently (unlike the desktop, which as we noted will still be hampered by corporate IT departments), we'll ideally see IE Mobile continue to advance in future releases. At the time of this writing, it still lags mobile Safari a bit but is generally as up to date as Mobile Opera, which is a huge improvement.

In the meantime, however, IE10 Mobile is another example demonstrating that the modern mobile world isn't just iOS and Android. At the time of this writing, Windows Mobile adoption is still pretty low, and Android and iOS are definitely the largest players, but Microsoft isn't going to let the mobile market get away easily. Additionally, it has been throwing huge amounts of money into marketing its Surface platform, which uses the full version of IE in sync with the desktop version. The unification of IE's code base across tablets and desktops means that, more than any other platform, developers are going to have to start treating the IE market as a single whole that works on multiple devices, rather than drawing a clear line between the mobile, tablet, and desktop versions. And viewed that way, IE is still a serious contender.

We also need to keep mobile use in perspective. Mobile, and particularly responsive web design, may be, *like, so hot right now*, but if only 8 percent of your audience uses smartphones to access your site, you need to weigh how you spend your time for that 8 percent versus the other 92 percent of users. (On the other hand, if your numbers are the reverse, go nuts!) Check your stats in Google Analytics or in (shameless plug ahoy!) Ninja For Google Analytics at `http://itsninja.com`, which I designed for web designers and developers so you can have the relevant Google Analytics data at your fingertips.

Firefox OS: Mozilla's Ambitious Mobile Platform, and the WebAPI

While companies like Microsoft try to push their own platforms, part of which involves the Web, Mozilla has been working hard at turning the Web into a mobile platform, especially with its Boot to Gecko (B2G) project, which was released in 2013 under the name Firefox OS for better brand recognition. You can find its impressive microsite online here: `www.mozilla.org/en-US/firefox/os/`.

At the time of this writing, Firefox OS phones are available in Spain, Venezuela, Colombia, and Poland. Seventeen operators support it, none of which are in the United States, and it's available on only two different devices. It hasn't exactly exploded out of the gate, but it does represent a unique innovation over other mobile platforms: it's entirely web-based. It's built on another Mozilla project, called WebAPI.

The WebAPI project has set its sights high and aims to fill the many large gaps in using web technology as a mobile platform and includes APIs for things like a phone dialer, SMS functionality, an address book, camera access, device settings, games, and more. It states its goal as "pushing the Web to include—and in places exceed—the capabilities of competing stacks."

This means you can have a phone powered entirely by web apps, and you can see how they run simply by *viewing the source*, just like any other web app or web site. The WebAPI project is beyond just supporting Firefox OS. Firefox OS is a great place for the WebAPI to bring itself to the forefront, but there's no reason that you couldn't build a host of web-driven applications on other platforms that use the WebAPI.

By all accounts WebAPI and Firefox OS are functionally doing quite well. For example, way back in 2012 The Verge reported the following from the Mobile World Congress (`www.theverge.com/2012/2/27/2827659/mozillas-boot-to-gecko-project-the-internet-is-your-phone-hands-on`):

[Firefox OS] is, in essence, a phone operating system that is entirely web-and HTML5-based. From the moment you turn the phone on, everything you see is HTML5. Even the dialer uses Mozilla's "telephony APIs," and is itself web-based. There are no native apps, just a series of the most impressive bookmarks you've ever seen. [. . .]

Sending messages, taking pictures, playing Cut the Rope, browsing the web, and nearly everything else we tried worked correctly, if not always gracefully. It was actually really hard to believe that we were using an entirely web-based device—we kept asking if they were lying, and it wasn't really HTML5. Of course, there was an easy way to prove it: you can see the source code of any app at any time, to see exactly what's behind what you're seeing.

This is "HTML5" in the broadest sense of existing and new (particularly Mozilla-invented) web technology, not the HTML5 specification per se. Nevertheless, it demonstrates the incredible potential for web technology beyond HTML5 and the power of the Web as a platform in its own right.

It also shows the development of web technology is not purely a matter of the WHATWG versus the W3C, as we saw way back in Chapter 1. It's possible for players such as Mozilla to do plenty of innovation in their own time (and on their own dime) and (as Mozilla is doing) take their work to the W3C to ensure it becomes a patent-free standard all can use and implement.

Whether adoption of the Mozilla platform will ever catch on is yet to be seen. At the time of this writing, it's not exactly tearing the market apart, but it's still early. What Firefox OS does show is that there are resources from large players on the Web committed to driving innovation in mobile and that open web technology, and thus eventually web standards, can play a big role in that.

HTML5 Mobile Compatibility

For more on the current state of HTML5 mobile compatibility on a wide variety of platforms, Maximiliano Firtman has put together an excellent chart with 15 mobile browsers, and a variety of HTML5 and related web technologies and APIs, that's available here: http://mobilehtml5.org/.

That wraps up our quick journey through HTML5 and mobile, so now let's get back to HTML5 and web app development.

HTML5-Powered Content Management

One key reason designers should have at least some interest in HTML5's web app features on desktop and mobile is content management systems. CMSs are the one category of web apps (broadly speaking) we *all* rely on for our client or company work.

For example, it would be great to see CMSs take advantage of the History API for fast page loads, local storage (for auto-saving form entries, perhaps), and maybe offline functionality for mobile blogging/content editing. (We'll touch on these features in a moment.) There's also the Mozilla HTML5 Image Uploader (http://hacks.mozilla.org/2010/02/an-html5-offline-image-editor-and-uploaderapplication/) that uses a bunch of HTML5 technology such as the offline application cache, local storage, Canvas, and drag and drop and that serves as a good indicator of how HTML5 can enhance the CMSs we (and our clients) use day in, day out. The sooner we suggest these features, the sooner they'll be implemented.

The JavaScript Age

While we may spend a lot of time in the trenches wrangling CMSs, it's worth keeping an eye on the big picture too. The overarching theme of these new features—and possibly the future direction of the Web itself—is they're all about JavaScript APIs and not hypertext per se. In a sense, hypertext is now the tail wagged by the JavaScript dog, especially in terms of web applications.

The problem of marking up documents has been solved. Over the next decade or so we'll see major improvements in writing applications, as HTML5 (and related) features for web apps become baseline standards. After all, HTML5 is largely a web apps spec from the mid '00s.

This is a (small) part of the reason we're perhaps entering the JavaScript Age, as Mike Driscoll puts it in "Node.js and the JavaScript Age" (http://metamarketsgroup.com/blog/node-js-and-the-javascript-age/):

> *[We need to shift] our view of the server from a document courier (HTML Age), or a template renderer (LAMP Age), to a function and data shipper. The principal role of the server is to ship an application to the client (JavaScript), along with data (JSON), and let the client weave those into a DOM. [...]*
>
> *The JavaScript age brings us closer to a web that is not a global digital library, but a global digital nervous system, whose implications we are only beginning to apprehend.*

Or, put another way, Jeff Atwood in "The Principle of Least Power" said the following (www.codinghorror.com/blog/2007/07/the-principle-of-least-power.html):

> *Atwood's Law: any application that can be written in JavaScript, will eventually be written in JavaScript.*

The question is, what will this mean for the humble web page?

JavaScript Killed the HTML Star

In a sense, we have been exploring this new frontier since the whole "Web 2.0" thing kicked off. So, we shouldn't be surprised that the thrust of new developments are JavaScript-related.

The humble web page has been incredibly robust and resilient. With billions and billions of them out there, and billions more being made, they're not going away any time soon. But the hugely inefficient *click - full-page refresh - click - full-page refresh* paradigm in high-profile sites may not be around for long in light of things such as the History API, which we'll look at in a moment.

We've achieved some pretty incredible things on top of the basic web page. Uber-nerds get excited about complex functionality (as is happening now with web apps–oriented HTML5 functionality), which then gets abstracted into a library, plug-in, or framework and becomes almost trivial for designers to drop into their sites.

While this is wonderful for us, it does mean the lines between web *page* and web *application* will continue to blur. Is a modern web site a JavaScript/Ajax/HTML5-powered *application* that serves content or a collection of simple, linked pages...something in between? Right now the answer is "all of the above," but it will be interesting to see at what point the amount of JavaScript on our site makes it more "app" than "page."

For example, consider the amount of functionality that can be bolted onto a traditional web page through JavaScript. JavaScript for animation; JavaScript for SVG (with Snap.svg and Raphaël, as we saw in Chapter 11); JavaScript for page state (which we'll look at later in the chapter); JavaScript for A/B testing your design; JavaScript for new CSS layout engines (for example, http://code.google.com/p/css-template-layout/); JavaScript for CSS preprocessing; JavaScript for graphics and games (Canvas and WebGL, as we saw in Chapter 9); JavaScript for audio and video controls (Chapter 10); and even JavaScript for decoding MP3s (http://hacks.mozilla.org/2011/06/jsmad-a-javascript-mp3-decoder/, which works around the patent issues we discussed in Chapter 9 and is pretty incredible in its own right).

Phew.

JavaScript is the wrapper around (or enabler of) all this functionality, some of which is HTML5, and some of which is not. But how long until we go all the way—if indeed we should—and launch bare-bones HTML pages with everything else abstracted into essentially one big JavaScript app? If some web apps are now being delivered as simply JSON data and a client-side JavaScript application (as we touched on earlier), why not web pages?

Well, there's SEO, but the situation is rapidly changing there. In November 2011 Google's Matt Cutts said the Googlebot was already spidering JavaScript/Ajax comment systems, at the very least (`http://searchengineland.com/google-can-now-execute-ajax-javascript-for-indexing-99518`); Google can crawl the (problematic) hashbang (#!) URL format; and the HTML5 History API provides new possibilities we'll look at next. (Apart from SEO, issues such as maintenance are, however, quite legitimate objections!)

It's clear which way the wind is blowing. Think how far we've already come from the days when JavaScript was synonymous with horrendous DHTML and clunky rollover scripts. Now it has become the de facto programming language of the Web.

Nevertheless, we shouldn't get *too* distracted by the technology. It's fun to explore all the possibilities that modern JavaScript frameworks have to offer, but the evergreens such as great copy, a great user experience (especially when measured in hard numbers such as conversion and/or engagement rates), and designing to generally *get the hell out of the way* will still matter above all else. Some things just never go out of fashion, and as long as our JavaScript frameworks are implemented in service of those larger goals, we'll stay on track with what the Web was meant to do. (We'll touch on this a little more when we look at performance-based design in the final chapter.)

But before we get there, let's quickly run through these new web app–oriented features and how we can detect them (along with some resources for further reading).

Modernizr, When Can I Use..., and Polyfills

Browser releases have become incredibly fast. As we touched on earlier, Chrome and Firefox aim to roll out updates in *weeks*. This alone makes it incredibly difficult, if not outright foolhardy, to try to detect which browser version gets which functionality.

Browser detection has never been a great idea. You still occasionally run into antiquated web sites that tell you to "upgrade" your bleeding-edge version of Chrome or Firefox to a "modern" browser like Internet Explorer 7, because that's all the developers could foresee at the time. It's hard to detect browsers that don't yet exist, but when the Web moves forward and your page is outdated, it's an embarrassment. Focusing on browser detection is a losing game that requires constant tinkering.

Modernizr

Instead, *feature* detection is all the rage, and that's what scripts like Modernizr do. They don't *add* any functionality. They simply tell you what features are supported in a given browser so we can tailor our page as appropriate.

Modernizr does this in one of two ways:

- By adding a class name to the `<html>` element (especially useful for CSS3 features) so we can write CSS for `.coolfeature {}` or fallback styles for `.no-coolfeature {}`.

- Through a global JavaScript object that contains properties for each HTML5 (and related) feature. Where those properties evaluate as true or false reflects whether the feature is supported. The built-in YepNope.js library allows conditional loading of supported scripts (yep, the feature is supported) and polyfills (nope, it's not, so load this polyfill).

Check it out at `http://modernizr.com`.
There's a full tutorial on HTML5doctor.com:
`http://html5doctor.com/using-modernizr-to-detect-html5-features-and-provide-fallbacks/`.

When Can I Use...

This is great for detecting features on a browser-by-browser basis, but how can we know what support is like for a given feature in the first place? To get an idea of global browser support for a given feature, I recommend Alexis Deveria's incredibly useful `http://caniuse.com` (which I've referred to in previous chapters).

Polyfills

Fallback functionality for unsupported browsers can be *sort of* enabled with "polyfill" scripts and hacks. Here's an excellent, near-exhaustive list of what's available: `https://github.com/Modernizr/Modernizr/wiki/HTML5-Cross-browser-Polyfills`. Keep in mind these are rarely get-functionality-for-free cards; there's always compatibility and performance issues to consider.

HTML5 Web App APIs

Let's jump into the new HTML5 (and thereabouts) web app functionality.

(Browser stats in this chapter come from `http://caniuse.com`, which goes back only to IE 5.5, Firefox 2, Chrome 4, Safari 3.1, Opera 9, iOS 3.2, Opera Mini 5, Opera Mobile 10, and Android 2.1. Windows Phone 8's current browser is IE10 with slight differences. I'm leaving out Opera's mobile browsers and Firefox Mobile for simplicity's sake, but keep in mind the rapid changes in the very broad mobile market we discussed earlier.)

History API (pushState)

Let's start with the HTML5 History API (also referred to as *pushState*). URLs have been abused to all hell for fun and profit in the Ajax era. This is especially true with the hashbang (#!) approach you may have seen on Twitter in the past, Facebook, and sites such as Gawker. (Typing `http://twitter.com/lukestevens` used to return `http://twitter.com/#!/lukestevens`, but Twitter is moving away from this behavior.)

Some people think this is, like, *the worst thing ever*, while others think it's the price of progress. See the debate, with links, here: `http://danwebb.net/2011/5/28/itis-about-the-hashbangs`. (That's from Dan Webb, who was in charge of *undoing* Twitter's hashbang URLs, as he tweeted here: `https://twitter.com/danwrong/status/171680703824662528`.)

In any case, the History API goes some way to solving this. With the History API we can still load a chunk of new content into your page with Ajax (or similar), but we can also update the URL in the user's location bar (*and* browser history) to make the whole process look like a very fast page request.

Mind you, it takes some work to fake the whole backward/forward page navigation thing. You can read Mark Pilgrim's detailed write-up and tutorial here: `http://diveintohtml5.info/history.html`. SEOmoz also covered the History API in "Create Crawlable, Link-Friendly AJAX Websites Using pushState()" (`www.seomoz.org/blog/create-crawlable-link-friendly-ajax-websites-using-pushstate`).

This would be a handy addition to the modern CMSs we offer our clients (at the very least). We'd get fast Ajax page loads without confusing not-necessarily-technical clients, who'd still see the new URL and have their back button work predictably.

It's also something we can consider implementing in a progressive way. There's no IE9 or older support (though it is in IE10+), Chrome support is good, Safari support is buggy, and Opera support arrived only in 11.5+. (On mobile, iOS 4.2–4.3 support was buggy, iOS5+ support is solid, and Android inexplicably dropped support in 4.0 but added it back in 4.2 and has maintained it since.)

But there is History.js (`https://github.com/balupton/History.js`), which aims to provide fallback support for unsupported browsers and smooth out the quirks in current implementations. The creator of History.js, Benjamin Lupton, discusses the pros and cons of the different approaches to handling URLs in "Intelligent State Handling" (`https://github.com/browserstate/history.js/wiki/Intelligent-State-Handling`).

(Remember, though, hashbang URLs are forever, even if used only as a fallback for older browsers. If someone uses a hashbang URL to link to your site, then that's a URL that needs to be maintained indefinitely. Falling back to full-page loads may be a better way to go.)

For current browser support stats for the History API, see `http://caniuse.com/#feat=history`.

HTML5 Web Storage (and JavaScript-Rendered CSS)

Web Storage (also known as *localStorage*) is often described as "cookies on steroids," given it can store up to 5MB of data (key-value pairs) on the client (the actual size limit is up to the browser and no longer specified in the spec, but 5MB was previously recommended and is still a good rule of thumb). Unlike cookies, the data isn't automatically sent back to the server, and it doesn't have an explicit expiry date. (Web Storage was originally part of the HTML5 spec but has since been spun out into its own specification, still edited by Ian Hickson: http://dev.w3.org/html5/webstorage/.)

This kind of storage could be used to save web app data locally, whether it's a saved game state (so the user can resume where they left off) or a document the user is working on.

In terms of web design, we could use localStorage to save the output of a CSS preprocessor. In the past few years, CSS preprocessors (such as LESS and SASS) have become all the rage, offering advanced CSS syntax and features such as variables, mixins, and better inheritance. You write the code using the new syntax, and the software spits out normal CSS a browser can understand. You can output the CSS as a one-off or automatically on the server.

You can also do it on the client side with JavaScript and Less.js (http://lesscss.org/). The Less.js script uses Web Storage to cache the outputted CSS, making subsequent requests for the CSS extremely fast.

This is a pretty profound development. We can now use JavaScript to generate CSS however and whenever we like and store it locally. No more faffing about with server-side scripts to do the parsing, during development at least. (For production it should be compiled to normal CSS; otherwise, those without JavaScript won't get your CSS either, and as we covered in Chapter 4, that's A Bad Thing™.) It's simple, it's powerful, and it works right now.

(By the way, I'm not advocating LESS over any other flavor of CSS preprocessor. If you decide to go down this route, use whatever floats your boat.)

For more on Web Storage, see the following:

- Mark Pilgrim's chapter from *Dive Into HTML5*: http://diveintohtml5.info/storage.html

- Opera's "Web Storage: easier, more powerful client-side data storage" article: http://dev.opera.com/articles/view/web-storage/

- Mozilla Developer Network's "DOM Storage" article: https://developer.mozilla.org/en/dom/storage

Web Storage is currently supported in IE8+ and all other modern desktop browsers. For current usage statistics, see http://caniuse.com/#feat=namevalue-storage.

Database Storage

Web Storage sounds great, for some kinds of data. What about database storage on the client side?

Politics, that's what.

The no-longer-maintained Web SQL Database spec (www.w3.org/TR/webdatabase/) has been implemented in some browsers using SQLite (Safari, Chrome, and Opera on the desktop), along with Mobile Safari and Android. But Microsoft never implemented it, and Mozilla is philosophically opposed to it (see http://hacks.mozilla.org/2010/06/beyond-html5-database-apis-and-the-road-to-indexeddb/).

Mozilla provided an alternative known as IndexedDB and implemented it first in Firefox 4 and in every version thereafter. Microsoft got on board with IE starting in version 10, Google started implementing it back in Chrome 11, and even Opera started support in version 17. Safari is the only holdout, seemingly committed to WebSQL, and mobile support at the time of this writing is limited to Android Browser 4.4 and IE Mobile 10.

Unfortunately, there's no single solution for this to date. Developers who want a client-side database must roll two solutions or not support Safari.

HTML5 Offline (Application Cache)

HTML5 allows developers to keep their web apps (or sites) running even if the client is offline—a common concern in the mobile world where a lost connection is just a tunnel away.

How? By specifying which URLs the browser should (and shouldn't) cache in a *manifest* file, which you reference by using the manifest attribute on the <html> element for every page of your web app.

It's one of those simple-in-theory-but-complicated-in-reality features that puts it beyond the scope of this book. So, if you want to know more, check out the following:

- The web developer edition of the HTML5 spec, which has a lengthy explanation and tutorial: http://developers.whatwg.org/offline.html

- Mark Pilgrim's chapter in *Dive Into HTML5*, which covers this feature in considerable detail, including debugging information: http://diveintohtml5.info/offline.html

- Dev.Opera's handy introduction: http://dev.opera.com/articles/view/offline-applications-html5-appcache/

- A List Apart's article "Application Cache is a Douchebag" by Jake Archibald, which covers many of the still relevant frustrations and issues with implementing the Application Cache API: http://alistapart.com/article/application-cache-is-a-douchebag

Bringing some of these features together (along with the Geolocation API that we'll look at soon) can create robust, mobile, HTML5-driven web applications. Now we just need to wait for the desktop to catch up.

And by "desktop" I mean Internet Explorer users, since IE didn't support HTML5's offline functionality in IE9 and older but does support it in IE10+. The other desktop browsers do support it, as does (importantly!) iOS , Android, and IE for Windows Phone. (For current usage statistics, see http://caniuse.com/#feat=offline-apps.)

Geolocation API

The Geolocation API provides a standard client-side way for a web site to detect the user's location. Geolocation on the Web isn't new. Plenty of sites use your IP address to work out your location (at least at the country level) so they can do the following:

- Serve you region-specific ads

- Lock you out of certain services (as anyone living outside the United States knows all too well!)

It can even be done on the client side when you load any Google Ajax API (which you may already use to load jQuery—see http://googleajaxsearchapi.blogspot.com/2008/08/where-is-my-current-user.html) or on the server side using something like www.ip2nation.com/.

The good news is you don't need permission to do old-school geolocation based on your user's IP. The bad news is it's not always that accurate.

The new Geolocation API, on the other hand, tries to use whatever location data is available, including the following:

- GPS

- Wireless network (as recorded by Google Street View)

- Cell tower locations

- IP address (it's agnostic as to where the data comes from)

It can then provide details about latitude, longitude, altitude, direction, speed, and even accuracy (when it's available). Previous locations can even be cached (to map out a trip, for example).

But you can forget about getting this data without anyone knowing. The device *must* ask for your permission before it can use it.

The Geolocation API isn't part of HTML5 per se. (You can see the spec here: `http://dev.w3.org/geo/api/spec-source.html`.) But it's cool and opens up some interesting possibilities with mobile web sites. The spec suggests the following:

- Blogging (or status updates) with location data attached

- Showing a user's position on a map

- Turn-by-turn navigation

- Tour-guide web apps

- Location-specific weather or news widgets

And remember, it all happens in the browser—no server-side IP detection required.

The Geolocation API is well supported in all modern desktop and mobile browsers, with the sole exception of Opera Mini. (For current usage statistics, see `http://caniuse.com/#feat=geolocation`.)

For more information, see the following:

- Mark Pilgrim's *Dive Into HTML5* Geolocation chapter: `http://diveintohtml5.info/geolocation.html`

- The "A Simple Trip Meter using the Geolocation API" tutorial: `www.html5rocks.com/tutorials/geolocation/trip_meter/`

- Firefox's user guide to "Location-aware browsing": `www.mozilla.com/ en-US/firefox/geolocation/`

Other APIs That May Be of Interest to You

Other new APIs in and around HTML5 allow developers to do the following, in the words of Remy Sharp (*Introducing HTML5*, 2011):

> *You can now create multi-threaded, multi-window, cross-domain, low- latency, real-time thingymegiggies using the simplest of string-based communication methods. Now go build something awesome.*

These APIs include cross-document messaging (IE8+ up, all modern desktop and WebKit mobile browsers), which allows documents on different domains to send information back and forth. This could be useful for a widget on one site that needs to pull data from another domain. This MSDN article provides a useful overview of the issues and technology: `https://developer.mozilla.org/en-US/docs/Web/API/window.postMessage`.

Web Workers (IE10+, Firefox 4+, Safari 4+, all recent Chrome and Opera, limited mobile) offers an API to run scripts concurrently in the background, instead of the one-at-a-time-while-everything-freezes-until-it's-done approach we have now. Wikipedia has a useful, brief overview: `http://en.wikipedia.org/wiki/Web_Workers`.

Web Sockets (supported across the board with the exception of Android Browsers before 4.4 and Opera Mini) allows efficient bi-directional communication between browser and server. At its most basic, this could be handy for a chat room application. For more resources, see `www.websocket.org/aboutwebsocket.html`.

The File API (supported by all platforms except Opera Mini and IE Mobile) lets us read and write files and directories, as demonstrated in this neat music player: `http://antimatter15.github.com/player/player.html`. There's also a useful tutorial here: `www.html5rocks.com/tutorials/file/filesystem/`.

Oh, and there's also the Drag and Drop API (supported by all major desktop platforms and only IE for mobile), which is, according to *every single person who has ever come into contact with it* (including Ian Hickson, who added it to the spec), pretty horrible. Drag and Drop (DnD) was added to IE5—yep, 5—by Microsoft in 1999, and other browser vendors also implemented it. So, Hickson reverse-engineered it (à la Canvas), documented it, and added it to the HTML5 specification in the spirit of documenting what already works. So, now we have widely supported Drag and Drop. (You can see Hickson's account of the process here: `http://ln.hixie.ch/?start=%201115899732&count=1`.)

Why not just use JavaScript for drag and drop? For on-page elements you certainly could, but the thing about the (somewhat brain-damaged) HTML5-via-1999 DnD API is it lets you drag and drop all kinds of content to and from *other applications*. There's a basic tutorial here: `www.webdesignerdepot.com/2013/08/how-to-use-html5s-drag-and-drop/`.

What Comes Next: HTML 5.1

So far, everything we've been talking about is included in the HTML5 spec, which at the time of this writing is fairly well locked in and should be finalized in 2014. Work on the next spec, titled HTML 5.1 (previously, and cutely, "HTML.next"), began in the middle of 2012 when the HTML5 spec was finalized.

5.1 is scheduled to itself to have a "last call" sometime in 2014 with a final recommendation going out in 2016. In the meantime, they'll have final revisions on a working candidate with all new work going into HTML 5.2. If the W3C follows this schedule, we should all be able to eagerly anticipate HTML6 by 2034 or so, and in the meantime, the rest of the Internet will have a field day coming up with other ideas on what HTML6 should be (my favorite: "The Spec that Brings us Freedom" at `http://html6spec.com/`).

HTML 5.1, to date, doesn't contain much to write home about with one exception: the encrypted media extensions (EME) specification, which allows for locking content (DRM) of not just video or video streams but images, text, and JavaScript files—anything that's served with a web page could be "protected" by EME and kept locked down from easy inspection.

This has obviously caused a lot of controversy, which we covered in more detail in Chapter 10. The Electronic Freedom Foundation is raising alarms and calling for boycotts of Netflix in response. The foundation summarized a valid concern for EME in a blog post (`https://www.eff.org/deeplinks/2013/10/lowering-your-standards`), saying this:

> *A Web where you cannot cut and paste text; where your browser can't "Save As..." an image; where the "allowed" uses of saved files are monitored beyond the browser; where JavaScript is sealed away in opaque tombs; and maybe even where we can no longer effectively "View Source" on some sites, is a very different Web from the one we have today. It's a Web where user agents—browsers—must navigate a nest of enforced duties every time they visit a page. It's a place where the next Tim Berners-Lee or Mozilla, if they were building a new browser from scratch, couldn't just look up the details of all the "Web" technologies. They'd have to negotiate and sign compliance agreements with a raft of DRM providers just to be fully standards-compliant and interoperable.*

Scary stuff. These are perilous times for the Web, and the next few years may drastically change the course of its future.

Along with EME in HTML 5.1 could be the Media Source Extensions spec, which is currently its own specification (`https://dvcs.w3.org/hg/html-media/raw-file/tip/media-source/media-source.html`) and, as you might recall, the other piece required to roll video products like Netflix into a 100 percent pure HTML `<video>`.

You can find the latest Editors draft of the HTML 5.1 spec here: `www.w3.org/html/wg/drafts/html/master/single-page.html`.

Wrapping Up

There you have it—a quick run through HTML5's web app–oriented features. As you can see, HTML5 is about introducing a native web apps platform. That isn't surprising considering the spec started as Web Applications 1.0 and Web Forms 2.0.

HTML5 is also just a stepping stone in the evolution of web applications, albeit a very important one and one that has been a long time coming. Post-HTML5 developments (especially from Mozilla in mobile, as we discussed earlier) are continuing at a break-neck pace. They'll continue to be called HTML5, as (I believe) Mark Pilgrim put it:

> *HTML5 will always be popular, because anything that's popular will be called HTML5.*

It's an exciting time for the Web. Hold on tight; it's going to be one hell of a ride.

The Truth About the Future of Web Design: Performance-Based Design

I will wrap up this book with a look into the future—not of HTML5, CSS3, or any particular technology, but the future of our profession. (And I want to pitch you on my web app at `http://itsninja.com`.)

Let's face it, we're nerds. We love technology. It's exciting, it's changing rapidly, and it's just plain fun to be on the forefront of one of the biggest technological and social phenomena in generations—the Web.

But cool technology is a means to an end. It irritates me to no end when web designers and developers breathlessly proclaim a new web site is "Designed with HTML5!" as though it means something. Technology *enables* design, but more/newer technology doesn't mean *better* design—sometimes it's quite the opposite. At the end of the day, web design is pretty simple. Users click or they leave. They engage or they bounce. They buy or they abandon. And it's the actual page design (and copy) that determines how often that happens.

So far, so obvious. But here's the kicker: *we can measure what users do with our design.* We can measure whether they click or buy or whether they bounce or exit. It's probably the most profound difference that separates our practice of designing on the Web from just about any other. We can measure *performance* in a way no other discipline has been able to in the history of design.

As the saying goes, what gets measured gets improved. And how:

- 37signals A/B tested the design of its Highrise marketing site and improved conversions by 102.5 percent: `http://37signals.com/svn/posts/2991-behind-the-scenes-ab-testing-part-3-final`.

- Conversion Rate Experts applied its methodology (explained in detail) to an SEOmoz landing page and made a cool additional $1 million per year: `http://www.conversion-rate-experts.com/seomoz-case-study/`.

- Digital Telepathy (a design agency that really seems to get it) redesigned the CrazyEgg marketing site and improved its conversion rate by 21 percent: `www.dtelepathy.com/case-studies/crazyegg`.

That's just a taste; there are plenty more examples at `http://abtests.com/` and `http://visualwebsiteoptimizer.com/case-studies.php`.

Operating in the Dark

It's just as well we can measure what we do because right now we're surgeons operating in the dark; we usually don't have a clue whether we help, hurt, or do nothing for our patients. We're operating on sites oblivious to design performance—whether people are reading more or buying more or bouncing less. We're not only operating in the dark, but we're doing so while experimenting with a bunch of crazy techniques that we've only just dreamt up and are all very excited by.

That's a scary thought.

Doctors in the 18th century once thought having grubby hands was a sign of professionalism, not a gross lack of sanitation. They thought they were doing the right thing. (The guy who tried to tell them otherwise, Ignaz Semmelweis, went mad—literally.) But when they started observing and measuring what was happening to patients, they figured out it wasn't such a good thing. Who knows what weird "best practices" we have in our profession that may turn out to be harmful?

Performance vs. Production

It's not all doom and gloom, though. The beauty of measuring what we do is that we can objectively find the best version of *any* given design. Don't you hate coming up with a bunch of cool designs only to have the client choose the one you like the least (or worse, something you're fairly sure will harm their business)? Wouldn't it be better if we could stop them from pulling the trigger when they point the gun at their foot?

We can do it now, and we can do it objectively, by changing the way we look at web design. I call it *performance-based design*, and I think it's the next chapter of web design after *standards-based design* (long may it continue!).

Standards-based design is about *how* we can achieve certain designs. It's production, and it's important. Much of this book has looked at how we can improve what we do when building sites (for example, use ARIA landmarks, use the new audio/video elements, use some new form features, experiment with Canvas and SVG, implement the History API, and so on). These are important developments in the *production* side of what we do.

Now, however, it's time to *also* start thinking about *what performs best* for our users, that is, what makes a real, measurable difference to how users interact with our site.

Measure When You Redesign

I imagine you've read this book because you're going to be rolling out HTML5 site features, or whole site redesigns, as part of your day job. Maybe you're going to use more CSS3 too. And maybe you've been following the Responsive Web Design tsunami and are about to put out a hot new responsive version of your site.

If that's you, please measure what happens and share the results!

Let's say you launch an "HTML5" site. It's fast thanks to the History API. There's some clever animation with SVG (or Canvas or jQuery or CSS3 or whatever). The video on the home page now uses an HTML5 media player.

What do you guess will happen?

Will bounce rates decrease? Does time on the site improve? Do more people convert or buy? We can measure all these things. If they do improve, great! We, as a community, need to know. We need data on what actually makes a difference for users—and what doesn't—so we can all learn from the evidence, not ideas or guesses or hopes or assumptions or "best practices."

We have the data; we just need to start sharing it.

The same goes for responsive sites too. If you roll out a responsive mobile version of your site, what do your mobile users do? Do they bounce less, stay longer, and read more? Or does the opposite happen? Or nothing at all? Do you know how to find out?

Or maybe it's a tablet site. Does a responsive tablet design make *any measurable difference* to user performance? And if so, which designs work best? Simpler or more complex? Desktop-like or mobile-like?

There are so many questions, and guess what? *We already have the answers.* They are sitting in your Google Analytics account. We just have to dig them up and share our data so we can learn what makes a real difference for users and what doesn't.

I've actually written a couple of books about this very topic and how to integrate these concepts into your workflow. They're sitting unpublished on my hard drive at the moment, and I'm keen to know whether you'd like me to put them out, so please let me know (e-mail me at luke@itsninja.com or tweet me @lukestevens).

Let's Get Objective

This problem of designers (including myself) not having the data front and center when we redesign has been bothering me so much I've actually developed a web app that goes some way to solving this problem. Ninja for Google Analytics dives into your Google Analytics data and bubbles up the most relevant performance stats for you in a simple, elegant interface: `http://itsninja.com`. Check it out; I think you (and your clients) will like it.

Objectively measuring design performance needs to become the *number-one priority* for every one of our projects. It's bigger than HTML5 or any other technology floating around (as interesting as they are). When you start thinking in terms of measurable performance (conversion rates and engagement rates especially), you'll see web design and development in a whole new way.

Until then, go nuts with the new stuff in HTML5, measure what happens, and publish the results!

Thanks for reading.

Luke Stevens

`http://itsninja.com`

`luke@itsninja.com`

`http://twitter.com/lukestevens`

Index

Get the eBook for only $10!

Now you can take the weightless companion with you anywhere, anytime. Your purchase of this book entitles you to 3 electronic versions for only $10.

This Apress title will prove so indispensible that you'll want to carry it with you everywhere, which is why we are offering the eBook in 3 formats for only $10 if you have already purchased the print book.

Convenient and fully searchable, the PDF version enables you to easily find and copy code—or perform examples by quickly toggling between instructions and applications. The MOBI format is ideal for your Kindle, while the ePUB can be utilized on a variety of mobile devices.

Go to www.apress.com/promo/tendollars to purchase your companion eBook.